VICTORIAN METAFICTION

VICTORIAN LITERATURE AND CULTURE SERIES
Herbert F. Tucker, Editor
William R. McKelvy, Jill Rappoport, and Andrew M. Stauffer, Associate Editors

VICTORIAN METAFICTION

TABITHA SPARKS

UNIVERSITY OF VIRGINIA PRESS
Charlottesville and London

University of Virginia Press
© 2022 by the Rector and Visitors of the University of Virginia
All rights reserved
Printed in the United States of America on acid-free paper

First published 2022

9 8 7 6 5 4 3 2 1

Library of Congress Cataloging-in-Publication Data
Names: Sparks, Tabitha, author.
Title: Victorian metafiction / Tabitha Sparks.
Description: Charlottesville : University of Virginia Press, 2022. | Series: Victorian literature and culture series | Includes bibliographical references and index.
Identifiers: LCCN 2022017037 (print) | LCCN 2022017038 (ebook) | ISBN 9780813948690 (hardcover) | ISBN 9780813948874 (paperback) | ISBN 9780813948720 (ebook)
Subjects: LCSH: English fiction—19th century—History and criticism. | English fiction—Women authors—History and criticism. | Authorship in literature. | Women authors in literature. | Novelists in literature. | Narration (Rhetoric)—History. | Fiction—Technique.
Classification: LCC PR878.A794 S63 2022 (print) | LCC PR878.A794 (ebook) | DDC 823/.8099287—dc23/eng/20220629
LC record available at https://lccn.loc.gov/2022017037
LC ebook record available at https://lccn.loc.gov/2022017038

Cover art: Letter courtesy of the Reading Library, Berkshire, UK

CONTENTS

Acknowledgments — vii

Introduction — 1

1. Metafiction in "Novel Guise": Charlotte Brontë's *Villette* — 49
2. Rhoda Broughton's *Cometh Up as a Flower*: "Like a Story-book!" — 70
3. "The Difference between Authors and Their Books": Charlotte Riddell's *A Struggle for Fame* and Margaret Oliphant's *The Athelings* — 91
4. Pseudonymity as Metafiction — 108
5. Neo-Victorian Victorian Novels: The Writer-Heroine as a New Woman — 127

Conclusion — 153

Notes — 159
Bibliography — 177
Index — 193

ACKNOWLEDGMENTS

This book has engrossed me since I wrote the first chapters during my sabbatical at Cambridge University in 2017–2018. That year of research was invaluable, and I am grateful to McGill University for preserving sabbatical leaves and to Pembroke College, Cambridge, for hosting me. On returning to McGill, I took an Associate Dean position in the Faculty of Arts, which delayed my writing until a research leave in Fall 2021 enabled me to finish the book. I am indebted to then Acting Dean Jim Warnick for arranging that leave and for his professional mentorship in general. Also at McGill, I have appreciated the support and example of Trevor Ponech as Chair of English and was helped in writing and finishing this book by colleagues including Allan Hepburn, Jo Nalbangtoglu, José Jouvé-Martin, Nicole Guedon, Iris Godbout, and Kathleen Holden. Several students read parts or all this book: MacKenzie Bleho, an undergraduate at the time and a formidable critic; Jeff Noh, whose knowledge of postmodern novels influenced my readings of metafiction; Sabrina Aguzzi, whose reading of metafiction in her M.A. thesis helped me to crystallize my ideas; and Holly Vested, who copyedited the whole thing—twice. Holly's sharp eye and even sharper intellect caught errors and weaknesses that I would have missed entirely. I also thank the students in two graduate seminars that were shaped, if indirectly, by this book: Victorian Fiction and Feminist Narratology (Winter 2019) and Victorian Fiction: Realism and Parody (Winter 2020).

Academic organizations and colleagues who heard or encouraged this work in its various stages include The Nineteenth-Century Seminar at Cambridge, and especially Ewan Jones, Jan Schramm, and Marcus Waithe; the Dickens Universe Summer Seminar conveners Sharon Aronofsky Weltman and Tricia Lootens; Graziella Stringos and the Victorian Popular Fiction Association; Helena Ifill and Dan Wall at the Centre for the Novel at the University of Aberdeen; Emily Senior and the Birkbeck Centre for Nineteenth-Century Studies; the Department of English at the University of Glasgow and the Erasmus Foundation; Tom Mole and the Centre for the Book at the University of Edinburgh; Jason Camlot at Concordia University; Cannon Schmitt at the University of

Toronto; and Mark Wormald at Pembroke College, Cambridge. The editors at the University of Virginia Press were gracious, efficient, and a pleasure to work with. Thanks go specifically to Editorial Director Eric Brandt and to the editors of the Victorian Literature and Culture series for their insightful and meticulous reading: Herbert F. Tucker, William McKelvy, Jill Rappoport, and Andrew Stauffer, as well as the anonymous reader whose critique significantly improved my final draft. When COVID restricted the world to the computer screen, I benefitted from the interpretive savvy, reinforcement, and humor of Dagni Bredesen, Louise Penner, Tara MacDonald, and Jessica Valdez. Thanks for being such great colleagues and friends.

Special thanks to Mark Elkin, who recovered chapter 5 from the ether one anxious Sunday morning.

As always, I am grateful to my in-house editor, Daryl Ogden, who generously and acutely read most of this book, and who always knows whether I am waving or drowning. Our children, Phoebe and Piers, accompanied this book (and their parents) to Cambridge in its early stages. Their school grounds were adjacent to the University Library where I started writing, and so we worked together, in a way. This book is for them.

VICTORIAN METAFICTION

INTRODUCTION

How did Victorian women establish themselves as writers of serious, literary fiction? With some important exceptions, it is arguable that they did. Through the end of the century, women writers grappled with the expectation that realist fiction reflected worldly experience and artistic objectivity, neither of which was readily cultivated in the middle-class home, the defining context of respectable femininity. Women writers thrived in lighter genres, which maintained lower expectations for objectivity or originality, but aside from George Eliot, even canonical and best-selling novelists like Charlotte Brontë, Elizabeth Gaskell, Charlotte Yonge, and Mary Augusta Ward were subject to affiliation in "lesser" literary camps: sensation, sentimentalism, didacticism, and a watered-down "domestic" version of realism.

Amid this social and generic bias, an increasing number of Victorian women chose to write novels about women novelists. These writer-heroines are often aspirants to a writing career instead of published authors, and in some cases their fiction is a deflective spinout from ambivalent autobiographical writing. Novels about novelists exemplify the literary form of metafiction, which features its own artistic construction as part of the story. Metafiction is dominantly identified with postmodern and postcolonial fiction, often representing a crisis of faith in narrative authority. Yet from the mid-nineteenth century through the fin de siècle, novels by Victorian women including Charlotte Brontë, Rhoda Broughton, Charlotte Riddell, Eliza Lynn Linton, and several New Woman authors share a common but under-examined trope: the fictional characterization of the woman novelist or autobiographer. These novels systemically dispute the assumptions that women wrote primarily about their emotions, or were restricted to trivial, sentimental plots; metafiction dislodges the narrative from these cultural prescriptions insofar as it presents the business and art of writing as the subject of the novel. Although it is a commonplace that late twentieth-century novelists (John Barth, John Fowles, William Gaddis) undermined mimetic authority by exposing the artifice of storytelling, the novels examined in this book are filled with self-referentiality and ironic representation. In *Worlds Enough: The Invention of Realism in the Victorian Novel* (2019), Elaine Freedgood makes this same point: "The Victorian novel . . . is riddled with key features of metafiction, although it is certainly rarely, if ever, accused of this, and it is conspicuously absent from discussions of metafiction that often begin with *Tristram Shandy* and then leap to the postmodern novel without pausing anywhere along the way."[1] *Victorian Metafiction* closes this diachronic gap, an absence also identified in the *Living Handbook of Narratology* (LHN): "One relatively unexplored issue is the development of metafiction and metanarration across different periods of literary history in different literary genres. . . . There are hardly any studies concerning functions that may be fulfilled by certain forms of self-reflexive narration in different historical epochs and literary genres."[2]

Victorian novels, by women and men, have long been identified with a materialist sensibility and teleological perspective. Conventional opinion maintains that their affinity for surface detail reveals a culture that was trying to encode the world in legible economic, racial, and gender-specific indices that would implicitly or explicitly allow them to better "read" and so organize their rapidly transforming society, suddenly crowded with an influx of people and goods through industrial development and colonial expropriation. Around or about 1910, the story continues, the artistic imagination changed and novelists like Virginia Woolf and James Joyce, tired of the superficiality of novels (and novelists) that described a world of surfaces, turned their attention to experimental representations of consciousness and other ineffable dimensions. They were helped along the way by Freud, a cataclysmic world war, and then another, all of which progressively eroded the collective sense of social stability that from the early twentieth century was associated with Victorian complacency. Finally, in the latter third of the twentieth century and concurrent with more social upheaval, this time underwritten by technological advancements like cybernetics and information theory, postmodern novelists such as Samuel Beckett, Alain Robbe-Grillet, and William Gass unmasked their own methods of representation as unstable, dynamic, and perspectival. Their metafictional self-consciousness moved us still further from the conceit of mimetic art.

But when we read the Victorian novel without an overdetermining future that frames its representational norms as backward or preliminary to the forms that follow, new critical insights and connections disrupt the conventional chronology summarized above. In a reversal of the mimetic tradition often attributed to nineteenth-century realist novels, in which novelists painstakingly render as accurate a "picture" of social reality as they can, the novels I am writing about imagine and *thus enable* the becoming of the serious woman novelist through the mirror of their own medium; the women novelists who emerged as a group in the twentieth century had to be preceded by their Victorian, fictional projections. Just as metafiction has been largely associated with the postmodern era, critics date the advent of women's narratological sophistication and artistic detachment, almost without exception, to modernists such as Virginia Woolf, Gertrude Stein, and Dorothy Richardson. Their Victorian predecessors, conventional scholarship maintains, were forced to write as honorary men (Eliot), in coded forms of personal protest (the Brontë sisters), or for a second-rate, mostly female audience (nearly everyone else). The feminist recovery of Victorian women writers beginning in the 1970s largely focused on the origin stories of the authors themselves, as titles like *Literary Women* (Ellen Moers, 1976) and *A Literature of Their Own: British Women Novelists from Brontë to Lessing* (Elaine Showalter, 1977) confirm. In its diachronic record of formal innovations in novels by Victorian women, *Victorian Metafiction* advances an argument that feminist criticism has either elided or attributed to modernism. The narrative basis of this argument, moreover, challenges the idea that novels by Victorian women testify to the suppressed or "silenced" emotions the novelists were unable to articulate directly. *Victorian Metafiction* reassesses many novels by Victorian women by examining an aesthetic register that eclipses their personal emotions or experiences with attention to literary form, and so credits them with metafictional, not biographical, self-consciousness—even in novels in which the literary heroine shares a resemblance to the novelist herself. My reading extends from a growing number of studies in feminist narratology that interpret narrative form as a revealing embodiment of historically situated perspectives.[3]

In the following sections, I move toward an analysis that discerns an animating power in Victorian novels. The novels I read, in addition to their intricate indices of social coding, use metafiction to stage a dynamic process whereby the heroine exceeds in art and social resolve the notional woman that a mimetic representation would attempt to "copy." The self-conscious, metafictional tension between the real woman authoring the novel and her fictional counterpart is, in the greater scheme of this book, a more pragmatic enterprise than it might first appear. The constructive agency I attribute to novelist-heroines follows two primary influences, one literary and one philosophical. Michael McKeon's 1991 essay "Writer as Hero: Novelistic Prefigurations and the Emergence of Literary Biography" convinced me of the social utility of the novelist-heroine in the Victorian age. McKeon argues that until the writer-as-subject was imagined in the modern novel, he or she could not occupy a professional role in history: "The novel coalesced as a genre once it was possible to conceive of the narrative subject as fundamentally separable from the external social, historical, and metaphysical forces that were traditionally taken not simply to condition but fully to constitute human existence. In fact, early novels tend to be *about* nothing other than this experience of disengagement—as well as the obstacles that may make it problematic."[4] Novels including Daniel Defoe's *Robinson Crusoe* and Samuel Richardson's *Pamela*, he explains, figured plots that gave the writer distinct power: Crusoe's heroic survival, in a world without witnesses, can only manifest in writing, and Pamela's letters imbue her with the sympathy that leads to her rescue and marriage. The novels about writers I examine tell very different stories, but, as in McKeon's examples, the descriptions of their subjects in fiction preceded—*and so made possible*—their historical emergence. The invention of a new social figure must be imagined before it can be put into practice.

Philosopher Agnes Callard's 2018 book *Aspiration: The Agency of Becoming* also helped me define the agency I am attributing to Victorian novels about novelists. Callard proposes that someone's professional aspiration may be driven by the values associated with that career, but these are projected values that the aspirant must acquire in practice. The process of self-transformation does not depend on inspiration or outside influence, but rather on *doing* the thing itself, and learning how along the way: "We aspire by doing things, and the things that change us so that we are able to do the same things, or things of that kind, better and better. In the beginning, we sometimes feel as though we are pretending, play-acting, or otherwise alienated from our own activity.... As time goes on, however, the fact (if it is a fact) that we are still at it is usually a sign that we find ourselves progressively more able to see, on our own, the value that we could barely apprehend at first."[5]

One of the novelist-heroines examined in this book exemplifies Callard's definition of self-creation. Charlotte Riddell's heroine Glenarva Westley, in *A Struggle for Fame* (1883), wants to be a writer. At first, her desire alone seems enough to transform her into a writer, but her setbacks in the publishing world gradually convince her otherwise. After many years and some unsuccessful novels, Glen finally writes a novel that satisfies her own artistic goals and attracts the praise of her critics. Glen's transformation into a writer dispels the romantic myth of a young girl's "calling" by showing her process of becoming a writer, and so focalizes *A Struggle for Fame* as a metafictional example of what Glen learns—especially since Riddell's novel mirrors many of the literary techniques and preoccupations of Glen's own breakthrough novel. The enactment of writing has more persuasive power than a social judgment ("women can be serious artists"), as it depersonalizes the activity of writing from an individual writer's own experience.

We have widely accepted the idea that a Victorian woman writer wrote "to express herself" in reaction to her repressive, circumscribed culture, and while that was no doubt often true, the intimacy of this lens discredits women's artistic labor as a skill that can be cultivated, taught, and reproduced by women in general. Metafictive portraits of women writers by women writers focus our attention on the work itself (both the fictional writer *at work* and the text in hand) and, in doing so, translate the individual writer's "voice" into a cultural product. Perhaps the most dramatic example of this Victorian phenomenon is Elizabeth Barrett Browning's *Aurora Leigh* (1856), which proleptically describes its own dazzling reception, until then unprecedented by the publication of a woman's poem. Aurora's epic autobiographical poem triumphs despite the critics who pronounced such work outside of a woman's scope. Her friend Vincent Cunningham writes from England to Aurora in Italy:

> We think here you have written a good book,
> And you, a woman! It was in you—yes,
> I felt 'twas in you: yet I doubted ...
> Forgive me. All my heart
> Is quick with yours since, just a fortnight since,
> I read your book and loved it.[6]

Vincent's conversion from skeptic to admirer and his description of "common critics, ordinarily deaf / To such fine meanings" who "praise your book aright"[7] forewarns *Aurora Leigh*'s own detractors not to be obtuse to Barrett Browning's own "fine meanings" in a categorical devaluation of women's poetry.[8] Circulated in periodical writing or criticism, partisan advice for or against a certain type of art or artist can feed a polemic. Narrative poetry and fiction, however, can influence opinion by simulating the social fortune of such a judgment—in this case, preemptively shaming those critics ready to dismiss *Aurora Leigh* based on its author's sex.[9]

The entry of a historically specific figure into narrative form is the central subject of this book. Metafiction's paradoxical combination of self-consciousness and detachment formalizes the evaluation of the Victorian woman novelist on the grounds of her gender—a phenomenon that she would confront by her own metafictional admixture of self-reference (novels by women about women writing novels) and artistic objectification (novelists writing about novel-writing characters in place of autobiography). Exposing novel writing as a process vulnerable to social and personal circumstances, the real novelists studied here slowly forged a professional identity out of the spectral properties of fiction. In the following sections, I set up the conventional understanding of Victorian realism as a historical project to explain why these novels (or others like them) have not been sufficiently acknowledged for their metafictional and experimental qualities. I then unpack metafiction and feminist narratology, contextualizing and separating their formal techniques from the twentieth-century novels they reference most often. In the final part of the introduction, I bring metafiction and feminist narratology into a specifically Victorian literary context, situating them as complementary processes that complicate the record on Victorian realism and women's writing.

Victorian Realisms, Then and Now

An emphasis on historical accuracy underwrites most criticism of the nineteenth-century novel in the twentieth century, with lasting traces into the twenty-first, and so can usurp approaches that employ formal or aesthetic lenses. As already noted, modernism cast realism as a relic of naïve representation, and in the postmodern period, an age that peeled away the surface logic of signifying language, historicized explanations of realism offered a seemingly straightforward example of an outmoded mimesis. Seminal twentieth-century literary histories including Georg Lukács's *The Theory of the Novel* (1916) and Erich Auerbach's *Mimesis: The Representation of Reality in Western Literature* (1946) characterize realism as the literary expression of a historical moment, the apex of which was the age of the "classic" novel of nineteenth-century authors like Goethe, Stendhal, Flaubert, Scott, Dickens, and Eliot. These novelists are said to achieve, especially in the closure of their novels, a totalizing logic that implies a coherent moral and historical perspective. For the Marxist Lukács, the realist novel exemplifies a material ideology that presents itself as coterminous with nature rather than provisional human design, and so its portrayal of bourgeois values effaces the political structures that produce the novel in the first place. The weightiness of these pronouncements, though not their political orientation, informs F. R. Leavis's *The Great Tradition* (1948), which declared the "greatness" of a novelist (Jane Austen, George Eliot, Henry James, Joseph Conrad) in absolute terms that cemented a twentieth-century canon. Pronouncements on realism are not the most obvious of Leavis's critical exertions, but his genealogy of the English novel as a record of "cultural continuity" and "organic interrelatedness" conforms to the representation of historical accuracy and totalizing vision attributed to realism by Auerbach and Lukács. Another formative contribution to the definition of the realist novel in the twentieth century was Ian Watt's *The Rise of the Novel: Studies in Defoe, Richardson, and Fielding* (1957). Watt explains the emergence of the novel in the eighteenth century as the literary distillation of contemporaneous reading practices, economic individualism, and the spread of Protestantism. He treats narrative methods developed in the novel (such as the interest in daily life, idiosyncratic characters and speech, and sociological detail) as formal expressions of the philosophical move toward empirical and individual experience. The novel, then, had a socially constructive role in imagining the consequences of individual actions in a transforming world.

The historical specificity of nineteenth-century realism effectively defines the study of Victorian novels, though inside the field challenges to the mimetic understanding of realism go a long way in destroying the image of the Victorian novel as smugly self-contained and empirically confident. Critics such as Felicia Bonaparte, Audrey Jaffe, George Levine, Harry E. Shaw, and Nancy Armstrong have defined realism as a hypothetical project without distancing themselves from historical context.[10] With clarity and precision, Jaffe's monograph *The Victorian Novel Dreams of the Real: Conventions and Ideology* (2016) articulates the difference between the Victorian attempt to represent the real, which few of us would question, and the assumption by the Victorians that such a thing was possible, which all of us should question. By arguing that "the real" is "an object of desire," Jaffe connects realism with a convention usually posed as its opposite: fantasy. Techniques that are commonly read as signs of materialist confidence, such as sociological detail, the evocation of solid and specific geographies and objects, and recognizable sequences of time and events, then, are not manifestations of a represented reality but an armory of tools for fantasy building.[11] Levine's important recalibration of nineteenth-century realism's imaginative complexity in *The Realistic Imagination: English Fiction from Frankenstein to Lady Chatterley* (1981) also facilitates a connection between the real and the hypothetical. Levine defines realism as a historical phenomenon, but insists that it was a method of representation, not the achievement of representation. More recently, Anna Kornbluh has urged an "enhanced attention" to "literary realism as the production of possible spaces rather than the document of existing places" as an antidote to the field's proliferations of granular history and (re)confirmations of Foucauldian ideological control.[12] Such versions and visions of realism, stressing its capacity for model building rather than its declarative power, prepare the ground for further work that can take realism's capacity for experimentation as a given, and apply narrative techniques not often associated with the Victorian novel.

Felicia Bonaparte's emphasis on creative power in *The Poetics of Poesis: The Making of Nineteenth-Century English Fiction* (2016) aligns especially well with my argument for the constitutive power of novels about writer-heroines. Bonaparte interrupts the conventional emphasis on nineteenth-century realism's mimetic efforts to insert the Greek understanding of *poesis*—or "making"—as integral to the art form. Nineteenth-century English novels, by this account, did not aim to reflect reality but rather "understood the end of art to be the creation of a new world."[13] Bonaparte credits the German Romantics and especially Schlegel with this visionary influence on nineteenth-century novels, and in their "fusion of real and ideal," she explains, they "cannot but become reflexive": "The self-consciousness Schlegel speaks of is the awareness of the artist in the very work of art that, to accomplish this remaking, he needs to create a kind of art that creates a kind of world. . . . Such self-consciousness in art tends to turn fiction towards metafiction."[14] Here Bonaparte accounts for the critical neglect of nineteenth-century metafiction: "So strong a grip has [a mimetic understanding of realism] had on the mind of the twentieth century and still, on the whole, on the twenty-first, that all too often when something disputes the hypothesis of 'realism,' it is rarely seen as a challenge to the hypothesis itself but as an error in the artist's execution of his purpose. . . . And whenever it has become overwhelmingly obvious that some individual work cannot be cataloged under 'realism,' it has been unceremoniously moved to a totally different period."[15]

Most of the metafictional novels that I write about in this book have not been missed through artistic error, because they have not garnered much critical attention at all. In the period of their original reception, however, Bonaparte's assessment holds. The metafictional elements in *Villette, Cometh Up as a Flower, The Autobiography of Christopher Kirkland*, and *The Type-Writer Girl*, as I explore later, were all identified by critics as aberrations, weaknesses, and in the case of Rhoda Broughton, evidence that she was "too much of a rattle . . . to build a careful plot."[16] Because women's fiction was consigned to a lesser status, these novels were more likely to be summarily dismissed than probed for points of artistic failure. Regarding Bonaparte's complaint that nineteenth-century novels that "cannot be cataloged under 'realism'" are moved "to a totally different period," I pursue the other side of this equation by comparing Victorian novels to novels by authors such as J. L. Borges, Kurt Vonnegut, and Margaret Atwood.

Victorian Metafiction differs from *The Poetics of Poesis* in the connections I draw between poesis and cultural production: Bonaparte's conceptions of novelistic "making" refer to a largely mythopoetic realm. To me, women's representations of women writers materially contributed to the serious or literary woman novelist, a figure that in the early and mid-Victorian era either escapes notice or courts mockery. That material contribution, moreover, displays metafiction's capacity to reflect and embody at the same time: as Barrett Browning writes in *Aurora Leigh*, "The artist's part is both to be and do."[17] My first chapter, "Metafiction in 'Novel Guise': Charlotte Brontë's *Villette*," examines narrator/writer Lucy Snowe's ambivalent self-disclosure against the long-standing interpretative tradition whereby women's novels are assumed to be autobiographical, a supposition that undermines artistic craft. With roots in the eighteenth century and repurposed in the 1970s as a mode of self-empowerment, this tradition wielded particular—and unwelcome—influence on the reception of Brontë's novels. Since the publication of *Jane Eyre* (1847), Brontë was dogged by a public fascination with her sex, morality, and personal life that often shaped the critical assessment of her fiction. In *Villette* (1853), writer-heroine Lucy Snowe answers this public scrutiny by writing a text that makes biographical and confessional interpretations discursively impossible. *Villette* in this way closely resembles Thomas Carlyle's *Sartor Resartus* (1836) in its deconstruction of autobiographical record and its self-aware narratological standoffs. Like Brontë's, Lucy's habit of deferring meaning onto fictional proxies likewise disrupts a biographical interpretation, and rather than signaling her own repressed emotions, emphasizes the fictionality of her writing. If Brontë could not control the attention she received in life, she could construct a novel that puts its withholding narrator in the seat of power.

My second chapter reads Broughton's controversial novel *Cometh Up as a Flower* (1867) in parodic reference to the same cultural and literary script that casts the Brontë sisters as tragic heroines instead of celebrated authors. Nell LeStrange, Broughton's autobiography-writing heroine, veers into fiction as she self-consciously borrows literary tropes. In seeking a kind of poetic justice, she enhances the story of her life with romantic conventions that lend it meaning and closure. But a parodic element inflects her tale, and Nell's conflation of the roles of a woman writer and tragic heroine gestures toward melodrama—as does her death from consumption at the end of the novel. This chapter closes with a reading of Broughton's final novel, *A Fool in Her Folly* (1920), which extends her satire of the Victorian woman writer, a victim of her own genius and obsessed with suffering, into the modern era. A metafictional reading of this little-known novel asserts Broughton's canny awareness of the naïve introspection attributed to Victorian women's writing. The links between Broughton's novels and the Brontë canon, too, contribute to metafiction's intertextual mode of critique, evidence of what Julia Kristeva calls a "hidden interior polemic," by which one literary discourse echoes and distorts another.[18]

In chapter 3, I focus on Charlotte Riddell's unjustly neglected *A Struggle for Fame* (1883) as a lesson in the critique of the novel as an art form, a reading that has been overshadowed by autobiographical interpretation. A comparable text, Margaret Oliphant's *The Athelings* (1857), anticipates Riddell's fully realized metafictionality. Where Oliphant's Agnes Atheling ends her writing career when she (presumably) marries a skeptic of "lady novelists," the marriage between Riddell's Glen and her husband is never fully reconciled to Glen's career, an ambivalence that enriches the portrait of her professional ambition. Success comes to Glen when she liberates her writing from the modest domestic sphere that comprises her life, and that, according to the publishing world, should also command the subject of her fiction. She teaches herself to write in the style of Eliot, developing her brand of realism in opposition to the generic prescriptions for feminine writing. Riddell's tacit implication that her own novel is a working example of Glen's efforts teaches the reader how to read serious realism by a woman writer in a book that becomes its own object lesson.

Chapter 4, "Pseudonymity as Metafiction," begins by analyzing a publishing trend that may at first appear peripheral: the woman writer's adoption of a male pseudonym. Instead of considering how the pseudonym silences the woman writer, I examine the opportunities afforded by a wholly fictional male perspective, first in two brief late-Victorian novels written under male pseudonyms, Julia Frankau's satire *Dr. Philips* (1887), published by "Frank Danby," and Margaret Harkness's deft social critique *A City Girl* (1887), published by "John Law." In the second half of the chapter, I turn to Eliza Lynn Linton's generically elliptical *The Autobiography of Christopher Kirkland* (1885). Where many critics seek to confirm Linton's life in her portrait of Christopher, my reading follows the cue of the (fictional) autobiographer and approaches the novel's experimental design through the example of postmodern novels, especially those that demand an erasure of what we know about the "real" author. Linton's novel fits Linda Hutcheon's designation of "historical metafiction" in its self-conscious use of both genres—a designation rarely attached to nineteenth-century novels.[19]

The final chapter in *Victorian Metafictions* takes a current genre—neo-Victorian fiction—and explores its precedent in two New Woman novels of the 1890s: *The Type-Writer Girl* (1897) by Grant Allen (writing as Olive Pratt Rayner), and *A Writer of Books* (1898) by Emily Morse Symonds (writing as George Paston). These novels deftly explore the marginalized stature of the woman writer to show her exclusion from serious realism, a challenge that the novelist-heroines comment on and correct with metafiction. In their self-conscious attention to constructed identity and marginal points of view, these novels align with contemporary neo-Victorian novels. They also make the process of invention, not representation, the crux of the plot; the writer-heroines cannot realize their own careers as novelists until they create fictional proxies for themselves—an irony subtly refracted on Rayner (herself a fictional novelist) and Paston (a proxy for Morse Symonds). When Paston's novelist-heroine Cosima Chudleigh aspires to write "the most precious and difficult thing of all[,] ... the effect of growth, change, and development,"[20] she encapsulates the plot of *A Writer of Books*.

The conclusion discusses the legacy of Virginia Woolf's dismissive treatment of Victorian women writers as narrowly sentimental and hostage to approved conventions. The robust history of metafiction by Victorian women that this book uncovers testifies to their contribution to the development of "the novel"—an achievement obscured by biographical interpretations of the writers' individual lives as well as a common focus on social history in fiction of the period. Ironically, by replacing efforts to "recover" these authors, metafictional analyses testify to a more triumphantly feminist understanding of their *novels*. The conclusion ends with a short study of Elizabeth Taylor as a modernist who reflects quite seriously on Victorian women's metafiction. Her

1957 novel *Angel* satirizes the trope of the self-absorbed "authoress" so cannily that it exposes metafictional self-consciousness to be the cultural burden of the late-Victorian woman novelist. While *Angel* is caustically funny, it also sympathizes with the intellectual alienation of the woman writer and, indirectly, testifies to her struggle to produce the art that Woolf derides.

Metafiction's Postmodern Determinants

The term "metafiction" is usually attributed to the novelist and critic William Gass or to the critic Robert Scholes,[21] and critical monographs about metafiction started to appear in the 1970s, sometimes using the related terms "self-conscious fiction," "reflexive fiction," "surfiction," and "historiographic metafiction."[22] As a narratological operation and without historically contextualizing details, metafictional novels refer to their own artifice, often making the assemblage of the novel a part of the story. For Mark Currie, metafiction occupies a border territory between fiction (the willing suspension of reality) and criticism (the insistence on objectivity).[23] As Linda Hutcheon explains in one of the early formal studies of its kind, *Narcissistic Narrative: The Metafictional Paradox* (1980), there are overt and covert ways to register metafiction. A novel might inspire the reader's awareness of metafictionality indirectly through the reader's interpretative work. For instance, Doris Lessing's *The Golden Notebook* (1962) examines the life of heroine Anna Wulf in sections named for color-collated notebooks, each with a different organizing feature (the black notebook describes Anna's success as a novelist, the red notebook her disenchantment with the Communist Party, and so on). In moving between these various framings of Anna's stories, the reader consciously tries to adjust their inconsistencies, thus modeling the very interpretive struggle and identity fragmentation that the collection of discrete notebooks represents. Metafictions that make their self-conscious operations more explicit may feature an author "interrupting" his or her own story, as we see in *The French Lieutenant's Woman* (1969), where the novelist John Fowles compares his role as narrator to that associated with nineteenth-century realism and the Victorian setting of his novel. A classic example of an overt metafictional presence is the narrator of Laurence Sterne's *The Life and Opinions of Tristram Shandy, Gentleman* (1759–67), wherein digressions on the expectations of fictional convention constantly interrupt the story.

A sample of critical studies of metafiction written between 1975 and 1988[24] by critics including Hutcheon, Robert Alter, and Patricia Waugh reveals several common patterns. These books often open with an acknowledgment that metafiction is not a historical phenomenon per se, and the texts usually carted in to demonstrate this are *Don Quixote* and *Tristram Shandy*.[25] Most critics single out the nineteenth-century realistic (or specifically Victorian) novel as a point when metafiction disappeared or was eclipsed by the positivistic sentiment of the day, which I discuss in detail below. Several cite Joyce, Beckett, and sometimes Woolf as modernist predecessors to the genre, and all but Christensen, who focuses on the mid-twentieth century, agree that the 1960s confluence of post-structural philosophy, a tumultuous historical age, and a probing self-consciousness across art forms led to the explosion of postmodern metafiction. In *Narcissistic Narrative*, Hutcheon notes an evolving tradition of self-consciousness but uses "postmodernism" and "metafiction" almost interchangeably; as she explains in the preface to the 1984 edition, she chose "metafiction" of the two terms for her title because it was "more descriptive" and because she was limiting her purview to literature and not other arts.[26]

The invincibility of the mimetic project in nineteenth-century realism is another critical commonplace in studies of metafiction. Waugh concedes that "metafiction is . . . a tendency [or function] . . . inherent in all novels" but singles out the nineteenth-century realistic novel as her counterexample to metafictional self-consciousness and irony. "In the case of nineteenth-century realism," she writes, "the forms of fiction derived from a firm belief in a commonly experienced, objectively existing world of history."[27] Currie claims that metafictional characteristics can be found throughout the history of the novel, but his examples skirt the Victorian age and include the elaborate framings of Chaucer's *Canterbury Tales*; Shakespeare's plays-within-plays; and novelists such as Fielding, Richardson, and Austen (though only in *Northanger Abbey*), whom he calls "precursors" to postmodern metafictionalists.[28] Using the nineteenth-century realist novel as a foil for metafiction is pervasive: "For the historian of the self-conscious novel . . . the nineteenth century was something of an aberration. It marked the triumph of the 'realistic' novel, which eschewed any suggestion of contingency behind the façade of its illusion"[29]; "[the realistic novel's] confidence in man's ability to know, to make sense of the universe, reaches a high point in the nineteenth century, which was not coincidentally the age of the great realistic novel."[30] Even Hutcheon, for whom the nineteenth-century novel participates in "a dialectical literary progression from one kind of novelistic mimesis to another," qualifies its representational reach: "The realism of the nineteenth-century [novel] . . . is based almost entirely on what will be called a mimesis of product."[31]

Perhaps the critic most invested in framing metafiction as the sophisticated inverse of nineteenth-century realism is Alter. In *Partial Magic: The Novel as a Self-Conscious Genre* (1975), Alter considers why metafiction jumps from Sterne and Fielding in the eighteenth century to Woolf and Joyce in the twentieth, without any significant contribution in between. For Alter, nineteenth-century novelists "under the urgent pressure of history" turned a politically conscious eye to "the sheer mechanics of contemporary life." The French Revolution's shattering of inherited hierarchies, which continued in early and mid-nineteenth-century revolutions elsewhere in Europe and intermittently threatened England, pushed novelists to "engage [with] historical reality" and so "reconstitute" in artistic form the fragmented post-Napoleonic world. The novels of the age, he continues, treat "society" and "the nineteenth century" as "clearly discernible entities, distinct and scientifically describable in the forces they exerted on individual lives."[32]

Beyond Alter, many critics of metafiction argue that history before the postmodern age was relatively transparent and so easier to represent. When Waugh, writing in the early 1980s, points to the boom of metafiction in the 1970s, she explains that "over the last twenty years, novelists have tended to become much more aware of the theoretical issues involved in constructing fictions," and also that "structures of contemporary society are . . . more diverse and more effectively concealed or mystified, creating greater problems for the post-modernist novelist in identifying and then representing the object of 'opposition.'"[33] Noting that Waugh's explicit reference to "nineteenth-century realism" defines her "past," we can extrapolate the following: in the nineteenth century there was (1) consensus in the fictional construction of good and evil, heroes and villains; (2) society was homogeneous and transparent; and (3) novelists did not probe or doubt their representational techniques. But no nineteenth-century scholar could agree with this summary. We might more readily concede a subversion of each point, with the novels of this period reflecting (1) the characteristics of moral ambiguity; (2a) a rapidly diversifying society; (2b) the advent of structural materialism and apprehension of relative value; and (3) an ongoing dialogue in novels about the capacity of fictional representation. If one were to mine the depths of nineteenth-century fiction to find illustrative examples of

Waugh's versions of points one through three above—the moralistic universe represented in a stable culture without any representational hesitation—the options are more limited. We might cite the following example: "I knew from every tone of his voice, every chance expression of his honest eyes, that he was one of those characters in which we may be sure that for each feeling they express lies a countless wealth of the same, unexpressed below; a character the keystone of which was that whereon is built all liking and all love—DEPEND-ABLENESS. He was one whom you may be long in knowing, but whom the more you know the more you trust; and once trusting, you trust forever."[34]

In this quote from *John Halifax, Gentleman* (1856), Dinah Mulock Craik's narrator, Phineas Fletcher, describes his new friend John Halifax with a moral clarity almost biblical in its repetitiveness. Through the many twists and turns of this novel, John never strays from being DEPENDABLE and, as one would predict, his sterling character is dutifully rewarded by "society." The novel fits Waugh's summary of nineteenth-century fiction—"nineteenth-century realism . . . derived from a firm belief in a commonly experienced, objectively existing world of history"[35]—but not realism or the canonicity she implies: *John Halifax, Gentleman* is a sentimental and didactic novel, known to scholars for these features and rarely taught in college or university classrooms. It is intermittently out of print (though used copies available on the internet and the inscriptions in them testify to its successful afterlife as a prize for Sunday-school attendance or graduation from parochial school).[36] Reading about nineteenth-century realism in criticism primarily devoted to postmodern-era metafiction inspires logical reversals, like the one of Waugh's summary posed above, or internal dialogues that refute the invariably confident claims with Victorian examples interjected: "Culture in the nineteenth century was charged with a positivistic optimism ["Dover Beach"] about its ability to find out what makes man and the universe tick [*Middlemarch*]. This optimism may have encouraged the literary culture to use the novel as a tool, one designed both to acquire such knowledge experimentally [*Jude the Obscure*], and to disseminate it confidently [*New Grub Street*]."[37] Nineteenth-century realism's positivist achievement is nowhere more triumphant than in the summaries of late twentieth-century critics who do not seem to have read it.

In *The Politics of Reflexivity: Narrative and the Constitutive Poetics of Culture* (1986), Robert Siegle explores self-conscious narratives under the heading of "reflexive fictions" in a way that avoids the historicized dismissal of nineteenth-century metafiction, though that is not his primary objective. He contends that the doubled-back cycle indicated by "reflexive" differs from an inward turn toward self-consciousness both narratologically and politically. If "narcissistic" metafiction retreats from the referential field of a text by myopically revisiting its semiotic roots, his more dispassionate "reflexive" allows for a self-conscious examination of a narrative as well as that narrative's inevitable reflection of a particular cultural and political perspective. The novels he studies, W. M. Thackeray's *Vanity Fair* (1848), Conrad's *Chance* (1913), Robert Penn Warren's *World Enough and Time* (1950), and Fowles's *The French Lieutenant's Woman*, all manifest the techniques of metafictional self-commentary, but also probe and critique the social assumptions of their ages and locales. Reading *Vanity Fair*, Siegle suggests that the narrative voice in the novel is not simply an individual narrator (and certainly not the historical individual Thackeray), but a perspective representing the same rising bourgeois culture the novel parodies. Siegle's designation of a wider cultural target accommodates the novel's generic mishmash (of the Newgate novel, the sentimental novel, the historical novel, and so on) and its many discursive sources (including theology, colonialism, and drama), and so illustrates the combustible and heterogeneous period of Thackeray's novel rather than the fitful thinking of an inconsistent novelist. This is a brilliant reading of the novel in part because Siegle insistently foregrounds how *Vanity Fair*'s erratic plot and destabilized perspective upset beyond recognition the staid "Victorian age" so often nodded to in studies of later novel forms.

Most of the critics I have been citing are not scholars of nineteenth-century literature, and most of my sources date to the period when metafiction was named, approximately between 1970 and 1985. Criticism of the Victorian novel today is rich in its approaches and critical innovations, and within it an oversimplification of the novel as a mimetic tool neither endures nor dominates. And yet a historical bias, or what Jaffe calls "the idea of a real behind realism" and underwriting methodologies including New Historicism, thing theory, and surface reading, is still present, and arguably dominant.[38] These methodologies have greatly contributed to our knowledge, but their recovery of historical knowledge and context does not challenge our period-specific understanding of "the novel" as often as it alerts us to deeper and deeper readings of Victorian history. Further, the scholars of metafiction that I have characterized as disserving Victorian and nineteenth-century fiction—not to be confused with current scholars with a material or historical focus—named and defined metafiction. As a description of a kind of novel, metafiction has therefore been overwhelmingly identified with later twentieth-century fiction based on an expedient understanding of nineteenth-century fiction. And while most of the critics cited here do nod to metafiction's status as a narrative technique rather than a historically specific definition, none of them does justice to the metafictional complexities of Victorian novels. Either they haven't read *Sartor Resartus, Vanity Fair, Wuthering Heights* (1847), *Villette, Great Expectations* (1861), *Dombey and Son* (1848), *Bleak House* (1853), *Adam Bede* (1859), *Middlemarch* (1871), or any of the novels of Wilkie Collins (to provide only a representative control group), or they have read them through the historical bias reflected in Alter and Waugh's work—an a priori lens of interpretation— without also considering the ontologically ambiguous narratological features that can complicate even novels heavy with information and detail.

The history of the era that was defining metafiction brings into relief another likely variable in the bias that linked "Victorian" to "unprogressive" and "naïve"—a bias still persistently attached to the period by peripheral literary eras and fields. In the run-up to her reelection campaign in 1983, Margaret Thatcher proposed that a return to "Victorian values" would steer the United Kingdom out of recession and extensive unemployment. The social resonance of "Victorian" echoed conservative principles, an austerity campaign, and certainly more of the blacking factory than the rise of mass literacy. Unhappily for Thatcherites, the historical evocation also resounded with sexual hypocrisy, as a wave of philandering MPs and the exposé of a pedophiliac sex ring linked to Downing Street and Parliament recalled the exploitative sexual hierarchies of the actual Victorian age. Postmodernists likely to be dismissive of totalizing histories on a theoretical level might nevertheless have been primed to assume an opposition between radically decentered metafiction and the narrowly conservative Victorianism, extending to the novel, evoked by Thatcherism.

Of the critical works I have cited so far, Siegle's study of reflexive fiction offers the most cogent critique of conflating a narrative operation with a particular historical period. He cites the "myth" that reflexivity is "a distinctly historical fad": "The worst form of this myth is one that views eighteenth-century fiction as emerging from satire and apologue through reflexivity towards nineteenth-century realism, when the novel reached its zenith as the revelation of moral truth and order; in the twentieth century, sadly enough, the novel lost confidence in itself and has gradually degenerated into such symptoms of unreliable narration, hopelessly reflexive disparagement of its own truth claims, fabulation, and the like."[39] Siegle's teleology of the development of the novel resembles mine until we get to the relative values ascribed to nineteenth-century and twentieth-century novels. For Siegle, the nineteenth-century assumption of realistic authority marks the apex of the novel's cultural status, with its twentieth-century antecedents unable to claim certainty and so cultural power. For me, the reductive treatment of nineteenth-century realism as a mimetic project credits modernist forms with awareness of language's inability to replicate life; I read Siegle's terms of disappointment (in modern and postmodern novels) as signs of sophistication: "reflexive," "disparagement of truth claims," "fabulation," and so on. But regardless of our disagreement about the loci of novelistic authority, we agree that narrative techniques like metafiction or reflexive fiction can be co-opted by one era or another and over-identified with the socio-history of a literary period. "Realism" so automatically registers "Victorian" (or "nineteenth century")—and thus an understanding of representational confidence (or naïveté)—that we are unlikely to subject it to analyses alongside postmodern literature. The historical approach has engulfed these terms on a functional, if not always consciously theoretical, basis.

As nineteenth-century realism defined itself against the popular forms more accessible to women writers, its perspectival assumptions were gendered accordingly. The assumption of a male subject position in descriptions of nineteenth-century realism is nowhere more explicit than in its purported relationship to history. When Alter argues that the momentous changes of nineteenth-century life demanded purposeful not reflective novels, he cannot be describing the work of a woman author: "There is an obvious fascination in the nineteenth-century novel with the sheer mechanics of contemporary life—in politics, commerce, class relations, industry, crime, education, entertainment, virtually every sphere.... One must not forget that in an age of rapidly expanding audiences and serial publication, the novel was enormously important as a source of information in a way it had not been before and would not be afterward."[40] To assume that a woman writer had the same access to and authority over any of the public spheres on Alter's list, or that she may have been able to simply channel her "fascination" with these subjects into an informative novel, is to ignore the historical record of women's experiences in publishing and the novels they wrote. The challenges a woman faced in writing about class relations, for instance, explain Gaskell's mollifying narrative voice in novels including *Mary Barton* (1848) and *North and South* (1854). Robyn Warhol has described this voice as the work of the "engaging" female narrator who must don her cloak of authority cautiously, as differentiated from the "distancing" male narrator, who can write declaratively.[41] I realize that in challenging Alter I'm arguing with someone who wrote what he wrote in 1978, but as with the critical definitions of metafiction and feminist novels, this logic gets archived in the vault of "the nineteenth-century novel" and continues, if invisibly, to shape the field. Because of such chronological norms, our interpretations often start inside of inherited historical barriers, and the juxtaposition of "Victorian" with "metafiction" or "experimental feminist fiction"—as I've found while writing this book—sounds incongruous and suspect.

Translated into narratological agency, the difference between a woman writer reflecting on her writing and anticipating how it will be received and a male writer writing something that speaks for itself—that when uttered, enters the universe impartially—is the very difference between the way that realism has been ascribed to "the Victorians" and the way Victorian women wrote. Women writers did not have the authority or privilege to write without looking over their shoulder at their writing and pondering its fate and their own as the very same. When *Jane Eyre* was deemed un-Christian, Charlotte Brontë was scuttled out from under the cover of Currer Bell and called amoral. In a preemptive public-relations move, she wrote semi-fictionalized portraits of her sisters to make their novels more palpable to a censorious audience that would judge *Wuthering Heights* and *Agnes Grey* (1847) through the docility-meter of their authors. Novelists as different as George Eliot and Mary Braddon scandalized their readers by living with married men, a sin with significant consequences on artistic reception. When the authority of realism is oversimplified in descriptions of nineteenth-century novels, it is a male novelist who constitutes the cultural ground zero that gets harnessed into statements about Victorian novels' "unselfconscious faith"[42] in representation, "confidence in man's ability to know,"[43] and a "firm belief in the commonly experienced, objectively existing world of history."[44] Susan Lanser's response to sweeping claims about nineteenth-century realism underscores the determining power of gender: "It seems likely that realism's conventions of powerful, public narrative voices authorized to mediate important contemporary questions at a time of particularly rigid separation between 'male' and 'female' spheres, supported a masculine authorial identity and legitimated the squeezing out of women from the ranks of 'serious' novelists."[45] Thomas Carlyle summarizes the masculine nature of nineteenth-century individualism when he writes that "the History of the world is but the Biography of great men."[46] In contrast is John Stuart Mill's observation that "all the education that women receive from society inculcates on them the feeling that the individuals connected with them are the only ones to whom they own any duty."[47] Victorian women's impersonal proclamations upon objective knowledge fields and genres, as Linda Peterson has shown in her extensive work on Victorian autobiography, are very rare.[48]

If the critics cited earlier (Waugh, Currie, Stonehill) use nineteenth-century realism to register a time when representational language and its object were fused, and attributed the fissure between a semiotic sign and its referent to the forward-thinking modernists or postmodernists,[49] Levine explodes that literary history, locating in realism a range of dissonant operations: "There is . . . a continuing tradition of self-consciousness in realistic fiction, a tradition formally initiated in *Don Quixote*. The self-consciousness marks realism's awareness both of other literatures and of the strategies necessary to circumvent it, and—at last— its awareness of its own unreality."[50] Self-consciousness, formative roots in *Don Quixote*, and awareness of artificiality . . . Levine could be describing metafiction. A formal allegiance between realism and metafiction sounds somewhat less incongruous than that between Victorian and postmodern fiction, if only because the former pair's chronological association is implicit rather than explicit.

Even so, comparing Victorian novels to postmodern novels is an unpopular but not wholly original activity. Jay Clayton makes a striking case for it in "Dickens and the Genealogy of Postmodernism" (1991). Clayton begins his essay by noting the virtual absence of references to Dickens, as well as other canonical Victorians, in a sample of forty-odd studies of postmodernism.[51] (My experience with a modest pool of a smaller field, metafiction, largely corroborates this absence, except for the all-purpose connotation of "nineteenth-century realism" that functions as metafiction's foil.) But when Clayton reorganizes our familiar entry points into Dickens away from the historical causality that periodization fosters, the picture changes. Dickens's proliferation of pigeonholed secondary characters, the encroachment of the marketplace on all facets of social and even emotional life, and the labyrinthine experience of the modern city all resemble facets of postmodernism. And because another theoretical underpinning of the movement is its radically unfettered-by-history existence, applying postmodern qualities "backward" should not be a conceptual problem. Clayton is not so much working to reorient Dickens scholarship as he is exposing the shaping expectations that we inherit from conventional literary history. Interpreting on a formal plane instead of through the connective tissue of a localized new historical approach does not change Dickens, but it can, as Clayton says, "help us rethink the relation that exists between his use of [postmodern narrative] technique[s] and the social world."[52] This kind of conventionally anachronistic pairing can also reveal the depth to which even Victorian literary scholars unconsciously decide what they will find before reading a new novel—or at least have in mind certain horizons of expectation.

Feminist Criticism and the Elision of Metafiction

If critics of metafiction ignore the Victorian novel in their history of the technique or single it out as metafiction's opposite, their contemporaries, second-wave feminist literary critics in the 1970s, devoted thorough attention to nineteenth-century novels written by women. Books like *A Literature of Their Own* and *The Madwoman in the Attic: The Woman Writer and the Nineteenth-Century Literary Imagination* (Sandra M. Gilbert and Susan Gubar, 1979) examined canonical authors such as Jane Austen, Mary Shelley, the Brontës, Elizabeth Gaskell, and George Eliot and lesser-known writers, too, such as Maria Edgeworth, Frances Trollope, Ellen Wood, and Olive Schreiner. The dominant interpretation of Victorian women novelists was that patriarchal culture forced them to submerge their language of protest and their challenges to the patriarchy into coded or symbolic plots. In *Breaking the Sequence: Women's Experimental Fiction* (1989), for instance, editors Ellen G. Friedman and Miriam Fuchs argue that nineteenth-century women novelists "expressed dissatisfaction with or ambivalence toward prevailing ideas of appropriate behavior in fiction and life through covert means—subtexts, minor characters, patterns of imagery . . . [—making] hidden or disguised challenges to patriarchal notions of fiction."[53] Were women to articulate their repressive condition directly, the argument goes, they would inhibit their chances of being published in an industry owned, managed, and primarily evaluated by men, and they would also likely compromise their personal relationships and social standing.

Two related critical discourses enriched this sociohistorical argument. The influence in the 1970s and 1980s of French semiotics led critics including Julia Kristeva, Luce Irigaray, Hélène Cixous, and Mary Jacobus to argue that the patriarchal basis of language prevented women from authentic discursive protest. Irigaray asked, "How can women analyze their exploitation and make their claims within an order prescribed by the masculine? Is a women's politics possible therein?"[54] Psychoanalytic criticism contributed to this approach by refuting text for subtext in an interpretive parallel of the Freudian search for the subconscious as the essence and agent of personal identity. Psychoanalysis enabled feminist critics to identify female subject positions that may only exist under the surface of normative culture, or in coded or symbolic form. Charlotte Brontë could gesture to gender inequality by making Jane Eyre testy and self-sufficient before soothing these energies in a happy marriage, but her real political act was the monstrous, vengeful Bertha, the repressed Victorian woman's id writ large. Ann Heilmann, in *New Woman Strategies: Sarah Grand, Olive Schreiner, and Mona Caird* (2004), reads the New Woman novel of the 1880s and 1890s through French feminist theory, which she finds an apt model for their mimicry, femininity, self-reflexivity, subversion, and libidinality.[55] In contrast and as I clarify in chapter 5, my historicized interpretation of metafiction treats these formal strategies as inextricable from cultural and literary politics.

Consensus about encoded political messages in nineteenth-century women's fiction did not stimulate a strong tradition of work on the textual level of these novels, although there are important exceptions to this rule—especially the work of Heilmann, Lanser, and Warhol—that I describe elsewhere in this book. Most feminist critics from this era situate narratological innovation in modernist writers, almost always starting with Woolf. Rachel Blau DuPlessis, in *Writing beyond the Ending: Narrative Strategies of Twentieth-Century Women Writers* (1985), typifies this chronology: "It is the project of twentieth-century women writers to solve the contradiction between love and quest and to replace the alternate endings in marriage or death that are their cultural legacy from nineteenth-century life and letters by offering a different set of choices. They invent a complex of narrative acts with psychosocial meanings.... Twentieth-century women writers ... who examine how social practices surrounding gender have entered narrative ... consequently use narrative to make critical statements about the psychosexual and sociocultural construction of women."[56] Blau DuPlessis's description of "narrative acts" in women's writing attributes formal transformation of the novel to historical feminist achievements, which other critics corroborate. According to Friedman and Fuchs, "twentieth-century women experimental writers" force the transition from covert to overt rebellion by making use of "radical forms—nonlinear, nonhierarchical, and decenter[ed]."[57] In the first volume of *No Man's Land: The Place of the Woman Writer in the Twentieth Century* (1988), a sequel to *Madwoman in the Attic*, Gilbert and Gubar offer tepid praise to the nineteenth-century women who "may have empowered twentieth century women writers to change the shape and scope of their fiction," if primarily by conceptualizing a mold to be broken: "Instead of the female author functioning, if at all, in women's narratives as a repressed or maddened figure who is eclipsed by the docile heroine, she now [in the twentieth century] appears in the work, though often ambiguously, as the representative of a powerful alternative to the plot which she nevertheless still fashions."⁵⁸

Other books tell the same story in their inclusion of who qualifies as a worthy subject of feminist narratology. Editor Kathy Mezei's selection of essays in *Ambiguous Discourse: Feminist Narratology and British Women Writers* (1996) opens with three essays about Austen, and then the chronology skips approximately 100 years and resumes with several essays about Woolf, and others about Mina Loy, Anita Brookner, and Angela Carter. Austen earns inaugural credit, the Victorians are eclipsed, and serious narratological innovations emerge in the twentieth century.

The twentieth century, moreover, is often the source of change—not the writers themselves. Nancy Gray in *Language Unbound: On Experimental Writing by Women* (1992) writes that

> [modernism] provided an especially active context for women writers seeking to break old bonds. . . . Modernism is generally regarded as a time of global upheaval that altered perceptions of reality, fragmented any preconceptualized reliance on coherence or stability, and produced revolutions in artistic form and intellectual thought. Writers sought word-forms for human consciousness, dispensed with linearity of plot and time, and created voices and styles that interrogated the very foundations of what constitutes meaning, perception, self-in-the-world, and art. Such innovations are potentially well suited to dispensing with fictional Woman and investigating a/any woman as herself.⁵⁹

Gray situates the narrative revelation of authentic womanhood during the tumultuous early twentieth century in an argument that, as with most definitions of realism, begins with the historical age and sees how a subject—here, the narrative construction of unfiltered feminine subjectivity—reflects it. In an earlier essay, Judith Kegan Gardiner writes about the manipulation of narrative as a critical literary move but also as a self-conscious evocation of a woman writer's own life that needed modernism to ignite it: "Twentieth-century women writers express the experience of their own identity in what and how they write, often with a sense of urgency and excitement in the communication of truths just understood."⁶⁰ Just understood? Were Mary Wollstonecraft and Charlotte Brontë unacquainted with subjection? The historicized nature of this argument creates another de facto Victorian world that is unrecognizable to a Victorian scholar: a time when women did not write to express their own opinions but presumably thought they were imitating "life," and when they were unaware of their alienation from social power, and when they experienced no pressure to instigate change. I doubt any critic would say this so starkly, but again I am illustrating the ease with which an overly simplified version of the Victorian novel, or the Victorian woman writer, is activated by revolutionary statements about the narrative forms and artists that followed.

In "Feminist Aesthetics and the New Realism" (1992), Laura Marcus lucidly addresses the conflation between modernism and feminist form, showing the way that the latter has developed out of a particular historical context. Feminist debates, she writes, tend to claim that a "feminist aesthetic" is intrinsically modernist or avant-garde. Among the diverse usages of the term "modernism," one can distinguish two in particular: (1) a focus on subjectivity and the complex workings of consciousness, with the often related claim that subjectivity is intrinsically fragmented; and (2) modernist writing as linguistically innovative, self-reflexive, and subversive of received wisdoms and traditional narratives.[61] In the same way that metafiction has been treated as equivalent to postmodernism, feminist aesthetics in the novel have been defined as an extension or invention of the twentieth century. Friedman and Fuchs's exploration of the epistemological assumptions that underwrite modernism and postmodernism corroborates the association between modernity and experimentalism in women's fiction, and they argue, like me, for a new chronology. But where I am locating experimental narratives in Victorian women's fiction, their charge of anachronism has a shorter history. Writing in 1984, they argue that "over 80 years of women's experimental narratives need to be recovered and recognized," which brings us to a new beginning of the experimental tradition: the work of Woolf, followed by that of Richardson and Stein.[62] Likewise, Lanser's chapter in *Fictions of Authority* (1992) on Eliot's appropriation of male power is followed by a chapter on Woolf's experimentalism, but there is no explanation of the passage from adaptation to innovation.[63] The connotations of "Victorian" and "modernist" seem to do this work in shorthand. *Victorian Metafiction* engages rather unfashionably with criticism on metafiction and women's writing from the 1970s and 1980s because it is this critical foundation, I argue, that still explains our disinclination to read nineteenth-century novels as metafictional. In other words, the reasons why we seldom put these genres together has a history, and by deconstructing that history we can better identify new connections between these novels and critical approaches less often applied to Victorian novels.

The metafictional approach in this book takes issue with the quest for an author's authentic voice so central to the second-wave feminist project. But how much influence, a reader might fairly ask, does the second-wave feminist critical tradition still wield today? The revolutionary spirit articulated in books like *The Madwoman in the Attic* and *A Literature of their Own* has faded, but some of the basic premises of these books—including the effort to find an individual writer's "voice" and particular experience—are still operative or have been redirected to more overtly progressive fields like queer, postcolonial, and disability studies. The publication of *Gilbert and Gubar's "The Madwoman in the Attic" after Thirty Years* (2011) testifies to the lasting influence of second-wave feminism. Even though many of the essays identify Gilbert and Gubar's ideas as outmoded and regret the narrow definition of Victorian women in the original book (white, middle to upper class), their turn to a wider pool of gendered and racialized subjects retains the original book's identity-based cathexis.

Victorian Metafictions has an obvious precedent in Joan Douglas Peters's *Feminist Metafiction and the Evolution of the British Novel* (2002), though the ways that Peters and I understand metafiction's influence differ significantly. Peters examines seven canonical novels—*Moll Flanders, Clarissa, Jane Eyre, Bleak House, Mrs. Dalloway, Lady Chatterley's Lover,* and *The Rainbow*—all of which have (or centrally include) a female narrator. These narrators enact, for Peters, a decentralizing effect that she compares to Bakhtin's dialogic reading of the novel: the inclusion of marginal perspectives challenges generic convention from the inside of the narrative. But where Peters's interpretation of marginal female voices differs from Bakhtin's theory of the novel can be difficult to pin down, as can her overarching argument that these voices subvert the tradition of British realism in general. How can novels both represent the canon and contest it at the same time? Metafiction offers an ostensible answer to this question in its formal reflexivity, but again, the distinction between the novels Peters identifies as feminist and metafictional and *the novel* as a genre lacks clear definition. Perhaps the most salient difference between Peters's book and *Victorian Metafiction*, however, is Peters's determination to isolate metafiction from its social foundations. The reading of a narratological technique outside of social history, in fact, prevents Peters from offering the kind of nuanced reading of "the feminine" that her argument rests on, which throws it back into the Bakhtinian territory we can link to any novelistic representation of conflict, argument, or alterity.

Over the past two decades, the most influential feminist work in Victorian studies has occurred in the domain of journalism and periodical writing. Novels are part of this field, given the frequency with which they were serialized, but the turn to print culture has emphasized the novelist's professional adaptation more than her novel's formal or aesthetic qualities. Deborah Wynne's *The Sensation Novel and the Victorian Family Magazine* (2001) and Beth Palmer's *Women's Authorship and Editorship in Victorian Culture: Sensational Strategies* (2011) both consider how magazine editors domesticated sensation novels, known for their salacious content, for the popular press. Adapting a type of reader to ideological norms also informs the study of literary criticism by and for women in Jennifer Phegley's *Educating the Proper Woman Reader: Victorian Family Literary Magazines and the Cultural Health of the Nation* (2004). Other scholars, such as Alexis Easley, Kay Boardman, Hilary Fraser, and Laurel Brake, have broken entirely new ground in uncovering the professional practices that enabled women's uneasy rise to careers in the print marketplace, broadly conceived.

Despite the vastly expanded field of Victorian novels facilitated by digitization, most noncanonical novels by women still are absent from the critical record. Writing in 2002, Nicole Diane Thompson elaborates on this selection bias: "Ideological agendas of many contemporary readers have blocked sympathetic and serious engagement with most Victorian women writers. . . . [Those] considered suitable candidates for critical rediscovery are usually those whose ideologies can be viewed as consistent with current feminist ideas or who can be interpreted as subversive in some way."[64] Patricia Zakreski agrees that feminist critics "have not considered the works of most non-canonical women novelists in depth. Or, when they do . . . they tend to evaluate the authors according to how apparently radical they seem from a feminist perspective."[65] We often find it easier to identify with the authors of dated and orthodox novels and the difficulties they almost invariably faced as women in the publishing industry than we do with their novels about sacrificial wives or pious schoolgirls, to name two character types who have not aged well. I do not question the value of such historical exegesis, but rather point out its potentially deflating effect upon the recovery of esoteric fiction.

The focus on Victorian women writers, sometimes in lieu of their novels, has recently focused on professionalization, including negotiation of the tricky business of fame. One of the most influential contributions to this literary history is Easley's *First-Person Anonymous: Women Writers and Victorian Print Media, 1830–1870* (2004). Easley elucidates the benefits for women who chose to write anonymously, which include protection from charges of impropriety, vanity, or dismissive associations with "feminine" writing—benefits that served women writers of fiction and nonfiction. Men as well as women published anonymously, but publicity carried far more serious risks to women, for whom a virtuous private life was the height and goal of respectability. Through a close analysis of the periodical writing and professional stature of Harriet Martineau, Christian Johnstone, Elizabeth Gaskell, George Eliot, and Christina Rossetti, Easley argues that "the suppression of individual identity through anonymous publication . . . enabled the development of new definitions of women's political subjectivity and liberal individuality."[66] Easley insightfully characterizes how each writer positions herself relative to the changing market and reveals the periodical archive to be a prodigious source for women's professional and subjective identity construction, and so brings added valence to the questions surrounding women's self-representation in (and with) novels. Author-organized studies like Easley's make centripetal arguments about literary culture more than they reappraise particular texts.

The novelists studied in this book had to embark upon a cumulative artistic endeavor. First, they had to imagine a serious woman writer conceptually rather than personally (or autobiographically), as any real or historical woman would be bound to the laws predicated by her sex. They were not making use of a transparently mimetic process; their realism required hypothetical models. The venue for this experiment was the novel, for where else could a woman's artistic labor be imagined and described incrementally, informed by her motives, desires, and particular experience? The novels examined here figure writer-heroines who function as creative proxies for an authorial identity not yet recognized in the first phases of the novel I study, or as a working model of the evolving professional opportunities concurrent with the New Woman of the later novels. In this way, the metafiction I am identifying has an anticipatory and even generative relationship to historical reality, not unlike Jaffe's description of realism as a method that conceptualizes fantasy, or Levine's insistence on nineteenth-century realism as an experimental method practiced in a pragmatic age.

Novelist-Heroines at a Glance, 1836–1899

In *Representing Female Artistic Labour* (2006), Zakreski suggests that the "smothered" autobiographical voice of Victorian women "could account for the relative paucity of representations of women writers in women's fiction of the mid-Victorian period"; "there are only a few narratives from [this period] that feature an authoress as their heroine."⁶⁷ When noncanonical novels are included in the count, the number of novels with novelist-heroines increases. But even if this expanded list can be considered limited, the claim that women's voices were "smothered" implies that women's true voices were repressed by a culture hostile to their self-interest and intent, whether consciously or not, upon their political and intellectual suppression. This explanation tacitly imagines that the woman writer's representation of the woman writer was *more possible* than the infrequency of its examples suggest. In an alternative view, women writers were in the process of incorporating their professional identity through the novels they wrote, learning what shape it took through the process of representing it. Their self-representations were unfolding in the real time of their narrativization rather than through actualizations that did or did not make it into print. The difficulty of defining a woman novelist at this time is borne out by the tortuous fictional plots that trace their attempts to become writers or maintain their careers. As the novels surveyed below show, novelist-heroines are punished routinely for assuming authority, fame, ambition, and a dereliction of feminine duty. Even when these novels fall in line with cultural prescriptions against professional women, however, their very creation subverts their stance against intellectual and/or ambitious women writers. A contradiction between a book and the story it tells, which would also include the many (mostly late century) novels about aspirant writers who try and fail to become novelists, encapsulates metafiction's interrogation of its own medium.

Novels by women about women writers complicate clear distinctions between subject and object, author and writer. Meanwhile, criticism that does not account for the Victorian woman writer's transitive status may inadvertently show how interpretive norms assume the objectivity and impersonality granted to artistic works by men. Alexander Nehamas's distinction between the historical writer and a book's author exemplifies the use and inference of this default position. For Nehamas, the historical writer is "firmly situated within a specific context, the efficient cause of a text's production."⁶⁸ These writers "exist outside their texts and . . . [so] are not in a position of interpretive authority over [them]."⁶⁹ In contrast, the novel's author, produced by the text's existence, is "manifested or exemplified in a text" but "not depicted or described in it."⁷⁰ But Nehamas's dissociation of author and writer loses its firm boundaries when applied to Victorian women, especially those writing novels before the 1880s and 1890s. As all the novels I survey here show, the patent insecurity of historical women writers in Victorian culture appears, again and again, in novels *about* a woman writer's disputed, hidden, or maligned identity. If historical writers did indeed exist firmly "outside their own texts," debate about a woman writer's place in society would not so consistently inform the plots of these novels. Furthermore, by concentrating on women writers, these novels dispute Nehamas's claim that an author is manifested by a book's existence, but not depicted in it: the very redundancy of author as subject *and* creator of a book exemplifies a metafictional tangle for which his categories do not account.

I am not proposing that identifiable and even stereotypical "lady novelists" did not exist at this time, in novels and in life, but rather that the techniques and conventions associated with their work limited its recognition as serious art. For Catherine A. Judd, when women writers, including Charlotte Brontë and Eliot, adopted male (or gender-neutral) pseudonyms, they were not indicating "apprehension of being silenced as women in the marketplace, but rather their dread of being judged by a 'class standard'" that treated women's writing more permissively than men's.[71] To break that standard, women novelists had to rebrand their fiction, and metafictional portrayals of women *at work* as writers helped to do this, even when they are overtly hostile to a woman novelist's ambitions or cynical about her success. Eliot, the most successful example of a woman writer who avoided classification as a lady novelist, did so as the exception that proves the rule. Her own denigration of "silly novels by lady novelists" at once categorized her as a serious artist and confirmed the lesser status of women writers in general. Had she written a novel with a novelist-heroine in it, she might have broken the illusion of *sui generis* genius born when *Scenes of Clerical Life* produced "George Eliot" in 1857. That illusion was certainly applied to Barrett Browning after the publication of *Aurora Leigh*. A critic for the *North British Review* dismissed that poem's championship of women poets by stressing Barrett Browning's originality: since "Mrs. Browning is herself almost the only modern example of such development, the story is uninteresting from its singularity."[72]

A short story by Anthony Trollope, "Mary Gresley" (1870), exemplifies the cultural and intellectual bias against women writers that the novels in this book contend against, particularly in the way that Trollope's story formally encapsulates a male narrator's perception of a woman writer. The narrator, unnamed, is the editor of a literary journal who meets the titular heroine when she moves to London in hopes of becoming a novelist. With very few exceptions, the narrator uses the first-person plural form to tell his story about Mary: "Child as she seemed to be, she had in very early years taken a pen in her hand. The reader need hardly be told that had not such been the case there would not have arisen any cause for friendship between her and us. We are telling an Editor's tale, and it is in our editorial capacity that Mary first came to us."[73] The editor broadcasts his professional clout in every use of the plural form, which sounds especially jarring in his evocations of clearly individual behavior, such as when he announces, "In love with Mary Gresley . . . we never were. . . . We were married and old; she was very young, and engaged to be married,"[74] or, at the end of the story, "We kissed her once,—for the first and only time,—as we bade God bless her!"[75] By loading every statement with the weight of anonymous consensus, these recollections diminish Mary's already subordinate status; they expose naïve and unprotected Mary to the scrutiny of all of "us," even as "we" kissed her.

Mary's appeal to the editor resides primarily in her difference from "women": "Of woman's vanity she had absolutely none. Of her corporeal self, as having charms to rivet man's love, she thought no more than does a dog."[76] This is a compliment. In reference to her modesty, the editor confirms that "it is the fact that all female literary aspirants are not 'modest-like.'"[77] Mary's self-effacement moves him to bestow his professional attention on her, as he explains: "We must not allow our readers to suppose that the intensity of our application [in helping Mary write her novel] had arisen from the overwhelming interest of [her] story. . . . It was simple, unaffected, and almost painfully unsensational. It contained, as I came to perceive afterwards, little more than a recital of what her imagination told her might too probably be the result of her own engagement."[78]

Mary must write from her own experience, he assumes, for "how was it to be expected that a girl of eighteen should portray characters such as she had never known?"[79] Despite her studied efforts, Mary's career hinges entirely upon an injunction issued by her fiancé, a curate, who disapproves of novel writing. When the curate's feebleness evolves into a fatal consumption, Mary promises at his deathbed that she will "make no more attempt at novel writing."[80] Her loyalty to her fiancé's wishes does not register much of a loss for art at the time, but her sacrifice becomes clear later. When Mary moves back to the country and dedicates herself to the poor, her letters to the editor—to his surprise—evince real talent: "From time to time we endeavored to instigate her to literary work; and she answered our letters by sending us wonderful little dialogues between Tom the Saint and Bob the Sinner. . . . [And] though that mode of religious teaching is most distasteful to us, the literary merit shown even in such works as these was very manifest."[81]

The circumstances around the emergence of Mary's talent conspire tidily against a writing career. When she is writing in London the editor does not "dream" of "anything but failure,"[82] and when her skills become "very manifest" her writing is foreclosed by her pledge to her fiancé. The impossibility of Mary's success furnishes the story with its charm by depicting a pure soul whose inoculation from worldly ambition seems more providential than circumstantial. Even the editor's show of encouragement is trumped by the sentimental futility that defines her: "We had told her frankly that we would publish nothing of hers in the periodical which we were ourselves conducting. She had become too dear to us for us not to feel that were we to do so, we should be doing it rather for her sake than for that of our readers."[83] The editor expresses Mary's dearness by ensuring that her work is not published. The absence of *Mary's* desires from this story, moreover, determines at every turn the editor's regard for her, a romance of attrition finally epitomized by her death as a missionary's wife in Africa.

"Mary Gresley," a minor story from a major novelist, consolidates most of the formally and ideologically entrenched prejudices with which the novelists in this book, real and fictional, grapple. The editor's confident summation of Mary's thoughts and motives explain, in kind, Lucy Snowe's aggressive privacy. His assumption that Mary could not imagine characters or plots beyond her personal experience presupposes the same autobiographical impulse that Brontë, Broughton, Riddell, Linton, and Paston at once advance and extricate themselves from through metafictional techniques. In fiction's inimitable contribution to history, artistic representations transmogrify into lived experience; real writers can imitate art and demand a room of one's own only after art consolidates a pattern to be imitated.

Trollope's focalization of "Mary Gresley" from the perspective of an editor does not map onto a straightforward scheme whereby male novelists objectify the experience of women writers and women novelists embody their writer-heroines more fully or sympathetically. Indeed, the fraught subjective overlap between a feminine narrator and her writer-heroine stimulates many—most—of the metafictional reflections and deflections that this book examines. As noncanonical novels about women novelists in this next section demonstrate, a feminized narratorial perspective does not guarantee sympathy for or even identification with its writer-heroine (or just as often, anti-heroine). Compared to the novels that constitute the subjects of my chapters, the novels skimmed here are less useful as examples of metafiction insofar as they largely follow a prescriptive social evaluation of women's writing and attend less than my focal examples to the writerly process itself. As these short summaries confirm, Victorian women's novels about women novelists predictably touch upon three themes, often in some combination: the allure and danger of fame, the woman artist's isolation from society and usually marriage, and the link between literary genius and suicide or self-destruction. For all the developments in women's novels across the period, these themes are strikingly consistent. The most dramatic shift in the content of these novels happens in the 1890s with the advent of New Woman novels that explore women's authorship as a form of socioeconomic independence. The 1890s are also the only decade in which novels about women novelists are notably prolific, a phenomenon I explore in chapter 5.

Caroline Bowles's *Fanny Fairfield* (1836) confirms the uneasy status of a woman's writing talent in this period and demonstrates how it often functions as a pretext for something else. The novel uses a literary vocation to propel the heroine toward fame and ruin: a simple girl from a country village, Fanny produces writing that seizes the attention of a local gentlewoman, Lady Gertrude, whose ambitions for Fanny obstruct the young writer's romance with a local man. Lady Gertrude introduces Fanny to a fashionable but dissipated painter; they marry; he proves to be a forger; is imprisoned in Newgate; and Fanny dies of consumption. Bowles, who published the serial in *Blackwood's* under the signature "A," was the wife of Poet Laureate Robert Southey, and the perils suffered by her celebrity-seeking poetess recall Southey's letter to a young Charlotte Brontë in which he warned her that a literary career was inhospitable to feminine life.[84]

Notoriety through a literary career leads to similar punishments in E. Owens Blackburne's *Molly Carew* (1884). Young Molly happens upon a gift for writing as if through friendly possession: "She has never composed one line of either poetry or prose during her life; it is, therefore, with no little surprise she finds thoughts resolve themselves into sentences in her brain."[85] Her writing habit provides the pretense for her move to London in pursuit of a famous author, Eugene Wolfe, with whom she has fallen passionately in love. Molly's love for Wolfe overcomes her better judgment when she lies on the stand at his murder trial, a crime for which she suffers five years of penal servitude.

Contributing to her public image as a criminal are "extracts from her writings" that purportedly testify that "her mind always had a murderous tendency."[86] There are passing references to corrupt publishers and plagiarism, but *Molly Carew*'s drama and suspense relies on its complex romantic and criminal plots rather than its portrait of a woman writer.

The literary talent of these writer-heroines (as well as less sensational ones) almost always implicates inborn, unbidden genius rather than the self-conscious cultivation of talent that metafictional novels about women writers can reveal. The more sensible heroines in this position couch their genius in unassuming and feminine personas, as we see in Clara Stanley, the title character in Grace Aguilar's short story "The Authoress" (1853). A suitor of Clara's, Granville Dudley, does not know she writes until his friend Heyward tells him: "'She does not display [her talent], Granville. No one would imagine she was a whit cleverer than other people; she has no pretensions, nor airs of superiority; but she writes, she writes, "there's the rub", and she loves it too.'"[87] While Granville eventually regrets marrying someone else, Clara remains contentedly single and devoted to her literary calling.

Eliza Meteyard's *Struggles for Fame* (1845) (not to be confused with Charlotte Riddell's *A Struggle for Fame*, 1882) also treats literary genius and marriage as incompatible. Heroine Barbara Leafdale's vulnerable orphanhood prefigures the marginal existence she leads as a young writer trying to support herself in the periodical marketplace. *Struggles for Fame* follows a Dickensian model whereby multiple plot lines, involving a kidnapping (of young Barbara), conniving criminals, a stolen fortune, and the eventual restitution of a family line, compete for dramatic effect. Also Dickensian is the reinforcement of genetic inheritance when Barbara turns out to be the daughter of a famous political writer. At the novel's end, she inherits a manor house with an extensive library, and tells her suitor that "the pursuit of literature, and the duties of a wife, rightfully performed, are things incompatible with each other, so I firmly decline your [proposal]."[88] But this proto-feminist declaration of women's independence leaves a much fainter impression than the novel's antic criminal and comic plots.

The literary exertions of the titular heroine in *Anne Sherwood, or The Social Institutions of England* (1857), by Fanny Aikin-Kortright, are also secondary to that novel's purpose. Dedicated to Harriet Beecher Stowe, *Anne Sherwood* exposes the plight of the "white [slave] of England": the governess. Heroines Annie and Ellen Sherwood, orphaned daughters of a clergyman author, suffer loneliness, exploitation, and humiliation in a number of governess posts. Determined to expose the abuses of the upper classes that she experienced as a governess, Annie becomes a successful author. By serving the novel's didactic purpose, Annie's vocation could have easily been ministerial or oratorical; her identity as a writer seems merely circumstantial. In the preface to *Anne Sherwood*'s second edition, Aikin-Kortright (writing under the name "Berkeley-Aikin") explains a similar motive. While she may be "obliged by the taste of the age to adopt the form of the novel,"[89] her intention is to document "the united testimony of some ninety or one hundred professional gentlewomen representing their class" of governesses. *Anne Sherwood*, Aikin-Kortright insists, evinces "neither fictitious scenes or fictitious characters, but individuals, groups, and tableaux from *real existence*."[90]

In Margaret Oliphant's *The Athelings* (1857), which I also examine in chapter 3, literary genius and a marriage plot find unusual alignment. Agnes Atheling possesses the "strange faculty of expression which is as independent of education, knowledge, or culture as any wandering angel," "yet genius, in some kind and degree, certainly did belong to her."[91] Early in the novel, Agnes's novel is handily accepted for publication and receives very favorable reviews; she avoids the unscrupulous publishers, contested authorship, or scathing reviews that befall so many of the writer-heroines discussed in this book. Agnes's writing develops over the course of the novel to better resemble a religious vocation than a professional career, which justifies her fitness for (an implied) marriage to a rector.

Except for the nefarious publishers that exploit Barbara Leafdale in *Struggles for Fame*, these novels largely ignore the cutthroat politics of the literary marketplace that so many historical accounts of the period describe. Fictional novelists who learn to navigate the industry are dominantly male, such as Charles Dickens's David Copperfield (*David Copperfield*, 1850), W. M. Thackeray's Pendennis (*The History of Pendennis*, 1849–50), Mary Elizabeth Braddon's Sigismund Smith (*The Doctor's Wife*, 1864), and George Gissing's Reardon and Biffen (*New Grub Street*, 1891). This pattern marks the exceptionality of Riddell's *A Struggle for Fame*, though Trollope touches upon a woman's reckoning with the commercial literary market in *The Way We Live Now* (1875). In that novel, Lady Matilda Carbury pursues a literary career to augment a meager living; her experience exposes corruption reminiscent of the novel's larger plot involving the rise and fall of tycoon Augustus Melmotte. "Absolutely and abominably foul . . . was the entire system by which [Lady Carbury] was endeavoring to achieve success, far away from honor and honesty as she had been carried by her ready subserviency to the dirty things among which she had lately fallen."[92] Unlike many of the writer-heroines described above, Lady Carbury lacks the talent that might compensate for publishing's craven practices.

Novels about women novelists repeatedly connect literary talent (or genius) to social alienation, some with profound consequences and others to no discernible purpose. In the latter camp is a curiously event-free novel of 1871, *The Diary of a Novelist* by Eliza Tabor. Excessive descriptions of nature are interspersed with a few basic facts about the diary-writing novelist: she lives alone in the country; her fictional characters are her "friends and companions";[93] she enjoys a picnic with neighbors that occasions more descriptions of her rural surroundings. A generous reader might characterize this novel as evidence of a woman writer's extreme sensitivity to nature; this ungenerous one is not sure what to think. Another novel that, more bleakly, associates the writing life with torpor and impotence is Beatrice Harraden's *Ships That Pass in the Night* (1893). Bernardine Holme, orphaned and solitary, hopes to become a writer when she checks into a Swiss sanatorium for tubercular patients. There she slowly becomes close to an older, withdrawn patient, Robert Allitsen, or "the Disagreeable Man," whose encouragement of her writing can hardly be recognized as such. "You are certainly getting better," he tells her. "I should not be surprised if you were able to write to write a book after all. Not that a new book is wanted. There are too many books as it is; and not enough people to dust them. Still, it is not probable that you would be considerate enough to remember that. You will write your book."[94]

Bernadine does get better and returns to London. There, poised to begin a writing career and a relationship with Allitsen, she is "knocked down by a waggon"[95] and dies in a hospital, alone. Anticipating the fruitless careers of Thomas Hardy's Jude Fawley (*Jude the Obscure*, 1896) and Gissing's Biffen and Reardon (*New Grub Street*), Harraden chooses an aspiring woman writer to characterize futility.

While the novels described above are more concerned with women's writing as a social thematic than a metafictional proposition, in no way do popular novels bypass metafictional sophistication in general. (Indeed, most of the novels at the heart of *Victorian Metafiction* are noncanonical and critically understudied.) The following section offers brief readings of four little-known novels about women novelists that engage just as fully with metafictional reflectiveness as the novels I write about in chapters 1 through 5. Despite the implication of its scholarly record, metafiction is not exclusively to conventionally "literary" or "important" novels. In each of the novels discussed below, the writer-heroine's generic choices, professional status, and reckoning with fame refractively implicate the author of the novel, whether those novels explicitly endorse women's writing careers or not. But from the Victorian era on, criticism has largely assumed that popular women's novels are formally and ontologically insignificant, though New Woman novels (including Mary Cholmondeley's *Red Pottage*, 1899, discussed below) have generated more critical and formal attention than their early to mid-Victorian counterparts. The value of these esoteric and often superficially trivial novels expands when they are read in large numbers; reading a few here or there to enrich a canon-based familiarity with Victorian fiction only serves to reinforce the formal and aesthetic criteria that underlie that canon. Literary criticism, which is pattern recognition, cannot recognize new patterns without substantial enlargement and disruption of the field. Without these examples, challenges to canonicity are largely hypothetical (or as we might quite hilariously say, *academic*).

Ruth Hall: A Domestic Tale of the Present Time (1854)

Sara Payson Willis (1811–72) was a popular American satirist, journalist, and novelist who published under the name Fanny Fern. *Ruth Hall*, her first novel, follows Willis's own experience closely (though it omits certain experiences like her divorce from her second husband).[96] As did Willis, Ruth loses her eldest daughter and (first) husband to illness in quick succession, and without help from her family, struggles to support herself and her two younger daughters. She starts publishing short articles under the name Floy in newspapers and magazines, and soon an editor hires her as a regular columnist. Her columns are so successful that a clamorous public seeks out her true identity, but her editor underpays her, and until another editor properly compensates her, she lives the life of a starving artist, barely supporting herself and her daughters. These events mirror Willis's young adulthood and her creation of the popular "Fanny Fern," though Ruth suffers much greater poverty than did Willis.[97] In the preface to the novel, Willis (as Fern) signals the complexity of its generic affiliation:

> I present you with my first continuous story. I do not dignify it by the name of "A Novel." I am aware that it is entirely at variance with all set

rules for novel-writing. There is no intricate plot; there are no startling developments, no hair-breadth escapes. I have compressed into one volume what I might have expanded into two or three. I have avoided long introductions and descriptions, and have entered unceremoniously and unannounced, into people's houses, without stopping to ring the bell. Whether you will fancy this primitive mode of calling, whether you will like the company to whic it introduces you, or—whether you will like the book at all, I cannot tell. Still, I cherish the hope that, somewhere in the length and breadth of the land, it may fan into a flame, in some tried heart, the fading embers of hope, well-nigh extinguished by wintry fortune and summer friends.[98]

Willis does not "dignify" her story (or "tale" in the subtitle) by calling it a novel, but the criteria she associates with novels (startling developments, hair-breadth escapes) are hardly dignified. They are, however, generically conventional, in contrast to the metaleptic description of her narratorial position as a "primitive form of calling." Because she invites us to imagine her physically navigating the story's progress and scenic changes, she undermines its literariness, including its illusion of taking place outside of historical time, as does her present-tense admission that she "cannot tell" if the reader "will like the book at all."

But this illusion of a candid interaction precedes a story in which Ruth's obscured identity is central to the plot. Ruth's readers variously identify Floy as a man ("because she had the courage to call things by their right names"), a "disappointed old maid," a "designing widow," a "moon-struck" girl, but "all said she was a nondescript."[99] Unusually for a novel about a famous woman novelist, Ruth does not have to fear public exposure as Floy: the few people who know her pseudonym are either protective of her (Mr. Walter), or in the case of her family members, horribly incriminated by Floy's autobiographical record of their neglect, which contributed to the penury that drove her to write in the first place. The diversity of social types ascribed to Floy testifies to the inchoate formation of the mid-century woman writer, and while the novel inflates this classificatory mystery through its characters' curiosity about the real Floy, Ruth's clear resemblance to Fanny Fern moves the debate from typology to an actual identification, barring the final strand that would connect Fanny Fern to Sara Payson Willis. Even so, Willis manages this sequential recognition in a way that preserves the appearance of modesty. One of

Floy's most avid admirers, the editor with whom she eventually contracts, correctly intuits that her poignant writing reflects "bitter life experience": "she did not draw upon her imagination," he observes. Willis cannily exploits the nested identities that implicate, in order, Floy to Ruth to Fern and ultimately herself in this editor's diffuse praise. "She is a genius, certainly, whoever she is": "What a singular being she must be, if I have formed a correct opinion of her; what powers of endurance! What an elastic, strong, brave, loving, fiery, yet soft and winning nature! A bundle of contradictions! and how famously she has got on too! . . . That first piece of hers was a stroke of genius—a real gem, although not very smoothly polished; ever since I read it, I have been trying to find out the author's name, and have watched her career with eager interest."[100]

Presumably Willis, even as Fern, would not publish claims to her own genius so effusively, and by displacing this praise onto her literary alter ego (and presenting it from the editor's point of view), she mitigates the autobiographical connection. More precisely, by transferring her experience to the character Ruth and presenting Fern as a distinctly physical presence ("I have . . . entered unceremoniously . . . into people's houses"), Willis erases easily discernible self-promotion through the creation of two third-person proxies. Ruth, then, appears to be Fern's alter ego, and the actual author (Willis) recedes to the background—a metafictional sleight of hand that allows her to write about herself without appearing to do so. Ruth's struggle, too, excuses Fern the famous writer from lionizing Floy, whose life very clearly mirrors her own. Even as inquiries as to Floy's identity flood her editor's office, "'Floy' scribbled on, thinking only of bread for her children, laughing and crying behind her mask,—laughing all the more when her heart was heaviest; but of this her readers knew little and would have cared less".[101] The replacement of Ruth with "Floy" in this passage suggests that Ruth thinks of Floy as a character in her own right—one whose success masks but does not erase the private struggle that conceived her. Late in the book, when Ruth enjoys great success, her daughter asks, "When I get to be a woman shall I write books, mamma?" Ruth's answer lays claim to the suffering that necessitated her writing career, not the fruits of its labor: "God forbid . . . ," she says, "no happy woman ever writes."[102] The tragedy that inspired Ruth's success makes her a "genius" to pity rather than envy. At the novel's end, Ruth, with Walter's help, moves to a new town with her daughters and seems poised to continue enjoying the remuneration that her career as

Floy makes possible. *Ruth Hall* may be sentimental, maudlin, and rife with clichés, but Willis's strategic depersonalization anticipates postmodern metafictions in which authorial perspective and a writing heroine are inextricable, like Carol Shields's *Swann: A Mystery* (1987) or Margaret Atwood's *The Blind Assassin* (2000).

A Woman's Story (1856)

The price of a woman writer's public exposure reaches high melodrama in Anna Maria Hall's (née Fielding) *A Woman's Story*, published under the name Mrs. S. C. Hall. Hall (1800–1881) was a well-known literary figure, keeper of salons, and friend to Oliphant and others. In Hall's novel, Helen Lyndsey, born to selfish and inattentive parents, endures a loveless childhood by writing poems and stories. In her young adulthood, Helen's household falls apart when her father proves to be a forger, her mother abandons the family, and Helen and her father abruptly disappear. Months pass, and Helen resurfaces in London after a mysterious writer, H.L., has caused a great stir of interest: all of fashionable London speculates about H.L.'s sex, age, nationality, and background in a plot reminiscent of the search for Floy in *Ruth Hall*. But Helen's eventual self-exposure as H.L. triggers her downfall: the specter of celebrity leaves her vulnerable to financial exploitation, most seriously in a blackmail scheme leveled against her by her purported half-brother. Woven into the story of Helen's authorship are numerous intrigues and crises: her father's descent into idiocy; a string of debts, bribes, and forgeries; the stain of illegitimacy; an uncommon number of "fits" among the chief characters; torrid passion, internecine conflict, and a few side plots involving Irish laborers in heavy dialect. The florid plot is narrated by an elderly friend of Helen's family whom they affectionately call "Nobody." Nobody embraces her name for the access it yields, explaining that Helen "had such faith in my secrecy, such perfect and entire confidence in my affection" that she "gave voice to her ideas freely" in Nobody's company.[103] Nobody has closer association with Helen than Nobody, who basks in Helen's fame and, later, tries in vain to preserve her reputation.

Helen's path from adulation to literary oblivion can be read as a punishment for confirming that she is the famous H.L. The public's fascination with H.L. depends on the mystery of identity rather than the writing talent that makes H.L. famous. In a scene in which Helen reads the latest speculations about

H.L. in the morning papers, she finds "the tone of knowledge and mystery" to be "most amusing":

> One [writer] declares that the identity of "H.L." has been known to them from the first moment, when the first poem appeared in a certain journal; another assumes that I am not myself, but a multiplature, a sort of literary Hydra, writing with the same pen and ink; . . . all but one profess to be well informed as to who I am, [another] declares that no woman could have written the more philosophic portions of the drama, the report that a *young* lady is the author, being too absurd to need contradiction, as the least practiced critic must know that the framework of the play is constructed by a master hand.[104]

Instead of convincing the public that a woman could write with a "master hand," the confirmation that H.L. is indeed a "young lady" only demonizes Helen, repurposing her writing talent to reflect an insatiable demand for fame.

Helen's vulnerability to the dangers of celebrity becomes the central problem in the novel and imitates the familiar plot of a young woman preyed upon by a designing suitor:

> Helen—Helen! who, without any planned or defined culture, intuitively, unconsciously, almost without self-striving,—during the dangerous part of her life without guidance . . . [;] with a mind superior in dignity to the outer world; with imagination giving to the visible an invisible power; admiration thrust upon her, in its enervating and seductive forms . . . [;] strengthened with her strength, having been so long her evil spirit, that she listened unconsciously to its suggestions as affording relief in small matters, until the demon grew into a hideous familiar—was *she* to have no thought given to her, no sympathy, in this melancholy triumph! Her punishment was just; but her penitence was true.[105]

According to Nobody, Helen cannot be held responsible for the lack of governance in her life, but her fall from the heights of fame "was just." The end of the novel documents Helen's "penitence" by borrowing stereotypes of a fallen woman reestablishing herself in society. She devotes herself to her cousin Florence, sickened by rumors surrounding Helen's (alleged) half brother, who was Florence's own fiancé. A plot whereby repentance follows moral weakness merely appropriates Helen's writing "genius" as the spark of her fatal notoriety.

At the novel's conclusion, Nobody situates Helen ten years after the main action of the novel living a quiet life with Florence and her uncle. A servant girl reports the local gossip about Helen to Nobody: "Mamma says that Miss Lyndsey's play held the stage [that] season, but *she* seemed quite forgotten. . . . Miss Lyndsey went abroad with the Middletons to nurse Florence, never leaving her day or night. I think it such a pity she should have wasted the best years of her life—in nursing."[106] Nobody responds to the servant girl by endorsing feminine sacrifice: "'Waste her life!' I repeated, indignantly, 'Helen Lyndsey has sanctified her life, by the holiest friendship that one woman ever felt for another. Young lady, you do not know what you are talking about.'"[107] By this estimate, Helen's devotion to Florence compensates for her ruined career and attenuated writing talent. Assigning women's art to an acceptable social form, the servant girl has the last lines of the novel. "Then tell [the story of Helen's life]," she commands Nobody: "tell it, that your experience may be useful to others: tell it—as 'A WOMAN'S STORY.'"[108] When Helen as H.L. displays prodigious writing talents, society perceives her as a "Proteus," a "phoenix," and a "Hydra"[109]—all mythical forms that defy the laws of nature and gender. In her feminine and voluntary descent into "penitence" and anonymity, however, Helen encapsulates the generic experience of "a woman's story." (And as a great writer, H.L. does not reflect the potential of women's art but, when exposed, the particularity of Helen's own experience.) Nobody's own anonymity, moreover, allows her to tell Helen's cautionary tale without implicating herself in it. Reproving fame in a form only actualized by public exposure is an irony finely captured by a young Fanny Burney in her private journal: "To Nobody, then, will I address my Journal! since To Nobody can I be wholly unreserved—to Nobody can I reveal every thought, every wish of my Heart, with the most unlimited confidence, the most unremitting sincerity to the end of my life!"[110] *A Woman's Story* also understands that only total discretion can ensure social respectability but lacks Burney's parodic understanding of this contract.

Nigel Bartram's Ideal (1869)

Florence Wilford's (1836–97) novel features a young woman, Marion Hilliard, who writes a sensational best seller anonymously. She works as her married sister's unpaid governess until she meets and marries another successful writer, Nigel Bartram, without telling him that she is the author of the notorious novel

Mark's Dream. An extravagantly talented and equally retiring young governess reaching best-seller status with her first novel recalls Charlotte Brontë's success with *Jane Eyre*. The debate about Currer Bell's sex that immediately followed *Jane Eyre*'s publication also emerges in Wilford's novel: early in their acquaintance, Nigel gets an assignment to review *Mark's Dream*, and Marion's suggestion that it could be the work of a woman writer astounds him. "Do you mean—is it possible that you think the book written by a woman?" Marion answers,

> "I did not mean to have advanced that theory, but *do* think so. My wonder is that you can ever have supposed it to be a man's work."
>
> "But it is so much more clever and well sustained—forgive me—than the general run of women's books, and the villain is not after the pattern of lady's villains. Besides, there are a thousand little things, the description of dress, for instance, in which a lady would have betrayed herself. What woman would have dressed her heroine so unbecomingly as the author of *Mark's Dream* has done?"[111]

One such author, of course, was Brontë in *Jane Eyre*; ignorance of dress was also cited as sure proof of Currer Bell's masculinity.[112] When Nigel learns of Marion's authorship, his vision of her changes so profoundly that they drift apart, and Marion struggles to convince Nigel that *Mark's Dream* does not accurately represent her character. In this effort and for much of *Nigel Bartram's Ideal*, Marion defends a separation between art and life, or, more specifically, her own morality and the sensational *Mark's Dream*. For instance, she balks at Nigel's suggestion that the woman who wrote *Mark's Dream* "must be one who had a strange and sad acquaintance with the darker side of life[,] . . . who had herself sinned and suffered, and had written out of the depths of her own miserable experience," but the narrator obliquely confirms this description of Marion's earlier life.[113] When Marion's sister, Blanche, discovers that Marion wrote *Mark's Dream*, she connects a character in the novel to "that clever wicked Mr. Myland whom papa was so fond of. What men we did see when we were girls. . . . What would Nigel have said if he could have seen your surroundings then?"[114] Blanche never suspected that Marion wrote *Mark's Dream*, but by recognizing the similarity between Marion's character and a person from their past, she ingenuously reveals what her sister will not: that the novel extends from Marion's life experience.

While Marion attempts to treat her own literary gifts as external and unbidden, she sees Nigel's writing as a material extension of his self. In a bookstore,

Marion happens upon a positive review of a respectable but bland "lady's book," and "before [she] had read many sentences, she felt sure that *this* review was also by Nigel; she could not be mistaken in his style."[115] What Marion extracts from Nigel's positive review of a mediocre novel previews her larger transformation: "So this was how he liked a woman to write!" she notes. "It might not be very wonderful or very clever, but he had praised it; it would help show her what women ought to be."[116] Marion's language exposes more about writers and writing than she professes to know: her slippage from how Nigel "liked a woman to write" to "what women ought to *be*" (my emphasis) indirectly contests her professed dissociation from her own novel. That dissociation, moreover, proves to be not only gender specific but genre specific: Marion aspires to "be" like Nigel's taste in feminine writing, which the narrative calls "truthful and natural, and well drawn enough to have some merit, even from an artistic point of view" with "graceful style" and "purity of . . . sentiments," in contrast to the "strange [and] unhealthy" *Mark's Dream*.[117] She recoils from a public and professional identification as a woman writer when she insists archly, "I am not an authoress. I published one book; it was the great mistake of my life: all that I wish now is to leave it behind me."[118] This claim recalls Nigel's reaction to learning that she wrote *Mark's Dream*: "I did not marry you as an authoress, and I do not choose that you should be one."[119] Later, he muses that she "might have been the queen of a literary circle; how you have been as it were *wasted* on me."[120] In these denials and qualifications from both Marion and Nigel, we see Wilford's narrator making an extraordinary effort to extract an acceptable form of fiction from the "morbid" variety.[121]

With her writing career seemingly behind her, the narrator assures the reader that Marion contentedly prioritizes wifehood over the call of genius: "Some women of the true woman-of-genius stamp might have thought that they owed it to themselves to write, that they were born authors and must fulfill their vocation, spite of a narrow-minded husband's prejudices. Such a notion never entered Marion's head. Obedience in all things lawful seemed to her so plain and obvious a duty, that there could not be two opinions about it. She obeyed even more than his literal commands; she respected what she thought his wishes—she never wrote a line of original composition, even wrote it to be torn up the next minute."[122] After such affirmations of Marion's wifely devotion, Wilford's narrator extends some lenience—even tolerance—to Nigel: "'I wish you to be your true self,' he said, sadly. . . . 'Who am I to efface your individuality?'"[123]

But Nigel's ambivalence about her genius becomes insignificant when a serious and debilitating illness strikes him, preventing him for writing for an income. The doctor warns Marion that "writing is the worst thing for [Nigel], the very worst. . . . I don't see what is to be done, unless you write the articles for him."[124] Under these terms Nigel accepts the doctor's practical suggestion and approves the publication of Marion's second book. Wilford's narrator, then, forges an expedient alliance between Marion's writing and her marriage. This resolution again recalls *Jane Eyre* insofar as the happy marriage of an exceptional woman hinges upon the relative incapacitation of her husband.

Red Pottage (1899)

Mary Cholmondeley's (1859–1925) *Red Pottage* has been the subject of more criticism than *Ruth Hall, A Woman's Story*, and *Nigel Bartram's Ideal*, which is to say that an MLA search of the novel generates a modest field of about fifteen sources, most of which are journal articles. *Red Pottage* tells the story of two women who try, mostly unsuccessfully, to define themselves outside of the social prescriptions of marital and familial duty. Hester Gresley, a writer, lives with her conservative brother Reverend James Gresley and his family in a provincial town. Rachel West was born into a wealthy merchant's family, but after her father's death and debts impoverish her, Rachel must make a precarious living in the East End as a typist. Hester's first book, *Idyll of East London*, is informed by Rachel's experiences. When the novel opens, Rachel has recently inherited a large fortune and returned to society, where she falls in love with Hugh Scarlett, who has seduced a married society woman, Lady Newhaven. When Lord Newhaven discovers the affair, he and Hugh forge a suicide pact, though its resolution is withheld from the reader till later in the novel. Hester, meanwhile, finishes her second novel, widely anticipated to cause an even greater stir than her first. The plot climax for both Hester and Rachel concerns a sudden and devastating blow to their imagined futures: Hester's brother burns her manuscript, and Rachel's trust in Hugh breaks when he lies about his suicide pact. Both these events force *Red Pottage*'s narrator to renounce conventional resolutions and guide the story into an experimental, metafictional self-consciousness.

In addition to Hester's writing career, the status and influence of *the novel* plays a significant role in *Red Pottage*, as fictional conventions and particular novels provide an intertextual field of reference, especially for female characters. Here, Cholmondeley's narrator compares a character from Eliot's *Middlemarch* to *Red Pottage*'s Lady Newhaven and Sybell: "Both exacted attention, and if they were in the same room together it seldom contained enough attention to supply the needs of both. Both were conscious, like 'Celia Chettam,' that since the birth of their first child their opinions respecting literature, politics, and art had acquired additional weight and solidity, and that a wife and mother could pronounce with decision on important subjects where a spinster would do well to hold her peace."[125] The quotation marks around "Celia Chettam," Dorothea Brooke's self-absorbed sister in *Middlemarch*, signal a narrative transfer from the descriptive to the ontological. By emphasizing that "Celia Chettam" is a fictive construct, that is, the quotation marks remind us that Lady Newhaven and Sybell, too, are pieces in *Red Pottage*'s characterological design. Where Celia's conventionality throws Dorothea's high-mindedness in relief, these characters offset the relative originality of Hester and Rachel, morphing *Red Pottage*'s constellation of female characters into a proto-feminist, text-based object lesson instead of the arbitrarily realized social circle that straightforward realism might imagine.

But while the narrator moves Lady Newhaven and Sybell around like chess pieces in her greater design, Rachel maintains a self-consciousness more narratorial than characterological. She resists, for instance, the literary overdetermination that defines other women in the novel. Realizing the intensity of her attraction to Hugh, for instance, she compares herself to "those conventional heroines of second-rate novels who love tremendously once, and then, when things go wrong, promptly turn into marble statues, and go through life with hearts of stone. . . . I am just like that."[126] Of course, by identifying her feelings with the clichés of bad fiction, Rachel escapes the myopia of the women in *Red Pottage* who enact these clichés unknowingly. When Lady Newhaven warns Rachel that their friend Dick Vernon hopes to marry Rachel for her fortune, Rachel responds ironically:

> "According to public opinion [marrying for money is] a very praiseworthy attachment," said Rachel, who had had about enough. "I often hear it commended."
>
> Lady Newhaven stared. That her conversation could have the effect of a mustard leaf did not strike her. . . .

> "Well, my dear," [Lady Newhaven] said, lying down on a low couch near the latticed window, and opening a novel. "You need not be vexed with me for trying to save you from a mercenary marriage. I only speak because I am fond of you. But one marriage is as good as another. I was married for love myself; I had not a farthing. And yet you see my marriage has turned out a tragedy—a bitter, bitter tragedy."
>
> *Tableau.*—A beautiful, sad-faced young married woman in white, reclining among pale-green cushions near a bowl of pink carnations, endeavoring to rouse the higher feelings of an inexperienced though not youthful spinster in a short bicycling skirt. Decidedly, the picture was not flattering to Rachel.[127]

In juxtaposing Lady Newhaven's intradiegetic and Rachel's metadiegetic perspectives, this exchange lends Rachel a relative detachment that, in turn, inflects the stagey "tableau" that parodies the scene it follows: a fiction inside a fiction. While Lady Newhaven inhabits the scene unselfconsciously, Rachel's awareness of its melodrama functions like free indirect discourse and aligns her with the narrator.

Despite Rachel's awareness of the novelistic conventions that inform her own romantic loyalties as well Lady Newhaven's posturing, *Red Pottage* does not portray a world where fiction and reality are easily divisible constructs. In her introduction to *New Woman Fiction* (2016), Carolyn W. de la L. Oulton explores their overlap in her description of Rachel and Hester as New Women figures in sensational and realistic plots, referring respectively to Rachel's embroilment in the love triangle (with Lady Newhaven and Hugh) that leads to the suicide pact (between Lord Newhaven and Hugh), and to the destruction of Hester's bold and progressive novel by her brother. But the disposition of the two heroines transposes these generic affiliations. As described above, Rachel routinely resists identification with fictional conventions, and Hester's immersion in her writing can lead her to confuse real and literary worlds. Complaining of the constant interruptions to her work in her brother's vicarage, Hester tells Rachel that during one such domestic intrusion she was "in a difficult place . . . because only the people in the book were real just then." She continues, "The scene in my mind which I had been waiting for for weeks was shattered like a pane of glass, I became quite giddy and spoke wildly. And then . . . I burst into tears of rage and despair."[128] When Hester describes her book, Rachel observes that her "face changed. Eagerly shyly, enthusiastically, she talked to her friend about the book, as a young girl talks of her lover."[129] The affiliations between Rachel and realism and Hester and sensation deepen when each heroine faces a crisis. Rachel, brokenhearted at Hugh's deception, forces herself to break their engagement despite still loving him, while Hester nearly dies of "brain fever,"[130] that all-purpose cliché of melodramatic heartbreak, when her brother burns her book. The misalignment between sensible Rachel and her sensational love triangle, and quixotic Hester and the crushing oppression that almost destroys her, confuses a logical order whereby characters are identified with their experiences or art imitates life.

Red Pottage predicates, of course, its own reception in and through the violent destruction of Hester's work. The scene in which Hester finishes the book also alerts us to the mode of authorship to which Cholmondeley lays indirect claim. When Hester puts down her pen, the narrator writes,

> The night was over, and that other long night of travail and patience and faith, and strong rowing in darkness against the stream, was over, too, at last—at last. *The book was finished.* . . .
>
> It seemed to Hester as if once, long ago, shrinking and shivering, she had stood in despair upon the shore of a great sea, and had heard a voice from the other side say, "Come over." She had stopped her ears; she had tried not to go. She had shrunk back a hundred times from the cold touch of the water that each time she essayed let her trembling foot through it. And now, after an interminable interval, after she had trusted and doubted, had fallen and been sustained, had met the wind and the rain, after she had sunk in despair, and risen again, she knew not how, now at length a great wave—the last—had cast her up half-drowned upon the shore. A miracle had happened. She had reached the other side, and was lying in a great peace after the storm upon the solemn shore under a great white star.[131]

The spiritualism of Hester's creative process contrasts to her brother's punitive decision to burn her book in the name of clerical responsibility, and like any conversion narrative, the "miracle" of her book's completion changes her into a different person. But Hester's small-minded village cannot accept transformative art. At the novel's close, Rachel and Hester have traveled to India, and the villagers at home are celebrating a near-cliché of sentimental fiction: a double marriage between two sets of minor characters. This ending oddly juxtaposes two fictional modes—a sort of amalgam of *Sense and Sensibility* and *A*

Passage to India—which speaks to *Red Pottage*'s larger reflection on the struggle of the New Woman caught between two incompatible worlds. *Red Pottage*, then, offers both a mission statement for the future (in its indirect rendering of Hester's masterpiece) and a realistic account—in the tradition of *Middlemarch*—of the power of bourgeois orthodoxy.[132] In a short postscript following the final chapter, the narrator explains that she has "copied out one little chapter of the lives of Rachel and Hester," and though she cannot see forward "plainly," she catches "glimpses of those other pages. I seem to see Rachel with children round her . . . and the old light rekindled in Hester's eyes."[133] Though the fulsomeness of these projected plots outpaces *Red Pottage* itself, in "copying out" a tumultuous period in Rachel and Hester's lives, the narrator succeeds where Hester does not.

In *Ruth Hall, A Woman's Story, Nigel Bartram's Ideal,* and *Red Pottage,* the novelist-heroine's *act* of writing competes with and often eclipses what and how well she writes. These heroines are *women writers,* not writers—a designation we still use today in Victorian criticism of the novel. Seen this way, second-wave feminist criticism's determination to put the woman writer back into her fiction is redundant as it reinforces her as a unique historical subject. When we talk about Impressionist painters or the poets of the Jazz Age, the force of the artistic tradition outstrips the individual contributors. Critics like Leavis and Lukács who included a few women's novels in the nineteenth-century canon were implicitly saying that Austen and Eliot wrote *as well as* men, which informs their art with a story about their own gender identity: a transformation or miracle that enabled its greatness. Instead, *Victorian Metafiction,* by leaving the qualification of *women* out of the title, uses the art form as its defining subject.

1

METAFICTION IN "NOVEL GUISE"

Charlotte Brontë's *Villette*

One of the effects of the metafiction I study in this book is its enhancement of the artistic status of Victorian women's novels, which counteracted a common assumption that women writers were less capable of objectivity than men, and so more likely to write fiction that closely followed their own experience. Novels written in the first person, by men and women, were particularly apt to be conflated with the voice of the biographical author, as Susan Lanser explains in *The Narrative Act: Point of View in Prose Fiction* (1981). This extended, she writes, "even [to] texts like *Jane Eyre* where the I-protagonist/narrator has a fictional name and history. Critics who believed that all I-narrative was autobiography considered the use of the I-voice egocentric, self-indulgent, and an inappropriate 'descent' of the author to the level of a character-marionette."[1] The presumption of autobiographical content was damaging to women writers as it could confirm cultural biases, including their intellectual inferiority to men or unseemly desire for public attention. But autobiographical readings of novels were neither a Victorian invention nor necessarily a sign of a novel's lesser value. In the earlier eighteenth century, women often invoked their public personas to pique interest in their work. The racy plots of novels by Aphra Behn (1640–1689) and Delarivier Manley (1663–1724), for instance, recall events in their own lives, and Paula R. Backscheider writes that Eliza Haywood (1693–1756) was "strikingly and unusually present in [her novel, *The History of Miss Betsy Thoughtless* (1751)]. Haywood counted on knowledge of her long career as an expert on relations between the sexes and her identity as the great 'arbitress of passion.'"[2] Because novel writing in the eighteenth century was for either sex a field under construction—linked to commercial interests, a preoccupation with "low life," and suspect individual morality—women writers walked an especially fine line between fictional representation and supposed biographical experience, but as these examples show, autobiographical reflections (especially notorious ones) could be selling features. At the same time, other women novelists strove to erase their autobiographical signature to protect their public reputations, and some writers, such as Behn, practiced forms of self-exposure and self-protection. Catherine Gallagher's illuminating discussion of women writers' identity vis-à-vis the public world in the eighteenth and early nineteenth centuries in *Nobody's Story: The Vanishing Acts of Women Writers in the Marketplace, 1670–1820* (1994) traces the woman writer's experimentation with rhetorical "disembodiment," or her complication of the link between personal identity and authorial signature from Behn to Maria Edgeworth. Gallagher's argument informs mine in the instrumental as opposed to sacrificial use of anonymity or pseudonymity. "Instead of bemoaning" the elusiveness of the woman writer at this time "and searching for their positive identities," Gallagher concentrates on the social and professional efficacy that these filters could activate.[3]

The novels of Jane Austen at the turn of the nineteenth century helped to propel the women's novel into more detached and impersonal territory, at least in terms of Austen's plots. Her own life was free of scandal, yet her artistic creativity was interpreted as an extension of her unique selfhood rather than a cultivated skill. In the "Biographical Notice" (long but only tenuously attributed to her brother Henry Austen[4]) at the beginning of *Northanger Abbey* (1817) and *Persuasion* (1817), Austen's personal attractions—her face, voice, and mannerisms—transpose perfectly with a description of her prose. "Her features . . . ," the writer notes, "produced an unrivalled expression of that cheerfulness, sensibility, and benevolence, which were her real characteristics." When the writer claims, "It might with truth be said, that her eloquent blood spoke through her modest cheek," physical features collude so entirely with idioms for expression that Austen's person and writing talent are indistinguishable from each other.[5] Austen, we understand, so embodied the grace and wit of her novels that describing them as external, artfully developed products of her imagination seems redundant: she *was* her novels.

The maturation of the novel in the nineteenth century expanded into new generic categories, often with ties to very particular subcultures and professions, such as Newgate, nautical, and adventure novels. Expertise in most of these genres was necessarily masculine, and as W. R. Greg explains in his 1859

National Review article, "Whole spheres of observation, whole branches of character and conduct, are almost inevitably closed to [the female novelist]."[6] Fellow journalist R. H. Hutton attributes such social barriers to nature when he writes in an 1858 essay for *North British Review,* "Our lady novelists do not usually succeed in the field of imagination . . . We are fully convinced that this is the main deficiency of feminine genius."[7] Even as evidence of "feminine genius" multiplied in the works of authors like Elizabeth Barrett Browning and George Eliot, many critics were still unconvinced that women's imaginations exceeded their personal experience. Leslie Stephen declaims in the later century that "most obvious of all remarks about [Charlotte] Brontë is the close connection between her life and her writings. In no books is the author more completely incarnated. She *is* the heroine of her two most powerful novels."[8] With similar assurance, critic W. L. Courtney asks in 1904, "Would it be wrong to say that a woman's heroine is always a glorified version of herself?" This is not a real question, as he goes on to assert with quite spectacular hypocrisy that "the neutrality of the artistic mind" is what "the female novelist seems to find . . . so difficult to realise."[9] In *The Rise of the Novel* (1957), Ian Watt perpetuates the descriptive fallacy attached to women's novels by characterizing them as apt in the transcription of real experience and relationships, but lacking imaginative and intellectual distance. He explains that the "feminine sensibility" was "in some ways better equipped to reveal the intricacies of personal relationships and was therefore at a real advantage in the realm of the novel."[10] The reasons why this is so, he continues, "would be difficult and lengthy to detail" (and in the absence of such tedious analysis, "feminine sensibility" can accommodate any measure of social transformation, including enfranchisement and reproductive control, without impact). Watt cites Henry James's description of women novelists as "'delicate and patient observers'" who "'hold their noses close, as it were, to the texture of life.'" Their observations, James writes, "'are recorded in a thousand delightful volumes'" which, as it were, he does not identify.[11]

Where these earlier (and dominantly male) critics treated the autobiographical imprint of the female novelist on her novel as the sign of a derivative or merely observational talent, later twentieth-century feminist critics repurposed personal experience into heroic origin stories. Despite the radically difficult conclusions attached to autobiographical influence on the novel, then, we see a shared interest in this interpretative horizon from the early eighteenth century through second-wave feminism. The 1970s criticism of Sandra M. Gilbert and Susan Gubar, Elaine Showalter, Ellen Moers, and Patricia Meyer

Spacks[12] (among others) resonated with scholars and readers in part because it was so richly infused with the lives of the novelists themselves. Historical vignettes like Charlotte Brontë's composition of *Jane Eyre* (1847) in her father's presence but without his knowledge, or Mary Shelley's conception of *Frankenstein* (1818) in response to Byron's invitation to write supernatural stories, rival the fictions themselves. For Mary Jacobus, the autobiographical interpretation of women's novels prevails over historicity; her "autobiographical 'phallacy'" is a male pattern of interpretation that locates "women's writing ... closer to their [own] experience than men's" and argues that "the female text *is* the author," or at least a "dramatic extension" of her consciousness.[13] Two quotations from Ruth Parkin-Gounelas's *Fictions of the Female Self* (1991) elucidate some of the stakes implicated by this continuum:

> Until recently, it has been a common assumption that women are "too personal," "too self-preoccupied" in both their lives and their writing.[14]
>
> ... Until very recently, women have been particularly inhibited in their efforts at self-inscription.... The history of their attempt to insert the female subject into the literary models available to them is one of unease, subterfuge, and dislocation, rather than self-revelation and self-discovery.[15]

Set side-by-side, "too personal" and "inhibited ... at self-inscription" set up a critical contradiction: women were faulted for writing too much about themselves but also constrained from writing about themselves?[16] By default, Victorian women wrote about their own spheres of experience because they had limited access to formal education and worldly knowledge and were dissuaded from certain literary forms that were identified as masculine, such as epic poetry, history, and autobiography. They turned to fiction as an ephemeral subfield with lower expectations for its practitioners. But it is the value-laden opposition between "unease, subterfuge, and dislocation" and "self-revelation and self-discovery" that interests me in terms of what it says about a tradition in feminist criticism. Bypassing the argument that self-discovery almost necessarily is a dislocating process, Parkin-Gounelas can assume as a matter of course that the history of women's writing *is* a history of women's efforts toward self-revelation, even if women's writing has been consistently devalued by complaints about the novelist's self-referentiality. The association between a woman writer and her novel that dates to the eighteenth century transforms in the later twentieth century into a means of consciousness raising. This political conversion, however, does not alter the determinants of the comparison: whether pre- or postfeminist, patronizing or empowering, the revelatory connections between a woman writer and her novel juxtapose a type of writer with a type of writing and put her life at the center of the interpretative process.

Charlotte Brontë, Currer Bell, and the Specter of Autobiography

Perhaps no Victorian woman writer resisted autobiographical exegesis more strenuously than Charlotte Brontë. As we know so well, the publication of *Jane Eyre* stirred a national debate over the identity and especially the sex of its author, Currer Bell, and as the summary above specifies, once a novel was identified with a female author, its reception suffered accordingly. A scan of early reviews shows that a critic's decisiveness on the issue was more consistent than attribution to either sex: "Though relating to a woman, we do not believe [*Jane Eyre*] to have been written by a woman"[17] (*The Examiner*); "The writer is evidently a woman"[18] (*Fraser's*); "It is no woman's writing . . . no woman *could have* penned the 'Autobiography of Jane Eyre'"[19] (*Era*); "Though we cannot pronounce that it appertains to a real Mr Currer Bell . . . yet that it appertains to a man, and not, as many assert, a woman, we are strongly inclined to affirm"[20] (*Quarterly Review*); we "cannot doubt that the book is written by a female"[21] (*Christian Remembrancer*); "We have not the shadow of a doubt [that a woman wrote the novel]"[22] (*Westminster Review*). These reviews confirm that an author's sex was a relevant analytic in evaluating a novel, and that, despite their confidence in determining it, the critics were wrong about half of the time. The signs used to confirm Currer Bell's masculinity include ignorance of female dress and a "clear, distinct, decisive style,"[23] while femininity emerges through "life-like" characters[24] and focus upon "the history of a woman's heart."[25] Evidence of a novelist's sex, then, ranges from the material to the aesthetic, but rarely do the reviewers explain why or how the criteria they call upon is a reliable indicator of sex.

When the dual publication of *Wuthering Heights* and *Agnes Grey* followed *Jane Eyre* two months later, reviewers and presumably the public again debated the sex of the authors, as well as if all three novels "might be the work of one hand."[26] Continuing to circulate around the publication of Anne Brontë's *The Tenant of Wildfell Hall* (1848) and Charlotte Brontë's *Shirley* (1849), the debate's most considered rebuttal is Anne's from her preface to the second edition of *Tenant*, issued just over a month after its initial publication: "As to whether the name [Acton Bell] be real or fictitious, it cannot greatly signify to those who know him only by his works. As little, I should think, can it matter whether the writer so designated is a man, or a woman as one or two of my critics profess to have discovered[.] . . . I am satisfied that if a book is a good one, it is so whatever the sex of the author may be."[27] Anne's reticence on the identity of Acton Bell was, or was about to be, either superfluous or a question of principle: in July 1848, after the June publication of her novel, she and Charlotte visited their publisher, George Smith & Co., in London to prove their separate identities, and so disclose their gender. But even after the disclosure, Charlotte explained to Smith, "Currer Bell . . . is the only name I wish to have mentioned in connection with my writings."[28] In her 1850 "Biographical Notice," included in the reissue of *Wuthering Heights* and *Agnes Grey* after her sisters' deaths, she writes that the three sisters "had a vague impression that authoresses are liable to be looked on with prejudice."[29] This "notice," and particularly her representation of her sisters and their novels (Emily as a barely civilized rustic, and Anne's searing portrait of alcoholism in *The Tenant* simply a "mistake"[30]), reads opportunistically, as a way to placate a public prone to disapprove of the intensity and "coarseness" of the women-authored novels. There is, after all, no indication in the novels or in Charlotte's letters that she (or her sisters) held "vague impressions" about the reception of women writers, and much that confirms Currer Bell as a canny interpreter of gender politics.

The public excitement stirred up by the Bell brothers' novels put Charlotte—the unofficial family spokesperson and soon its last surviving member—at the center of two mutually reinforcing judgments: first, that the sex of a novelist determines whether its content is acceptable or not, and second, that the content of a novel likely translates the opinions and experiences of its author. For women authors, then, controversial content necessarily compromised the novelist on a personal level, which helps to contextualize Brontë's initial and continued use of a pseudonym. "Currer Bell" signals one instance of a methodical attempt to deflect critical and public attention away from either the historical individual "Charlotte Brontë," or from platitudinous claims about *woman*, and direct attention to the writing itself. In contrast, some earlier critics have interpreted the adoption of male pseudonyms as a form of wish fulfillment or deference. As Ivan Kreilkamp writes, "[Brontë's] career as Currer Bell is generally regarded as a phase she passed through on the way to full authorship, an unfortunate moment of self-concealment required by the sexism of the Victorian literary marketplace."[31] But the choice at hand was not a question between an authentic female or inauthentic male self (and the arbitrariness of distinguishing a female author from a male one, as the above reviewers show us, hardly outlines a transparent choice). Rather, Brontë was aspiring to the agency of "writer."[32] She sought the neutral authority that male writers could take for granted. In *Shirley*, she appears to confront the bias against women writers head-on through the mouthpiece of the progressive Shirley Keeldar and her narrator's command to readers to "Calm your expectations; reduce them to a lowly standard. Something real, cool, and solid, lies before you."[33] But *Shirley* generated tepid reviews and to Brontë's frustration only perpetuated the conversation about Currer Bell's gender. "Why can they not be content to take Currer Bell for a man?" she wondered. "I imagined—mistakenly . . ." she continues, "that *Shirley* bore fewer traces of a female hand than *Jane Eyre*: that I have misjudged disappoints me a little—though I cannot exactly see where the error lies."[34]

Perhaps aware that determining "where the error lies" is impossible when reviewers identify the sign of male and female writing with great confidence and no consensus, Brontë's final novel, *Villette* (1853), offers her most sustained challenge to artistic analytics determined by a writer's sex. *Villette* recycles the form of autobiography that Brontë already used in *Jane Eyre*, but Lucy Snowe's resistance to self-disclosure challenges the register of personal confession so often assumed in women's writing, and the wryly evasive *Villette* can be read in light of Brontë's exasperation with the enduring interest in her sex and personal identity. In drawing attention to *Villette*'s elisions, inconsistencies, and departures from fictional conventions, Lucy's narrative is not a realistic transcription of her experience but a piece of experimental writing. Its form and presentation systemically frustrate a causal sequence between "author" and "novel": Brontë attributes the novel to her known proxy, Currer Bell, whose name at once announces "not Charlotte Brontë" and "not a real person at all"; then there is the conceit of the autobiographical experience of a woman named Lucy Snowe; and finally, there is fictional Lucy's purported and incomplete narration of that experience, which is not named for her but for the site of its main action, the imaginary city of Villette. In the social critique explicit in the text and implicit in its metafictional deflections, *Villette* resists the critical and popular evaluation of a novel that starts from its author's identity and gender, and, as Brontë knew all too well, filters the reception of the novel accordingly. Late twentieth-century feminist criticism tended to follow this same causal logic, though as a recuperation and not an exposé of the "real" Brontë. To Janice Carlisle, "Lucy Snowe is the mask under cover of which Brontë conceals her identity in order to reveal the unappealing reality of her emotional life and its central figures,

M. Heger and George Smith."[35] Even if this were true, which seems outside the evaluative scope of fiction, why would Brontë *want* to reveal her own romantic disappointments? Doing so implies that her fiction provided her with a kind of therapeutic value, or it recalls Victorian-era pronouncements on women writers being confined to material that they experienced firsthand.

Reconciling (Auto)Biography and Metafiction, with Help from Thomas Carlyle

Now, a necessary interruption: my readers will have noticed that a book that professes to examine metafiction's supersession of the biographical has just reconstructed in some detail a historical period in Brontë's life, as if in preparation for an argument that links these events to Brontë's novels. I do contend that the public attention fixed on Brontë after *Jane Eyre* and *Shirley* provides an animus for *Villette*'s tendency to withhold or delay information from the reader. Biographical experience thus led Brontë to impede, in *Villette*, the novel's projection of its authors' (both Brontë's and *Villette*'s purported author, Lucy's) lives, even as many thematic details accord with Brontë's life: teaching in Belgium, isolation from friends and family, an attraction (or more) to a French "Master." Stein Haugom Olsen's distinction between historical and critical practices of literary biography can be helpful here. As a historical discipline, Olsen writes, "biography will make use of any work an author may have written . . . to give a historically correct presentation of the author and his environment." The author's works of art, he continues, "will be source material, among other types of source material, for drawing conclusions about the author's personality, opinions, emotional life, etc." In contrast, critical biography corrals that information to better understand the writer's works.[36] Alexander Nehamas makes a related distinction between interpretation that searches for meaning within a text, and that which seeks to understand the writer's intentions and experience.[37] The inferences I am drawing from Brontë's experience in the literary marketplace predicate the resistance I locate in *Villette* on a textual level: Lucy's aggressive self-protection formally rebukes the assumption that a woman's novel might be confessional and in so doing offers a metafictional rejoinder to those critics and readers who look for Brontë in Lucy. Charles LaPorte likewise reads *Aurora Leigh* as an indirect response to a specific critical appraisal. In its command of a poetic genre identified with male poets, "*Aurora Leigh* gives voice to a long struggle between Barrett Browning and her reviewers . . . [who] regularly urged her to write poetry that was more discernibly feminine".[38] An anecdote from Elizabeth Gaskell's *The Life of Charlotte Brontë* (1857) also integrates biographic material in this critical mode. Gaskell describes Brontë's lessons with M. Héger at the pensionnat where she studied in Brussels. After preliminary lessons, she writes, "M. Héger took up a more advanced plan, that of synthetical teaching. He would read to [the students] various accounts of the same person or event, and make them notice the points of agreement and disagreement. Where they were different, he would make them seek the origin of that difference by causing them to examine well into the character and position of each separate writer, and how they would be likely to affect his conception of truth."[39] Throughout *Villette*, Lucy prevaricates between interpretations and invites the reader to do the same; exploring multivalent lines of thought corresponds to the lessons Gaskell describes.

Inferring that Brontë's education shaped her novel(s) uses biographical experience to interpret a method employed in the fiction. A bio-historical approach, in contrast, might use this example to deduce Lucy's feelings about M. Héger ("she thought he was an excellent teacher"; "his lessons affected her profoundly") and in so doing flesh out a picture of Brontë as Lucy's direct prototype. In examining metafiction, my emphasis follows how Brontë's novel *works*, how its figuration of narrative authority, for instance, tells a story about power dynamics in the novel and relative to the "woman's novel" as a developing genre. Toward this emphasis on craft, information about Brontë's analytical training can illuminate her formal choices in *Villette*. Meanwhile, Brontë's feminist critics, as Patricia E. Johnson points out, have been relatively inattentive to "female writing as a thematics" in their discussions of the novels. Johnson explains this omission by proposing that sexual desire surmounts the identification of other types of desire in Brontë's novels, including allusions to female creativity and self-expression. Johnson asks, "How can a Victorian woman openly admit not only that she desires pleasure, but that she finds that desire most satisfied through writing," when the "Victorian woman's desires often cannot be directly named[?] The prohibition against such desires and ambitions was one that all Victorian women felt, but," continues Johnson, "Brontë met with it in an unusually blunt form," starting with Southey's patronizing advice to her in her teens and continuing through the frequent reception of her novels as unfeminine and improper.[40]

An important distinction between *Villette* and the other novels I examine relates to Lucy's objectives as a writer. While she identifies herself as the writer of the text we read as *Villette*, she does so as an autobiographer, not a novelist. Unlike Nell LeStrange's text in *Cometh Up as a Flower*, the subject of the next chapter, Lucy's text does not gradually slip from autobiography into fiction, though instances when *Villette* formally imitates or parodies "the novel" are telling forays into metafiction's capacity to eclipse the biographical with the aesthetic, as I describe later in this chapter. The complicated network that consists of Lucy the writer of *Villette*, the heroine of its central action, Brontë the *actual* writer of *Villette*, and "Charlotte Brontë" the famous novelist whose own life seems identifiable in many of *Villette*'s plot elements, dislocates any linear or causal path from life to fiction. It does not deny the autobiographical so much as call into question where a distinction between autobiography and fiction lies, and if it can be made at all. Lucy's ambivalence between self-disclosure and self-censorship makes her identity formation among the overlapping positions of writer-character-autobiographer *Villette*'s central problem, for in trying to disentangle these positions, the reader must acknowledge their ontological basis in text. In this way, *Villette* resembles no other early Victorian novel so much as Thomas Carlyle's astonishing *Sartor Resartus* (1836). First serialized in *Fraser's* (1833–34), *Sartor Resartus* was not identified explicitly as fiction or nonfiction. Its narrator, an English editor, happens upon a text written by a mysterious German academic, Herr Teufelsdröckh; that text, "Philosophy of Clothes," promises no less than total social reform. The Editor understands that Teufelsdröckh's own character and history will be interrogated in connection with so transformative a project, so as he attempts to translate and organize the "Philosophy of Clothes," he also grapples with the fragments of the philosopher's autobiography, which only exists as "masses of Sheets" that scatter like "Sibylline leaves," "without connection, without recognizable coherence."[41] As Carolyn A. Barros writes, *Sartor Resartus* "uses the devices of autobiography to create a fictional narrative and introduces the elements of the genre absent of the central personage, 'I,' that is characteristic of autobiography."[42] A text that invokes but fails to satisfy the norms of autobiography anticipates *Villette*, as does *Sartor Resartus*'s deconstruction of its author. Barros explains that "since autobiographies identify the narrator persona with the actual author, *Sartor Resartus* serves to highlight the persona as a rhetorical construct."[43] *Villette*, too, draws attention to the constructedness of autobiographical writing; both texts highlight the inventive (as opposed to synthetic or corrective) power of editorial decisions. *Sartor Resartus* is narrated by the Editor but about Teufelsdröckh, and *Villette* is Lucy's narration of her own life, but in each case the central subject remains elusive. Orbiting *Villette,* moreover, is the spectral presence of Brontë, who knows by this third novel that her own persona and her fiction are fatefully entwined.

Villette: Wherein Lucy Snowe Wears Teufelsdröckh's Vestural Tissue

Villette's cryptic plot merits a quick review. Lucy Snowe, mysteriously and tragically the sole descendent of her family line, arrives in Villette (a disguised Brussels) hoping to start a new life and needing to support herself financially. She becomes a teacher in a convent school and interacts with members of the school, the local gentry, and, somewhat discouragingly, Dr. John—a local physician who also treats her for nervous exhaustion. Coincidentally, she reunites with her godmother and godbrother, Louisa and Graham Bretton, whom she knew and loved in her childhood. Toward the end of the novel, her somewhat rancorous friendship with a fellow teacher, Monsieur Paul, unexpectedly blooms into a romance, just as he leaves the country to work abroad for a few years. In his absence and through his bequest, Lucy happily runs her own small school, waiting for his return. But finally, she obliquely refers to his disappearance in a real or metaphorical shipwreck, and the novel ends. It has been narrated by a much older Lucy, looking back on this time in her life; but beyond a general reference to her success with her school, no bridge is constructed between the period of the story and the later, undisclosed time and place of its writing. Lucy's only parenthetical description of herself at the time when she is writing her story also makes a suspiciously expedient connection: "(for I speak of a time gone by: my hair which till a late period withstood the frosts of time, lies now at last, white under a white cap, like snow beneath snow.)"[44] Her iterative "white" and "snow" allude to her last name as a representational choice, not a patronymic. To quote Jane Eyre, "This is not . . . a regular autobiography." But where Jane finishes that sentence by explaining that she is "only bound to invoke Memory where [she] know[s] her responses will possess some degree of interest,"[45] Lucy's uneven invocation of memory follows a less intelligible course, as many of the trophies of interest (what tragedy marked her early life, whether Paul died) are never written. *Villette*'s reader finds herself in a position aptly summarized by *Sartor Resartus*'s Editor when he takes stock of his scant information about Teufelsdröckh: "Now for [the] Biography . . . there were no adequate documents, no hope of obtaining such, but rather, owing to the circumstances, a special despair."[46]

The critical explanations for Lucy's inconsistency and reticence are too numerous to recount, but many confirm either Lucy's rebellion against her repressive life or an attempt to gain control over that life story. As Anna Gibson perceptively explains, both of these claims invoke "a definition of narrative authority rooted in Susan Gilbert and Susan Gubar's feminist account as a power of control over both self and story in which authorship is equated with autonomy, self-knowledge, and, most importantly, self-definition."[47] While we can agree with Gilbert and Gubar that female authorship at this time lacks autonomy, the mode that Brontë puts forward in *Villette* better reflects the ontological dispersion described by Carlyle's Editor than the figuration of a believable self, whether repressed or vengeful. Knowing that his scattered evidence cannot yield any decisive interpretation of his subject (Teufelsdröckh) or his subject's subject (the philosophy of clothes), the Editor issues this invitation to his readers: "Let the British reader study and enjoy, in simplicity of heart, what is here presented him, and with whatever metaphysical acumen and talent for meditation he is possessed of. Let him strive to keep a free, open sense; cleared from the mists of prejudice, above all from the paralysis of cant; and directed rather to the Book itself than to the Editor of the Book. Who or what such Editor may be, must remain conjectural, and even insignificant."[48] Telling his readers to "keep a free, open sense" and directing their attention to "the Book itself," the Editor registers his text in a continuous present, something to tailor and re-tailor as interpretation wills. Thus Teufelsdröckh, as a coherent character, becomes more and more remote: his history in Weissnichtwo ("know-not-where"), Germany, cannot be fully tracked, his various addresses are untraceable; the "river of his History," complains the Editor, "flies wholly into tumultuous clouds of spray!"[49]

In her reading of *Villette* and fictional autobiography, Heidi L. Pennington accepts, as I do, the "impossibility" of Lucy's "essential identity."[50] But for Pennington, the gaps in Lucy's story prompt readers to "try unsuccessfully to fill in the major fictional realities of [her] world," so that readers are co-creators of her discourse, identity, and story world, even though Lucy's "past and present selves reciprocally construct one another so completely that they demonstrate her exclusively discursive nature."[51] Pennington's reader-focused interpretation of Lucy differs from mine in its loyalty to the premise of a centripetally directed selfhood: even as readers understand that Lucy does not transcend the page, they are inspired, in this account, to imagine a coherent Lucy by way of their own projection, empathy, and desire. The Lucy that Pennington describes, while not "real" in any material sense, aspires to the concept of personhood, her difference from Teufelsdröckh analogous to the difference between believing in a ghost and in a magnetic field. But Lucy cannot simultaneously register in the reader's mind as a disembodied field of signifiers *and* inspire a conception of unique selfhood that, in Pennington's argument and along with other fictional autobiographies of the period, readers then take as a hermeneutic example for their own lives. To put it another way, my reading of Lucy teases out how her ambivalent self-reflectiveness severs the connection we might imagine to an actual self, whether in the shape of a woman named "Lucy Snowe" or "Charlotte Brontë." Following the example of *Sartor Resartus* and its lesson in metafiction that *Villette* continues, Carlyle gradually shows his readers that constituting Teufelsdröckh is not only hopeless but also epistemologically misguided; the tailor deconstructs into an aporia. As Meghan Freeman writes, in language that recalls the tailoring metaphor underwriting *Sartor Resartus*, "Lucy Snowe treats her past life as a potential exhibition of which she is curator, tasked with excising, adding, and manipulating materials with an eye towards the expectations, abilities, and desires of her hypothetical audience."[52]

If the reader's awareness of Lucy's missing parts challenges the conceptualization of a coherent self, it also inspires a formal consciousness more commonly tied to postmodern fiction, though also evident in *Sartor Resartus*. As the Editor becomes progressively aware that his written version(s) of Teufelsdröckh cannot adequately capture the person himself, he concentrates on the act of creation as more meaningful than the object it chases. To be human, in his account, is not to determine truth but to use "Tools," as exemplified by "the poet and inspired Maker; who, Prometheus-like, can shape new symbols."[53] *Villette*'s metafictional challenge to coherent selfhood, too, posits fiction-making as more elastic and productive than any (auto)biographic goose chase. Lucy's identification with the great actress Vashti, whose performance she sees with Dr. John, illustrates how artistic creation trumps the myth of unified selfhood in *Villette*. The performance, Lucy writes, was "a marvellous sight: a mighty revelation. It was a spectacle low, horrible, immoral."[54] In stark contrast is Dr. John's "branding judgment" of the actress "as a woman, not an artist."[55] Trained in the representational analytics that reduce *woman* to superficial and socially determined stages, as his early flirtation with Ginevra and marriage to Paulina show, Dr. John cannot appreciate Vashti's transcendent power that Lucy construes as both revelatory and, in its mockery of womanly restraint, convention-shattering.

Vashti's performance, in embodying such extremes, is "set down in characters of tint indelible" in Lucy's "book of life,"[56] which she means both descriptively—the third-person account of Vashti's art—and literally: Vashti's artistic example helps Lucy to constitute in "letters indelible" her own particular literary self-fashioning that is *Villette*. Other references to aesthetic representations in the novel fall short of this animating metaphor and linger in the margins of bad art. In her visit to the gallery, she muses that "an original and good picture was just as scarce as an original and good book,"[57] a metafictional announcement of her own representational self-consciousness. Recalling the first class she taught in Madame Beck's school, she writes, "I shall never forget that first lesson. . . . Then first did I begin rightly to see the wide difference that lies between the novelist's and the poet's ideal 'jeune fille,' and the said 'jeune fille' as she really is."[58] Reading this observation *in* a novel about a *jeune fille* situates Lucy's odd and incomplete story closer to a realism unmediated by gendered distortions. But realism, in this case, is not portraiture so much as the studied refusal of false consciousness. As Lucy the writer often tells us, she is *as* trapped by art and literature's failure to appreciate female complexity—to see women as more than "heroines" or "idols"—as she is by the claustrophobic environment of her convent school in the city of Villette, where she is spied upon, provoked by secret notes, mocked by students and colleagues, "haunted" by the simulation of a ghost, and—most stinging of all—ignored.

Villette's most ontologically revealing scene exemplifies how fiction enables Lucy to seize and appreciate what Carlyle's Editor describes as that "Prometheus-like" ability to "shape new symbols." One day as she sits in class, Paul bursts inside and propels her into the school's *grande salle*, seats her in front of two gentlemen, and announces that her "business is to prove to these gentlemen that I am no liar. You will answer, to the best of your ability, such questions as they shall put. You will also write on such theme as they shall select." Lucy realizes that "M. Paul has been rashly exhibiting something [she] had written" and the two gentlemen, Messieurs Boissec and Rochemorte, "dandy professors of the college," have accused him of forging her name on the composition. The "show-trial" Lucy describes is humiliating. "They began with classics. A dead blank. They went on to French history. I hardly knew Mérovée from Pharamond. They tried me in various 'ologies, and still only got a shake of the head, and an unchanging 'Je n'en sais rien.'" When the inquisitors move to "matters of general information," Lucy's "mind fill[ed] like a rising well": the "ideas were there, but not words. I either *could* not, or *would* not speak—I am not sure which."

Lucy interrupts her narration of the trial scene by recalling the assignment that provoked it: "The subject was classical. When M. Paul dictated the trait on which the essay was to turn, I heard it for the first time; the matter was new to me, and I had no material for its treatment. But I got books, read up the facts, laboriously constructed a skeleton out of the dry bones of the real, and then clothed them, and tried to breathe into them life, and in this last aim I had pleasure. With me it was a difficult and anxious time till my facts were found, selected, and properly jointed; nor could I rest from research and effort till I was satisfied of correct anatomy."[59] The order in which Lucy organizes her memories in this scene, and the success she ascribes to writing over speaking, enhance our broader understanding of Brontë's narrative choices in *Villette*. Under the cold scrutiny of the professors and in the interest of disproving Paul's forgery, Lucy is interrogated first on unfamiliar subjects, and by the time the material turns more "general," she has no reason or will to gratify her examiners. Her memory of writing the essay begins with a similar frustration: Paul assigning her a theme she knows nothing about. But in that case, she satiates her ignorance by researching and reconstructing "the facts" that she uncovers—a process she likens to an origin myth (constructing a skeleton of the "dry bones of the real," clothing and animating it). Despite the pleasure in this work, Lucy notes the shallowness of her knowledge: it was "not there in [her] head, ready and mellow; it had not been sown in Spring, grown in Summer, harvested in Autumn, and garnered through Winter; whatever [she] wanted [she] must go out and gather fresh."[60] Brontë makes a similar observation in a letter to her editor when she compares her authority with that of the great male novelists of the day. She "must guess, and calculate, and grope [her] way in the dark and come to uncertain conclusions unaided and alone," while "Dickens and Thackeray hav[e] access to the shrine and image of Truth, have only to go into the temple, lift the veil a moment and come out and say what they have seen."[61] Lucy's trial confirms her exclusion from the realm of authoritative writing by betraying the professors' incapacity to connect Lucy-the-author-of-the-essay with Lucy *authoring the essay* unless they see this feat performed live. The woman of their imagination does not write so well and can be sloughed off as collateral damage in a fight between men.

The next assignment the professors give Lucy, an essay on "Human Justice," recalls Brontë's sense of estrangement from intellectual expertise. As Lucy thinks of what to write, she suddenly recognizes the two professors: they were the same men who "half frightened [her] to death on the night of [her] desolate arrival in Villette" by trailing her as she tried to follow directions to an inn. "If 'Human Justice' were what she ought to be," Lucy thinks, "you two would scarce hold your present post, or enjoy your present credit."[62] But the recognition inspires her essay:

> An idea once seized, I fell to work. "Human Justice" rushed before me in *novel guise,* a red, random beldame with arms akimbo. I saw her in her house, the den of confusion: servants called to her for orders or help which she did not give; beggars stood at her door waiting and starving unnoticed; a swarm of children, sick and quarrelsome, crawled round her feet and yelled in her ears appeals for notice, sympathy, cure, redress. The honest woman cared for none of these things. She had a warm seat of her own by the fire, she had her own solace in a short black pipe, and a bottle of Mrs. Sweeny's soothing syrup; she smoked and sipped and she enjoyed her paradise, and whenever a cry of the suffering souls about her pierced her ears too keenly—my jolly dame seized the poker or the hearth-brush: if the offender was weak, wronged, and sickly, she effectually settled him; if he was strong, lively, and violent, she only menaced, then plunged her hand in her deep pouch, and flung a liberal shower of sugar-plums.[63]

Lucy's Human Justice, allegorical and female, relishes her very human pleasures and keeps the dissenting voices of beggars and children at bay. This is not justice in the hypothetical sense, which Lucy can neither access nor define ("Human Justice! What was I to make of it? Blank, cold abstraction, unsuggestive to me of one inspiring idea").[64] Lucy's Human Justice is a fantasy woman specially equipped to defend herself against the social forces that empower the two professors: arrogance, patronage, intellectual supremacy.

In this essay and the one Paul assigned to her, Lucy embodies in text (or in "novel guise") a concept that she cannot lay claim to directly or impartially. She recalls that writing the first essay "was a difficult and anxious time till [her] facts were found, selected, and properly jointed," and she could not "rest from research and effort till [she] was satisfied of correct anatomy."[65] The figure of Human Justice transcends this Frankensteinian labor and springs fully formed into Lucy's imagination, its confidence integral to the justice it enjoys. Lucy must transmogrify political concepts into fictional characters if she wants to contribute to a conversation that excludes her, and her vengeful delight in doing so is reiterated in Human Justice's refusal to respond to the questions posed to *her*. This metafictional dodge, of course, transpires in Brontë's invention of Lucy, who embodies *Brontë's* feminine exclusion from intellectual authority, and like Human Justice and the clamoring children, ignores her readers' presumed "appeals for notice, sympathy, cure, redress."[66]

"A Fictitious Form" . . . "I Can Accept"

Metafictional corrections to women's social and educational deficits are frequently attributed to late twentieth-century feminist novels. Gayle Greene, for instance, ascribes the origin of feminist metafiction to four novelists: Doris Lessing, Margaret Drabble, Margaret Atwood, and Margaret Laurence.[67] Almost simultaneously in the late 1960s, Greene writes in *Changing the Story: Feminist Fiction and the Tradition* (1992), these novelists turned to metafiction to probe and demonstrate the creative predicament of late twentieth-century women artists:[68] "Whether these novelists make their protagonists readers who speculate about how literature has shaped them or writers who seek new forms in their fiction, they use metafiction to challenge the cultural and literary tradition they inherit."[69] Drabble's *The Waterfall* (1969), one of the novels that Greene examines, begins as a third-person account of Jane Grey, but after a few chapters Jane interrupts the story and exposes herself as its narrator; thereafter, her third-person perspective regularly alternates with her first person. Jane's analogy for her writing echoes Lucy Snowe's: "I will reconstitute [my life story] in a form that I can accept, a fictitious form: adding a little here, abstracting a little there, moving this arm half an inch that way, gently altering a dead angle of the head upon its neck. If I need a morality, I will create one: a new ladder, a new virtue. . . . I will invent a morality that condones me."[70]

Jane likens her fictional process to bodily rearrangement, recalling the essay that Lucy "breathed life into" after assembling "the dry bones" of her classical research, an animating process she then repeats in her conceptualization of Human Justice as a vengeful woman. In correlating writing with person-making, these fictional authors make themselves creatively redundant: Jane does not simply transcribe her story into language but imagines it as a human shape that itself embodies the story. (Carol Shields captures this process in *Swann: A Mystery*: "(Pick up a pen, and a second self squirms out.)")[71] Lucy, too, does not describe "human justice" in the abstract but personifies her and then describes her as if she had her own will. The authors thereby efface their authorship with a metafictional genesis. Furthermore, the analogies of human creation or manipulation are doubly refracted through the writer-heroines before they implicate Drabble's hand, and in the case of *Villette,* cycle through Currer Bell's (at least while the novel was still published under that name) before arriving at Charlotte Brontë's. Jonathan Culler represents women readers performing a similar dislocation: "For a woman to read as a woman is not to repeat an identity or an experience that is given to her but to play a role she constructs with reference to her identity as a woman, which is also a construct, so that the series can continue: a woman reading as a woman reading as a woman."[72] As she reads, Culler's subject apprehends the social construct of "woman" that literature captures, a fragmenting process that underscores the woman reader's false equivalency to the literary subject that purportedly represents her. But Lucy and Jane's personifications of writing help externalize women's writing as an activity or discipline that they shape to their own advantage.

While her analysis does not identify metafiction, Alison Case also explores disconnections between female narrators and the stories they narrate in *Plotting Women: Gender and Narration in the Eighteenth- and Nineteenth-Century British Novel* (1999). The style that Case identifies as "feminine narration," usually but not exclusively attributed to female narrators, negotiates between a narrator's active control over her story and the cultural presumption that women should be passive and artless in their social participation. *Jane Eyre,* one of Case's most compelling examples, attests to this contradiction "in Jane's struggle against the negative image of her as a plotting woman and the projection of those qualities onto Bertha Mason" as well as Jane's tendency to move her plot forward by invoking "an external, supernatural force."[73] Case's recognition that the position and power occupied by a narrator were *formally* unfeminine (and therefore required compensatory adjustments) aligns with my proposal that metafiction enabled women writers to externalize "women's writing" as a mode of art rather than an extension of self.

Albeit it to a lesser degree, Brontë's sporadic replacement of Lucy's I-narrative with Lucy's invocation of herself in the third person anticipates the fiction-writing heroines studied in my subsequent chapters. In instances where Lucy refers to herself as a character, she does so with a framing context that topically engages with the operations of reading and writing. Her third-person status, then, is self-consciously literary, as it is her own projection and not that of an omniscient narrator, while her first-person narrative maintains an illusion of an older Lucy recounting her "real" past. We see an example of this self-characterization at the end of the novel, when Lucy describes the letters she received from Paul during his three-year absence from Villette.

> Do not think that this genial flame sustained itself, or lived wholly on a bequeathed or a parting promise. A generous provider supplied bounteous fuel. I was spared all chill, all stint, I was not suffered to fear penury; I was not tired with suspense. By every vessel he wrote; he wrote as he gave and as he loved, in full-handed full-hearted plenitude. He wrote because he liked to write; he did not abridge, because he cared not to abridge. He sat down, he took pen and paper, because he loved Lucy and had much to say to her; because he was faithful and thoughtful, because he was tender and true.
>
> There was no sham and no cheat, and no hollow unreal in him. Apology never dropped her slippery oil on his lips—never proffered, by his pen, her coward feints and paltry nullities: he would give neither a stone, nor an excuse—neither a scorpion, nor a disappointment; his letters were real food that nourished, living water that refreshed.[74]

After her description of Paul as "tender and true," the subject subtly changes from Paul's habit of letter writing to the letters themselves, and as befits a narrative where his ultimate fate remains unwritten, his significance to Lucy transfers to a purely textual medium more contiguous with literary reading and rereading than a historically bound relationship. In contrast is Lucy's response to Graham Bretton's promise to write to her when she leaves convalescence at his house to return to Madame Beck's: "He may write once[,]" Lucy reasoned. "But it *cannot* be continued—it *may* not be repeated. Great were that folly which should build on such a promise—insane that credulity which should mistake the transitory rain-pool, holding in its hollow one draught, for the perennial spring yielding the supply of seasons."[75] By comparison, Paul's letters are "food that nourished" and "living water that refreshed"; their efficacy bypasses the finite past tense she attaches to Graham's single letter and renders regenerative power. But most striking in this passage is Lucy's detached observation that Paul "loved Lucy": by avoiding the subjective and confessional taint of "he loved me," she excises this emotion from the autobiographical frame of the I-narrative and enters it into fiction's more plastic temporality. The slippage into a fictional register, moreover, prepares the reader for Lucy's mystification of Paul's fate a few lines later. As she commands the reader, "Here pause: pause at once. There is enough said. Trouble no quiet, kind heart; leave sunny imaginations hope. Let it be theirs to conceive the delight of joy born again fresh out of great terror, the rapture of rescue from peril, the wondrous reprieve from dread, the fruition of return. Let them picture union and a happy succeeding life."[76]

Lucy casts this passage into a provisional and allegorical mode that translates the event she has been leading to—Paul's expected return to Villette—into imprecise states of relief after trauma, and she imitates the fairy tale's "happily ever after" in "union and a happy succeeding life." This reverie-like state abruptly inverts autobiography's pretense of historical reportage. The novel's much-debated final lines also thwart autobiographical expectation with a crisp realism. In a hurried sign-off that suggests the omniscient narrator of a novel accounting for all of his or her characters, these lines simply announce that "Madame Beck prospered all the days of her life; so did Père Silas; Madame Walravens fulfilled her ninetieth year before she died. Farewell."[77] While the words themselves are not parodic, their discordance in relation to the rest of *Villette* conveys a generic glitch: How does an autobiographer end a story that must be ongoing for her to write the ending? Lucy's fictional closure solves this problem, though with a tonal shift that emphasizes its formal dissonance.

Once again, *Sartor Resartus* offers an intertextual analogy. When the faint trail on Teufelsdröckh finally vanishes and the Editor can only hope that "Time, which solves or suppresses all problems" may one day "throw glad light" on the fate of the mysterious philosopher, he parts company with his readers: "To one and all of you, O irritated readers, he, with outstretched arms and open heart, will wave a kind farewell. Thou too, miraculous Entity, who namest thyself YORKE and OLIVER, and with thy vivacities and genialities, with thy all too Irish mirth and madness, and odor of palled punch, makest such strange work, farewell; long as thou canst, *fare-well!* Have we not, in the course of Eternity, travelled some months of our Life-journey in partial sight of one another; have we not existed together, though in a state of quarrel?"[78] The Editor's repeated "farewells," also the final word of *Villette*, figure closure in *Sartor Resartus* as leave-taking, not resolution. Reflecting on the "Life-journey" he has shared with his reader, the Editor inscribes *Sartor Resartus* as dynamic ("a state of quarrel") and suspended (a state during which "we" "existed together"), a contradiction that anticipates the paradoxically present-tense intermission of *Villette*'s "Pause. Pause at once. There is enough said." By acknowledging an end in the story world *and* a text's capacity to infinitely regenerate, *Sartor Resartus* and *Villette* comprehensively break the pretense of critical biography and autobiography; in the story world, Carlyle's Editor admits he has lost his subject, and Lucy swerves to the fates of minor characters in her inability to conclude her own. Finally, the reader's consciousness of the textual apparatus commanding these decisions further dissolves Teufelsdröckh and Lucy into fictional phantoms.

Given the autobiographical subtext so often projected onto women's novels and so unwelcome to writers like Brontë, who sought a public for her art and not herself, choosing a writer-heroine for one's character may have seemed an unnecessary temptation of this critical fate. *Villette* offers a working model of a writer whose ambivalent autobiographical narrative is ruptured by metafictional scenes or passages that draw attention to Lucy's writing process and shift into present-tense and third-person perspectives. Lucy, unable to draw on her own intellectual and political experience to define Human Justice, alights on a female rendition of the concept. This is not an example of Lucy, or Brontë, "finding her voice" as a writer, but one in which she creates a figural voice that did not before exist. It emerges, moreover, when she retreats from her perspective into one mediated by fiction. Later, when Lucy approaches and then pulls back from the story of Paul's fate, she uses the letters he writes her to move from a finite past tense to a literary frame that can perpetually repeat. The final lines of the novel reinforce this distance from her autobiographical narrative by signaling other types of fiction—allegory, and then a dispassionate realism—that in their generic familiarity disengage from a narrative that seemed, as autobiography, to be propelled toward personal trauma. These instances of literary remediation do not help render a more coherent or "real" Lucy as much as they depict the dynamic process of literary self-*making*.

2

RHODA BROUGHTON'S *COMETH UP AS A FLOWER*

"Like a Story-book!"

In Rhoda Broughton's (1840–1920) *Cometh Up as a Flower: An Autobiography* (1867), heroine-narrator Nell LeStrange begins her fictional autobiography on an inauspicious note: "When I die, I'll be buried under that big old ash tree over yonder—." In the same scene, Nell clambers over gravestones in a church cemetery, considers writing an elegy, and reads the inscriptions on the graves in "a reverie."[1] When a strange man appears, Nell coughs to alert him that "there was a young woman perched, ghoul-like, on a gravestone in his vicinity."[2] But the man's presence diverts her from a preoccupation with death to the potential for a fictional encounter: "There was nothing impudent in his gaze, none of the fervent admiration with which, at a first introduction, the hero in a novel regards the young lady, who at a later period of the story is to make a great fool of, or be made a great fool by him. It simply expressed the moderate amount of curiosity with which a young Englishman regards a young Englishwoman whom he sees for the first time." Despite her disclaimer, Nell's chance meeting with Richard M'Gregor, whom she will soon know as Dick, calls attention to the fictionality of the scene that the reader might take for granted while reading a novel. The contrast she draws between "real life" and novels is signified by her alleged experience and her interest in fiction, as in this quotation, but also by *Cometh Up as a Flower*'s purported status as Nell's autobiography. The movement traced above from death imagery to fictional potential corresponds to the greater arc of the text. Nell's brief but passionate romance with Dick is quickly foreclosed by familial and economic obstacles, and she faces—as an autobiographer—a narrative and literal dead end when she succumbs to illness and a broken heart. But the autobiographer cannot write her own death, and Nell's gradual transformation of her story into fiction is both ontologically expedient and personally rewarding. Fiction offers Nell a far more satisfying scope than the allegedly "real" events that she transcribes.

As discussed in the previous chapter, *Villette*'s Lucy Snowe writes a selective account of her past that complicates the reader's attempt to "know" her, withholds information (sometimes until late disclosure, sometimes altogether), and restricts her account to the medium of writing instead of the illusion of a more candid telling. But where Lucy identifies and dismantles conventional representations of women as de-individualizing and reductive, Broughton's Nell works in an opposite direction: she finds fictional tropes and genres superior to her autobiographical experience. If autobiography formally connotes record over creative invention, Nell's strategic slippage into fiction literalizes her process of self-making, making it constitutive, rather than representative, of selfhood.

An Unconventional Autobiography

The frame that opens Nell's story differs from exemplary fictional autobiographies like *Robinson Crusoe* (1719) ("I Was born in the Year 1632, in the City of York, of a good Family"[3]) or *David Copperfield* (1850) ("Whether I shall turn out to be the hero of my own life . . . these pages must show. To begin my life with the beginning of my life, I record that I was born"[4]). Nell neglects to mention her birth date, her parents' full names, and her own full name at birth, instead beginning with her introduction to her future love Richard "Dick" M'Gregor, when she is nineteen. This point of initiation symbolically positions all earlier events as a kind of plotless and prelapsarian prelude to real life—not a subject for representation. Some details of Nell's past do surface throughout the story, but they do so as asides to a narrative that revolves around her doomed relationship with Dick. In her digressive and anecdotal style, Nell's autobiography—as claims the subtitle—resembles what Linda Peterson has explored as the *res gestae* mode, which diverges from chronological autobiography in its organization by recollection and reminiscence.[5]

Raised in an ancestral manor as the second of two daughters, Nell's position at the straggling end of a cash-poor family isolates her from society. The LeStrange family has fallen in status, becoming "but too well known at Epsom and Newmarket." Nell cannot pay the bills to the village tradespeople; the family manor crumbles around them; her clothes are inadequate and unfashionable—something she feels acutely when she visits neighboring families "at whom fifty years ago [her family] turned up [their] noses, [who] now tur[n] up their [own] noses"[6] at her. At one house party, she observes that "all the other ladies knew each other very well, lived in the same circle, had the same pursuits, objects, interests. I, alone, shivered chilly outside the magic ring. I was like a ghost come back, after the lapse of a century, to the house where he used to be lord and master and darling, who hears language that he understands not."[7] The archaic construction of this last phrase and Nell's identification as a ghost and a man dramatizes her separation from the convivial social world of the "other ladies." Her older sister, Dolly, determined to marry a wealthy man, forces an engagement with the world, but Nell anchors herself to their elderly father (their mother is dead), who divides his time between a withdrawal into his memories and an immersion in scholarly subjects like "epigrammatic French essayists and German metaphysicians."[8] While he does read the newspaper, his political loyalties are retrogressive, as we see when he sympathizes with the Confederate side of the American Civil War—a position that would be identified by readers in 1867 and since as the side of the vanquished. Nell manages the day-to-day operations of the house and tries to shield her father from their debts, but when the butcher tries to recoup his money for the ninth time, for instance, she decides in desperation that she must sell something of value. "The sole thing which I possessed . . . was a large unwieldy old watch, which had belonged to my maternal grandmother—a watch with a jeweled case with queer figures chased in gold upon it, and which I wore every day for want of a better, though it kept a time of its own, or, as often as not, no time at all."[9] Dick takes the watch from her to sell in London, discovers that it is quite valuable, and returns to Nell with some badly needed cash. Everything about this anecdote reflects Nell's relationship to modern life. She wears a watch that she does not recognize as valuable, which keeps irregular time or no time, until she must sell it, at which point she is out of time altogether.

Her disconnection from the modern world is mirrored by frequent meditations on a larger ontological uncertainty.

> Is it possible that one is through the whole course of one's life the same individual being? Is one possessed of but one individual soul? Does it not rather seem that each man or woman is in himself or herself a succession of individual beings, possessing, one after another, several successive souls? . . . Our estimate of things and people, our habits, tastes,

dispositions, at certain periods of our life are so radically different from, and totally antagonistic to, what they are at other such periods, that I think it is hardly possible that their variations should be accounted for by any of the alterations that it is within the province of time, sorrow, or any change of inner or outer life to effect.[10]

Nell's struggle to imagine how successive experiences cohere into a single life mirrors her unstable narrative perspective and its shifts between present tense and historical present, first and third person, and, as discussed later in this chapter, autobiography and fiction.

Many critics have written about the rise of the autobiographical subject—roughly synonymous with the rise of the novel—as a formative source (and sign) of modern individualism. Recent theories of autobiography that assume a mingling of historical and fictional modes better account for Nell's life story than earlier models that consolidate the autobiographical subject as autonomous and (appearing to be) self-directed.[11] As Martin Löschnigg explains, "The distinction between fact and fiction no longer seems to be the overriding concern" in postclassical narratology's theories of autobiography. Rather, these recent theories emphasize "narrativity as a vital factor in the construction of identity, i.e. a view that autobiography, in narrative terms, stages the drama of creating the autobiographer's identity."[12] Löschnigg's consideration of autobiography as "an experiential site, as a re-living of experience rather than as an attempt by a detached subject to interpret itself as an object" aligns with Nell's disrupted chronology and habit of representing past events in the present tense.[13]

Nell's purported autobiography also registers doubts about the value and significance of her story. For instance, when the novel opens, Nell is talking to herself in the family graveyard and musing about where she would like to be buried. As she relays to the reader, "These remarks I made to no other audience than myself, consequently they were received without any marks of dissent."[14] In the story she narrates about her past, her choices and desires are consistently challenged, if not rejected outright. Her family does not approve of Dick, as he has no money. Her rebuffs to Sir Hugh Lancaster's persistent courtship are ignored or overridden. Dolly scorns her opinions and Nell is looked down upon by local society. Even in the nonconfrontational sphere of written narration, Nell often disparages her "little bitter story" and "foolish little tale."[15] She questions whether her story has any value: "Will any one care to read it? Is a dissected heart worth looking at, even though it be rather a foolish one?"[16]

Later she skips over six uneventful months in her account with exaggerated deference: "I think even the patientest among you would go to sleep, or at least would yawn very widely, were I to test your powers of endurance with such an infliction."[17] In contrast is Jane Eyre's deft handling of a similar move: "This is not to be a regular autobiography," she coolly explains; "I am only bound to invoke memory where I know her responses will possess some degree of interest; therefore I now pass a space of eight years almost in silence: a few lines only are necessary to keep up the links of connection."[18] Where Brontë's heroine manages the inclusions and exclusions of her story with editorial confidence, Nell doubts she can hold the reader's interest and finds her method of self-expression inadequate: "I am afraid I am painting the little cabinet pictures of my life too minutely, too elaborately; like a Dutch painter, I am reproducing the cabbages and onions, the pots and pans of every-day life, *exactly*, and without elevating them."[19] An autobiographer who suspects that she is writing *too much* about her life and yet not imparting significance approaches generic confusion, if not contradiction. Nell also echoes George Eliot's famous definition of realism in *Adam Bede* (1859) as the "rare, precious quality of truthfulness" found in Dutch painting, but "despise[d]" by "lofty-minded people."[20] Degrading Eliot's technique as mere detail, Nell inadvertently reveals her own unsophistication, and in doing so, she prompts the reader's awareness of her autobiographical blind spots.

Nell's Formal Manipulation of Time

Nell's unpredictable sequencing of her life story emerges more dramatically in her habit of narrating past events in the present tense, a form also called the historical present. She occasionally references the time when she writes the account, a few years after the central events take place, but most of the recent past she writes about unfolds *in medias res*, as if she were watching her former self in real time instead of managing the representation herself. The energy of this presentist focus suddenly clashes, in the third chapter, with her announcement that she is writing the account from her deathbed—a diegetic sabotage of the suspenseful love story. A more benign version of this distorted perspective occurs in the first chapter when she observes that the story of her family history has caused her to neglect her own character's movement through space and time: "But all this time I am keeping myself waiting at my own hall-door while detailing my family's genealogy."[21] Later in the text, in a late-night conversation with Dolly, Nell wonders, "Why upon earth don't I go to bed, instead of sitting swinging my small slippered feet, ill-temperedly, to and fro?"[22] Nell-the-character seems to be unreliably connected to Nell-the-narrator. Charles Dickens also uses the historical present, but in the case of *David Copperfield*, for instance, he is careful to distinguish between the historical present of the revivified past and the present tense that connotes his narrative activity and differentiation between young David and mature David. In contrast, Broughton omits qualifications and asides that would explicate the moment of writing from the recalled event, disconnecting Nell from a specific time frame.

A challenge to linear time that invokes a specifically metafictional self-consciousness occurs when present-Nell narrates past-Nell fantasizing about "writing a book" to pay the bills—and so the text we are reading collides with this prospective text. They conceivably are the same, and just as conceivably, the one Nell imagines proleptically stays imaginary. Her second fantasy in this same passage is similarly ambiguous: she envisions "marrying a certain snuffy old bachelor uncle of the Coxes, and making him settle three-fourths of his income on papa."[23] This projection turns out to be a near summary of Nell's decisions later in the novel: when she believes that Dick has abandoned her and she decides to marry the older, wealthy Sir Hugh, immediately upon their engagement she asks him for a settlement for her father.[24] Because the older Nell, as autobiographer, would already know this turn of events, its glib presentation as a youthful daydream from her past has at once a double meaning and a self-canceling effect: it expresses the naïve idealism of the younger Nell *and* conveys the older Nell's ironic dissimulation of the story she is writing. But Nell's eventual participation in the kind of clichéd marriage she mocks early on makes it more pathetic and suggests that tired conventions are her lot in life.

Perhaps the novel's most formally significant manipulation of time happens in a passage near the end. Nell, married to Sir Hugh, is dreading Dolly's imminent visit. She sets the scene: "I am buried in an arm-chair in my boudoir, reading a novel. It interests me rather, for it is all about a married woman, who ran away from her husband and suffered the extremity of human ills in consequence.... The naughty matron is just dying of a broken heart and starvation in a Penitentiary, when I hear carriage wheels."[25] Nell's description of the novel she is reading makes her use of the historical present especially revealing. Her summary of the novel ("The naughty matron is just dying of a broken heart") is formally equivalent to that of her own experiences ("I am . . . reading a novel"; "I hear carriage wheels"). It is conventional to describe novels in the present tense, which acknowledges that the artistic time frame of the novel is extraneous to "real" life, and so a novel's present is whatever part of the whole one is reading or describing. But by treating her own past in this way, Nell undermines its status as an archived event in favor of the impression of its action. Nell has already explained that she is writing about a period about two years before, but in using the present tense, her narrative demands to be interpreted like a novel rather than a history.[26]

"I Know Absolutely Nothing"

What appears to be Nell-the-character's mutinous escape from Nell-the-narrator is complicated by the mounting evidence she provides about how ill prepared she is to narrate a coherent account, even of her own life. Hannah More's argument that women were generically unfit for autobiography previews Nell's dilemma by connecting organizational principles to nature rather than education. In the late eighteenth century, More writes that women "seem not to possess in an equal measure the faculty of comparing, combining, analysing, and separating [their] ideas; that deep and patient thinking which goes to the bottom of a subject; nor that power of arrangement which knows how to link a thousand connected ideas in one dependent train, without losing sight of the original idea, out of which the rest grow, and on which they all hang."[27] Nell's example suggests women writers lack not the native capacity to organize an autobiographical account, but the formal education and authorial confidence that would provide them with its shaping construct. Her organizational weakness reflects a social deficit, not a "natural" defect. Nell's imprecision and her collusion between past, present, and projection can be attributed, at least in part, to her faulty education, her shaky grasp of history, and her isolation from the modern world. (She has never been to London; she refers to her life at home with her father as living in "Castle Rackrent."[28]) When Dick asks her about her studies, she answers, "There's nothing to be told about nothing. . . . Papa knows everything; Dolly knows most things, and I know nothing. That's the state of the case."[29] Elsewhere, she confesses in more detail:

> Truth to tell, I was deeply dissatisfied with myself, and with the weedy unstocked condition of my mind's fair garden. Dolly did well to despise me; I was but a poor creature, and despicable; foolishest, childishest, among women. I knew absolutely nothing; I had not the least idea what

the Bill of Rights was about, nor who fought the battle of Fontenoy, or any other battle either. Dick would despise me too when he came to know me better; would get tired of me, and find me insipid. Whether a more accurate knowledge of dates would make me a more original companion, I did not stop to inquire.[30]

Yet Nell's professed ignorance accompanies a narrative so crowded with literary, historical, theological, and classical references that she also reveals a comprehensive exposure to knowledge. She is not, that is, unacquainted with a startling range of texts and subjects, but she lacks the training that could organize them into instructive information.

The references Nell makes in just one chapter illustrate the juxtaposition between her immersive reading and her lack of a formal, classifying education. In chapter 13, she veers from the Bible's Song of Solomon to a love poem by Alexander Smith, inserting words in French, Latin, Italian, Scottish dialect, German, and baby talk. She quotes from a play, refers to Thomas Babington Macaulay's "Ranke's History of Popes," Sir Walter Scott, *The Pilgrim's Progress*, the Divine Right of Kings, Alfred Tennyson's *Idylls of the King*, Thomas Parr, Roman history, Mother Goose, the book of Exodus, an essay by "Artemus Ward," the Gospel according to Mark, and the book of Lamentations. When Dick asks her if she ever reads poetry, she answers enthusiastically: "Oh, yes; very often. I have read 'Lara,' [Byron] and 'We are Seven,' [Wordsworth] and the 'Lord of Burleigh,' [Tennyson] and the 'Needy Knife Grinder,' [a burlesque of Robert Southey's pro-revolutionary verse written by the politician George Canning] and 'Samson Ago—Ago—something'" [Milton, "Samson Agonistes"].[31]

Dick observes that her "pieces of poetry seemed to have about as much relationship to one another" as Homer, Plutarch, and Nicodemus, after jokingly quoting from a piece of doggerel that humorously relates the three.[32] Dick's observation exemplifies the dizzying patchwork of Nell's entire narrative, and were her narrative squarely based in the past, it would align with the postmodern sense identified with Fredric Jameson, for whom "pastiche" imparts parodic language but lacks parody's awareness of its subversive effect. For Nell's references to history, languages, and literature to be parodic, she would have to be aware of the humor their juxtaposition imparts—as Dick is when he teases with the doggerel. But our proleptic awareness of the older Nell, in noting Dick's gibe at her younger self's poetic choices, transports the narrative to parodic ground: she sees the joke in retrospect.

Because she does not know the order of public or official history, Nell arranges the world according to her own linguistic networks, drawing from a huge range of subjects, languages, and genres. Adding to their discord, Nell's constant stream of quotations, epigrams, and references are seldom attributed or contextualized for the reader. On the day of her wedding to Sir Hugh, for instance, Nell explains "how it came about" by inserting these lines: "'The Queen laid her white throat on the block, / Quietly waiting for the fatal shock.'"[33] These lines on the death of Anne Boleyn are misquoted from William Harrison Ainsworth's *The Tower of London* (1840).[34] Not only does Nell misquote the original, but she neither attributes it to its source nor provides its original context. For Valérie Baisnée-Keay, "the attribution of authorship to a text . . . lends it certain social characteristics that an anonymous text does not possess,"[35] characteristics that Kate Flint describes in *The Woman Reader* (1995) when she proposes that "to employ a literary reference is to assert one's place within the cultural assumptions of that society. Quotations could thus be a means for women to claim . . . their right to be considered on equal terms with other, male writers."[36] Eliot asserts this right in her novels, where she makes prodigious use of (attributed) epigrams and so exhibits the intellectual armory associated with male scholarship. Nell's motley quotations assert no such right to cultural status and reflect instead a mind unaided by classificatory norms. In a more extreme interpretation, Nell's constant inclusion of quoted but unsourced material into her own writing eclipses the distinction between an author and a reader: the material circulates in her imagination separately from the canonical history that could impart its authority.

Hayden White has described historiography as a subject indebted to language systems and genres that can shape or even determine the "reality" of the events that are the subject of a historical account. His *Metahistory: The Historical Imagination in Nineteenth-Century Europe* (1973) emphasizes constructedness and perspective over concrete phenomenology, a significant contribution to postmodern understandings of history. White contends that nineteenth-century history was underwritten by conventions of realistic writing, not the reportage of facts. Nell's understanding of history is similarly based upon writing and written conventions, but without the structuralist imposition of order on the world that White describes. Her idiosyncratic vision of history reveals her alienation from the master narratives of history and literature that determine mid-Victorian reality. Nell is not a skeptic of narratological authority in the manner of postmodernists who have absorbed the existential fractures of late twentieth-century history, but a solitary mouthpiece of a rich body of knowledge that, in the style of postmodern fiction, follows no organizing narrative. For this reason, *Cometh Up as a Flower* strays from Linda Hutcheon's description of "historiographic metafiction" as "novels which are both intensely self-reflexive and yet paradoxically also lay claim to historical events and personages"[37] because the historical world that Nell evokes is so unauthoritative. When a late twentieth-century, postmodern novelist like Kurt Vonnegut in *Slaughterhouse-Five* (1969) irreverently situates history on the same level as fictional inventions, juxtaposing the former's truthfulness with the latter's absurdity and investing Billy Pilgrim, his time-traveling protagonist, with his own personal experiences in World War II, he is writing from a "post-authoritative" position—one where dismissing the conventions of representation is an artistic posture. Broughton's Nell cannot reject discursive authority because she does not occupy that territory to cede: her implausible grasp of history and her failure to provide citations reflects a genuine deficit of knowledge rather than an artistic imprimatur.

"Like a Story-book!"

If Nell is an unconvincing historian, her facility with the conventions of fiction convinces us that she is not writing *about* her life but rather composing a literary version of a life. As the novel nears its end, Nell's narration reads more and more extravagantly like fiction. In one example, she has been unhappily married to Sir Hugh for several months. Sir Hugh and his mother make a social visit that takes them from the house overnight. Nell sits alone in the parlor, amid a howling windstorm and utter desolation, when "suddenly there comes a lull between two rain-bursts; the moon comes sweeping out from behind a great cloud shoulder; the Portugal laurel beside me shakes and rustles; and from behind it a man steps out suddenly—steps out into the moonlit gravel walk, where the pebbles are glittering like so many diamonds."[38] After a chapter break that establishes this apparition as a true cliff-hanger, Nell continues: "Need I tell you who the man was?"[39] She need not. Dick himself emerges from the dark and stormy night. In the fervid conversation that follows, Nell learns that Dick did not ignore her letters, nor fail to write his own. Dolly intercepted his letters so that Nell never saw them, and worst of all, Dolly forged a letter from Nell that broke off the relationship and requested that he never contact her again. Dick's visit is a desperate attempt to seek explanation from Nell on the eve of his military departure to India. Their rash exchange hits all the marks of a melodrama: it establishes a conniving traitor in Dolly; Nell begs to run away with Dick at once; Dick honorably refuses to compromise her virtue; they kiss; the storm surges; Dick leaves Nell prostrate on the parlor couch. The Shakespearean twist whereby both lovers learn too late of each other's devotion reads conspicuously like bathetic convenience. In a reference to fictional convention that Nell articulates directly, she positions writing as a means of identity assimilation. Imagining her marriage to Dick, she considers, "Married at nineteen! How interesting, and like a story-book! Mrs. M'Gregor! Nelly M'Gregor! Major and Mrs. M'Gregor! I would write it down in my blotting-book as soon as I got home, to see how it looked."[40] Nell's slippage among projected writing, memory, and memoir casts the book we read into uncertain ontological status—that is, casts it as fiction.

Broughton's playful transit between a readerly awareness of fiction ("like a story-book") and the unacknowledged fictiveness that we suspect in Nell's ostensibly "real" autobiography (Dick's midnight visit to Nell) makes *Cometh Up as a Flower* an exceptionally sophisticated narrative. A contemporaneous, more celebrated novel by Louisa May Alcott, *Little Women* (1868–69), also uses metafictional references but does so with a more discernible cultivation of realism. In the following scene, Meg March confesses to her mother that she has received a semi-covert engagement, in the form of a letter, from John Brooke. Meg explains, "'I received the first letter from Laurie, who didn't look as if he knew anything about it,' began Meg, without looking up. 'I was worried at first, and meant to tell you; then I remembered how you liked Mr. Brooke, so I thought you wouldn't mind if I kept my little secret for a few days. I'm so silly that I liked to think no one knew; and, while I was deciding what to say, I felt like girls in books, who have such things to do. Forgive me, mother, I've paid for my silliness now; I never can look him in the face again.'"[41]

Meg's embarrassment that she acted like "girls in books" establishes a shared critical detachment with *Little Women*'s readers and so obscures Meg's status as a fictional character. In her eagerness to resemble girls in books, whether by marrying Dick or by writing her romantic autobiography in the first place, Nell distances herself from her readers. They must evaluate her through the conventions of fiction and melodrama instead of autobiography. Nell also resembles "girls in [a] book" when her health rapidly declines after Dick's surreptitious visit. With all hope of their relationship lost, the news that he has died of a fever in Lahore seems almost redundant. Nell's response is a wasting consumption conventional to heartbreak: "Hollow cheeks; the corners of the mouth drawn down, and the lines about it puckered up, as if with continual weeping; dark deep shadows under the eyes, the great wistful blue eyes that seem to see everything now mistily, dimly through unshed tears; the hair twisted up with such negligent untidiness, as if nobody cared or thought about it any longer; and the figure, the pretty, tall figure drooping and nerveless."[42] Here, the perspective of a fiction writer encroaches upon present-Nell's appraisal of her own features—not "my mouth" but "the mouth"; not "I no longer cared about my hair" but "the hair twisted up . . . as if nobody cared." With no more plot to wrest out of her sapless marriage to Sir Hugh, the onslaught of a tragic illness offers archetypal fictional closure—a formula she has prepared the reader for already. At the height of her romance with Dick, Nell previews the utility of a death plot as the only alternative to a future with Dick. Imagining how she would feel if he were to die, she reflects that her own survival "would be a physical impossibility. But if, by some miracle, I were to be unable thus to rid myself of life; if it were still to keep its undesired hated hold upon me, why—I'd take poison. Nothing could be simpler; arsenic, for instance."[43] But even simpler than arsenic is the trademark demise of a lovelorn heroine: "As I write, myself tottering on the verge of that last bed I so tiredly long for, Dolly is in the heyday of health and prosperity. Dolly will have that tear difficulty to contend with in my case; not I in hers. She will vanquish it, and will weep plentifully over this poor thin carcass, which indeed is ugly now."[44] The contrast between Nell's alleged decline and the romantic vigor of its description maximizes emotional impact at the expense of credibility, and Nell the tragic heroine effectively eclipses Nell the autobiographer. This is a dramatic instance of the present tense that Nell has used throughout the book—a narrative choice that foregrounds the agency of writing by featuring Nell as the conscious heroine of her own story instead of the conscientious recorder of history.

Nell's autobiographical future approaches a dead end when she "sacrifice[s] [herself], in order to prolong [her] old man's life,"[45] by marrying Sir Hugh. She foresees "long dreary years, forty, fifty, sixty perhaps, flash before my mind's eye, years of a bondage whose full horrors my innocent young soul but vaguely takes in; years *with* Hugh, and *without* papa."[46] The period directly before and after her father's death tracks a grammatical shift from the "I" narrative of autobiography and first-person fiction—"Oh, why could I not die of consumption, like that girl I took the jelly to yesterday? Why could not I cough myself out the world, as she was doing so fast?"[47]—to a flat and deterministic third-person past tense:

> Nelly LeStrange, with her light heart, her tumbledown Spanish castles, and her silly little tender jokes, has gone away, not from that room only, but from the world.
> They buried her yesterday in that dull chamber, where Death is holding his carnival among the LeStranges, and have left only a very heavy-hearted Nell Lancaster in her stead.[48]

In a novel riddled with premonitions and prognostications of death, Nell's desolation after the death of her father, the apparent abandonment of Dick, and the "dreary years" she anticipates with Hugh herald a turning point. Her wish to "die of consumption" like the "girl I took the jelly to yesterday" (a set piece Alcott also uses for *Little Women*'s doomed Beth March) gives her formless future a romantic shape.

Rather than pin down a specific juncture where Nell's narrative relinquishes autobiography for the more fertile grounds of fiction, I am interested in the way that fiction's subjugation of autobiography in *Cometh Up as a Flower* tells a story of its own, a story that pivots upon the failure of a woman's life history to render the personal agency, excitement, and artistic coherence that she can wrest from fiction. Nell's intellectual aimlessness, the family loyalty and improvidence that convince her to marry Sir Hugh for his money, and the impossibility of her relationship with Dick can only be made sense of in melodrama (the torrid reunion with Dick on the night of the storm) and tragedy (the heroine who withers away from heartbreak): that is, fictionality imbues her experiences with a symbolic integrity that autobiographical reportage does not.

A brief exchange between Nell and Sir Hugh before their marriage illustrates the emotional resonance that a literary reference can unfurl into metafiction, independently from its local context. When Sir Hugh balks in the face of Nell's reluctance to marry him, she assures him that she "'mean[s] to be [his] wife, and [she] suppose[s] [they] shall manage to scratch on pretty much as other people do.'" She continues, echoing the refrain from Tennyson's "Mariana": "to my own heart I say that 'I would that I were dead.'"[49] Nell's words to Sir Hugh transmit the assurance he needs, but her address "to her own heart" and to the reader conveys in shorthand the desolation of Tennyson's "Mariana," forever expecting a lover who "cometh not." This invocation turns out to predict the end of Nell's "autobiography" more closely than her breezy pledge to "scratch on pretty much as other people do." And finally, the contradictory meanings of Nell's reported speech and inner feeling testify, in exemplary metafictional form, to her ambivalence as a narrator.

Cometh Up as a Flower was serialized in *Dublin University Magazine* from July 1866 to January 1867 and published by Bentley & Son, in two volumes, in 1867. The ending of the serial version differs significantly from the Bentley edition. The serial ends after chapter 28, before Dolly's marriage and Dick's death, and is followed by a brief addendum, ostensibly written by an anonymous editor: "The M.S. ends here; a stronger hand must put 'Finis' to it, for the Almighty hand has written Finis to the poor life it tells about."[50] The editor then describes the scene of Nell's death. Sir Hugh comes into her sickroom, and gently tells her,

> "I have just heard such an awfully sad thing; I cannot tell you how cut up I am about it; poor M'Gregor is dead—died of cholera at Lahore; not a soul he cared about with him." . . .
>
> "Dead, is he?" said Nell, softly, and her voice sounded very sweet and clear, and she half rose from her chair, and stretched out her slight arms, while a very tender smile came rippling over her face. And then she sank back quietly, with eyes closed, as one that slept—but it was that sleep from which there is no waking here—and, her weary course at last ended; Hugh Lancaster's fair wife was not.[51]

While Nell could not believably narrate her own death, the anonymous editor bears a suspiciously close resemblance to the Nell that has been writing the autobiography all along. In accordance with her repeated prediction, the news of Dick's death neatly precipitates her own. The editor's resigned and sympathetic acceptance of her death ("her weary course at last ended") removes from the list of obvious suspects those who might find themselves at Nell's deathbed—Hugh's mother or Dolly. The use of the archaic inversion and vocabulary we see in the phrase "Hugh Lancaster's fair wife was not" is an ironic technique that Nell has used throughout the narrative. As if aware that a young woman's tale of romantic love almost inevitably sinks into literary overdetermination, Nell frequently offsets this generic pull by identifying it as parody, as we saw above at her first meeting with Dick: "Our eyes met. There was nothing impudent in his gaze, none of the fervent admiration with which, at a first introduction, the hero in a novel regards the young lady."[52] Nell's mock-heroic language—such as her names for Dick, who is large and blonde: "King Olaf" and her "strong fair Norseman"[53]—ironizes her romantic conventionality and yields to it at the same time; realism, she suggests, cannot compete against the shaping power of genre, even when the genre is clichéd. The appearance of this formal characteristic in the epilogue therefore posits not an editor who contributes the final scene, but Nell's continuity of voice in writing as a third-person narrator and formalizing the distanced appraisal of her story that she has experimented with throughout her text: formalizing, then, the transference of autobiography to novel.

Again, this is a reading of the ending of the serial version. The two-volume form includes ten new chapters and no editorial postscript. In its last chapter, Nell anticipates imminent death: "*June 20th.*—I am going so fast! oh, so fast! These are the last words I shall ever write; it is hard, laboursome to me to hold the pencil, but I do not want to leave the story of my poor life incomplete; incompleter at least than the story of all lives must be. Some other hand must put 'Finis' I know."[54] The last paragraphs of the two-volume edition focus upon Nell's contrition about the "intense earthly passion" "eating up body and soul." Her fears that she might not be going, in death, to "a good place"[55] alternate with her expectation that she would soon "with great gladness . . . be with [her] beloved for evermore."[56] While Nell's narrative bricolage compromises the piety of the theological and biblical quotations in the rest of the book (a critic in the *London Review* complains that "there is something far from agreeable in [Broughton's] vague transition from flippant jesting to prayer"[57]), these last pages impart an uncharacteristic religiosity, especially in Nell's repeated anxiety about entering "the City of the Saints of God!"[58] The function of the sympathetic editor at the end of the serial version has been usurped by a repentant Nell, here fully conscious of the sins of extramarital love and perhaps forestalling disapproval of her hope of seeing Dick beyond the grave.

The usually irreverent Nell here makes a dramatic shift toward religious judgment, especially the fear that she might face punishment after death for loving Dick. This anxiety could be a response to paratextual demands as well as intradiegetic logic. In transforming the serial version into two volumes, Broughton was evidently required to expand the original novel. Nell's extensive religious mediations at the end of the latter version might reflect Broughton's "padding" of the original, more economical ending. Alternately, Nell's fear about her afterlife could indicate Broughton's own apprehension about the reception of her novel by functioning as a preemptive defense against *Cometh Up as a Flower*'s frank portrayal of passion. Contemporary reviewers who described Nell's plea to run away with Dick as "simply abominable"[59] and critiqued the novel's "sensual sentimentality"[60] confirm that Broughton was writing on the margins of respectability. But far from exploring the possibility that Broughton's artistic choices were influenced by market forces and standards of reception was Michael Sadleir's dismissal of her as "too impatient, too much of a rattle, to build a careful plot."[61] Perhaps confusing Broughton with Nell, Sadleir's observation treats *Cometh Up as a Flower* like a spontaneous eruption on the page rather than an artistic construction.

"Intense Feeling" as a Basis for Reality

One of the underlying arguments of *Victorian Metafiction* is that the Victorian literary establishment challenged if not precluded, in overt and covert ways, a woman's ability to be a serious novelist. Familiar challenges included the suspicion that a woman's novel was *really* penned by a man, as the curiosity surrounding the Bell "brothers" exemplifies so well. The publication of *Cometh Up as a Flower* also incited scrutiny of the author's gender. A reviewer in the *Athenaeum* resolved "that the author [of *Cometh Up*] is not a young woman, but a man, who, in the present story, shows himself destitute of refinement of thought or feeling, and ignorant of all women either are, or ought to be."[62] The *Spectator* surmises that although the author "cannot be a man, . . . she may have learnt much from some man's mind," which would help to account for "certain audacities of expression, sometimes witty to an enjoyable degree, sometimes profane."[63] In an interview with Broughton first published in the *Lady's Pictorial* in 1890, Helen C. Black relays "an amusing anecdote" about the novel's publication: "'It was claimed by other people,' [Broughton] says; 'a lady told an acquaintance of mine that her son had written it, which diverted me much.'"[64] The false attribution of a woman's novel to a man could signify its value (the novel is so good it must be a man's work) and signpost gender transgression (if a woman wrote so bold and masculine a novel, she must be very *irregular*).

Other challenges to the serious woman novelist include more subtle denials of her agency as an artist. Black exemplifies this position in her description of how "the idea of writing occurred" to Broughton: "[Broughton] says she remembers a certain wet Sunday afternoon when she was about twenty-two; she was distinctly bored by a stupid book which she was trying to read, when 'the spirit moved her to write.'" She complied with the spirit and "delivered her soul of the ideas which poured in on her brain," and "at the end of six weeks . . . found a vast heap of manuscript accumulated, to which she gave the title of 'Not Wisely, but Too Well.'"[65] Black positions Broughton as a willing but passive recipient: the "spirit" "poured" ideas "in on her brain," and thus she "found" a finished manuscript. The title of that first novel, an allusion to Othello's description of himself after murdering his wife, echoes the heedlessness of Broughton's inspiration story. Toward the end of her article, Black shifts her characterization of Broughton's writing to a different form of tacit depreciation. "The home of Miss Broughton's ancestors, Broughton Hall . . . ," she writes, "is so well depicted in 'Cometh up as a Flower,' that none who have read the book and seen the place can fail to observe the absolute truthfulness of the description."[66] If Broughton is an empty vessel filled with inspiration in the beginning of this article, by the end her skills have morphed into a mimeticism seemingly best appreciated by her readers who happened also to have seen her ancestral home.

A more theoretically important elision of Broughton's artistic agency surfaces in a review of *Cometh Up as a Flower* published in *The Times*. The reviewer, who mostly commends the novel, admits that he or she does prefer "the authoress in her calmer and more serious moods—when she is sitting by her poor old father, weighed down with debt and disappointment."[67] The substitution of Broughton for Nell's character can appear to be a logical consequence of Broughton's choice to write, in first person, about a heroine who ostensibly has written the text we read. That text is inferentially framed for distribution by Nell's unnamed, posthumous editor, following the premise of the autobiographical novel, which is itself a fiction created by Broughton. The complexity of these successively embedded registers and their socio-historical significance to the woman writer contends against the equation of the first-person narrator with the biographical author, as described in the previous chapter.[68] Finally, the relative isolation of the Victorian woman writer creates a parochial feedback loop: a woman's respectability and moral authority depend on that isolation, and yet it predisposes her to charges of a narrow, overly personal focus. Broughton works out the dilemma facing a respectable woman who wants to write but lives in social isolation by inventing, in Nell, a character whose ungoverned transmission of a miscellany of texts and discourses mingles with her own observations and experiences. Thus, the "autobiography" seems so indebted to literary and other intertextual influences that its obtrusive constructedness overwhelms its illusion of realism or reportage. Nell's death, for instance, invigorates the impression of fiction; dying from heartbreak by way of consumption exceeds in its formal convenience and generic familiarity what we can allow in autobiography. In this way, Nell's imaginative reality trounces her (purported) historical reality, and she appears as the heroine of her own (tragic) novel.

Triumph through a formulaically fictive death script is not, of course, very triumphant. But a comparison between *Cometh Up as a Flower* and Broughton's final novel, *A Fool in Her Folly* (1920), reframes the former novel's conception of the woman writer's agency. The later novel, which Tamar Heller calls Broughton's "metafictional novel,"[69] is narrated by eighty-year-old Charlotte Hankey and takes place in 1859, when Charlotte is twenty. Young Charlotte lives with her parents and sisters in a comfortable house in the country. Her greatest excitement is "the arrival of the book box from Mudie's," and after reading *Guy Livingstone* her love for reading suddenly transforms into an ambition to write: "I must begin at once—begin to create—a thought whose splendour took my breath away."[70] Charlotte shares Nell's breathless enthusiasm but lacks her sense of irony. For Charlotte, the delusions of youth have been informed by sixty years of distance, whereas Nell's awareness of her own idealism allows her to be sincere and arch at the same time. Charlotte decides that her future "masterpiece"[71] should untangle "the biggest theme—incomparably the biggest theme—in all the compass of the round world": love.[72] Undaunted by her total unfamiliarity with the theme, she begins to write: "If Keats could project himself into a world of passionate mediaeval romance out of his Cockney surroundings," she observes, she too should "be able to hurl [her]self out of [her] tamely happy, matter-of-fact existence."[73] But when Charlotte's parents discover the manuscript, they are so horrified by the "wicked" ideas[74] therein that they burn it and dispatch her to an aunt, with whom she must stay until she can promise to give up writing altogether. At her aunt's house, she falls in love with a fascinating, flawed, and devastatingly handsome neighbor; he breaks her heart; she finally experiences passion and heartbreak; and, at the novel's end, she complies with her parents' wishes and returns home.

The obstacles that Charlotte faces as an aspiring writer recall Nell's, yet lack the genuine anxieties of looming bankruptcy, a dying father, and family pressure to marry for money. Charlotte's "copy," for most of the novel, comes to her through books. When her parents inquire how she conceived of her romantic material, she answers, "You should have locked the library door.... I learnt what you think so wicked from the greatest writers, the deepest thinkers, of all time! You *never* forbid me to read them."[75] As Charlotte points out to a writer from London she meets at a dinner party, other women writers have managed to extract remarkable art from quiet lives. "Isn't it astonishing, considering what Charlotte Brontë's life was," she asks the man from London, "that she should have been able to write [*Jane Eyre*]?"[76] She continues:

> "[Brontë] had no means of knowing—I mean personally—at first-hand, how [Rochester] felt when under the influence of so overwhelming, so scorching a passion as that with which Jane had inspired him.... Do you think—do you suppose it possible—I should be glad of your opinion—that it is possible to describe anything of which the writer is quite ignorant, quite without experience of their own, but about which he or she feels very, *very* strongly, so as to make it *real*—intensely real—to their readers?"[77]

Charlotte's dinner companion is silent, so she continues:

> "I mean," I said, excitement sweeping away all the maiden reticencies that should have tied my tongue, "do you believe that a woman—supposing that the writer happened to be one—could, by sheer force of imagination, put herself so much in the place of a man desperately, recklessly, overwhelmingly in love that people might think—if they didn't know, if the book was anonymous—that she was one?"[78]

These feverish questions consolidate socio-structural challenges to Victorian women writers very efficiently. Starting with the formative example of Charlotte Brontë and *Jane Eyre*, this Charlotte grapples with the assumption that a writer must have firsthand experience of the material she writes about, which conflicts with the sheltered life imposed upon proper womanhood. Charlotte wonders if an artistic projection of feelings beyond one's acquaintance can really achieve realism, and if a woman writer can authentically sound like a man "by sheer force of imagination." But her dinner companion's response crowns the list of impediments to the woman novelist that I have been examining. He answers, "'Of course, women have written under pseudonyms,'" and then shuns her openly.⁷⁹ After a few moments of confusion, Charlotte realizes, "[he] to whom I had appealed for information on a subject of abstract interest had at once perceived that I was speaking of myself, and had believed that I was asking him for the passion I was so anxious to describe."⁸⁰ Failing to identify her "abstract" search for "information," this man substitutes for her subject—a writer's abilities—a convoluted interpretation whereby he locates *himself* as the source of her fascination. He diminishes her question about a woman writer's authentic imitation of a male point of view to a superficial nod to male pseudonyms.

Charlotte's wish to understand writing as an art form and technique is reduced finally to the scope of her falsely projected, personal feelings. At the end of *A Fool in Her Folly*, she wistfully recounts her decision to give up writing and reunite with her family of philistines. She marries for convenience and relegates the dream of authorship to youth. In comparison, the end of Nell's tale in a rush of religious and melodramatic entreaties appears oddly empowered. In narrating a heroine's dramatic exit, the closure of the novel prioritizes the creative agency of the novelist over the referential duties of the autobiographer. In her essay "One Sister's Surrender: Rivalry and Resistance in Rhoda Broughton's *Cometh Up as a Flower*" (2006), Lindsey Faber similarly identifies a productive energy from Nell's death, writing that Nell "has longed for death as an escape from a miserable future, and it is in death that she finds acceptance and recovery," and that "Nell's narrative achieves a sense of continuity and perpetuity, for while it ends with her death, it opens with thoughts on her burial."⁸¹

Critics have identified the similarities between *A Fool in Her Folly* and Broughton's own life. Charlotte Hankey is born in 1839 and writes, as an eighty-year-old, in 1919; Rhoda Broughton lived from 1840 to 1920. Black's description of Broughton's inspiration to write ("ideas . . . poured in on her brain"; "day after day, night after night, she wrote swiftly and in secret"⁸²) anticipates the intensity of Charlotte's early inspiration. Sadleir imposes a biographical metatext on several of Broughton's novels when he writes that he had "no shadow of a doubt that the ill-fated love-affair of Char and Bill Drinkwater [of *A Fool in Her Folly*] is the love-affair of Nell and Dick McGregor in *Cometh Up*, of Kate and Dare Stamer in *Not Wisely*, and of Rhoda herself, in her excited book-stimulated teens, and some discreditable unknown."⁸³ But the contrast between Charlotte and Nell, and the endings of their stories, transfers whatever source material comes from Broughton into the more theoretically significant and enduring record of women's writing and metafictional reflection, the latter a manifest solution to the very dilemma it identifies. If we read Charlotte and Nell through the determining lens of Broughton's own life, we perform the same reduction as Charlotte's self-absorbed dinner companion: we move abstract representation to personal confession, and a professional dilemma becomes an isolated complaint.

3

"THE DIFFERENCE BETWEEN AUTHORS AND THEIR BOOKS"

Charlotte Riddell's *A Struggle for Fame* and Margaret Oliphant's *The Athelings*

The previous chapters argue that *Villette* and *Cometh Up as a Flower* use metafictional strategies to identify and critique barriers facing Victorian women writers. This chapter continues to examine how women novelists positioned themselves in an artistic marketplace through fictional portraits of other women novelists, but my emphasis shifts from the exigencies of personal circumstances to consider two fictional novelists who represent opposing types of the professional woman writer. Where the chapters on Brontë and Broughton identify roughly coterminous moments in the woman novelist's artistic detachment from her own life, this chapter posits a symbolic "before" and "after" in its examination of the female novelist as a figure of her age. As mentioned in the introduction, Margaret Oliphant's (1828–1897) heroine-novelist Agnes Atheling in *The Athelings* (1857) possesses an inborn talent for writing that neither her history nor her education can explain. Agnes, the narrator explains, was "not wise; she had no particular gift for conversation, and none whatever for logic; no accomplishments, and not a very great deal of information."[1] Her writing career develops in harmony with her personal life, with very little influence from the marketplace. Charlotte Riddell's (1832–1906) heroine in *A Struggle for Fame* (1883), Glenarva Westley, begins her literary career with a similar notion of a divine gift. But Riddell's meticulous description of Glen's adaptation to a fluctuating market, and the artistic flexibility that she learns to cultivate in response to it, consigns the idea of the literary "gift" to an obsolescent past. While both novels begin in the 1850s, Riddell's pragmatic understanding of the rise of literary professionalism inserts into her mid-century London a prescience that her heroine experiences but cannot yet articulate.

As Glen teaches herself to write serious novels, Riddell positions *her* novel—*A Struggle for Fame*—as the working example of Glen's lessons, using metafictional self-consciousness to explain its particularities of plot and style and its departures from a conventional fictional script. In contrast, Oliphant's choice of a woman novelist for her heroine fulfills a very different end. While Agnes is called a "genius," her novels eventually lead her to marriage, and so the end of her writing career. Written during a time when Oliphant was decrying progressive ideas in women's fiction,[2] this portrait of the woman writer is appropriately feminine and largely removed from the competitive publishing industry. All portraits of novelists in novels are metafictional, but where Riddell uses the form to expand the horizons of women's art, Oliphant's version is ironically self-canceling.

Myths of Genius

Unjustly overlooked by canonical and popular readers, *A Struggle for Fame* exceeds the domestic realism of *The Athelings* by virtue of its own demonstration of critical interpretation. Riddell's novel equivocates between the type of fiction her heroine is authorized to write by society and her actual literary achievements. *A Struggle for Fame* begins in the early 1850s, when Glen and her father leave their family estate in Ireland—lost to his financial imprudence—and move to London, where she hopes to become a famous novelist. Where the progress of the Atheling family is measured by their retreat from bustling London and actualized in their eventual home ownership in the country, Glen moves toward a precarious urban life. She and her father travel alongside a fellow Irishman, Barney Kelly, whose literary career evolves in parallel with Glen's, but which reflects a vastly different professional trajectory. In London, Glen meets and later marries Mordaunt Logan-Lacere, but the story of Glen's fluctuating success as a novelist overshadows the story of their marriage.

Linda Peterson examines *A Struggle for Fame* in conversation with Charlotte Brontë, especially as Elizabeth Gaskell shaped her posthumous reputation in *The Life of Charlotte Brontë* (1857). Riddell's novel, argues Peterson, "reinscribes myths of female authorship made famous in Gaskell's *Life* and other early Victorian memoirs of women authors: myths of genius and vocation, of solitude and loneliness, of domesticity and inspiration."[3] The example of

Brontë informs my reading of *A Struggle for Fame* too, but where Peterson finds in Glen strains of the Romantic genius and inspiration that Gaskell attributes to Brontë and Oliphant attaches to Agnes, I emphasize Glen's distinctly unromantic responses to the demands that the publishing market made upon women writers. In forging a career based on realism, Glen's novels emphasize process, technique, and application over a pure and almost arbitrary inspiration, such as that attributed to Agnes. Glen's teenage decision to become a famous novelist undoubtedly echoes the romantic Brontë myth, though not the Brontë sisters' actual experience with the world of publishing. As her family fortunes sink, she and her father must leave the family estate, also named Glenarva, for a small cottage on its grounds. "There came on her suddenly a mighty change," and she becomes consumed with the family's abrupt decline: "What could she do? If she had been a man there were fifty things to which she might have turned her attention; but being only a woman, which way would it be best, or indeed possible, for her to face the world?"[4]

As "fac[ing] the world" in this instance means the chance to earn an income, Glen decides on writing as her only possible solution. "For many a long day Glenarva Westley thought the idea which sprang into birth as she looked out on the quiet sea and that broad track caused by glittering moonbeams was one conceived under the spur of the moment; but in after years she comprehended how differently the matter actually stood. During the whole of her young life there had never been a time when to every look and tone of nature she failed to respond with the deep sympathy of an imaginative and poetical temperament."[5] The narrator's description of this temperament accompanied by its mature correction casts it into youthful fantasy; Glen's romanticism seems more juvenile than divinely transmitted. "In fancy [Glen] had peopled each lonely scene her eyes rested on. She dreamed of heroes and heroines, of great deeds of courage, endurance, devotion," and her moment of revelation comes to her "in a flood of moonlight": "'I will write,' she said."[6] Peterson attributes "cultural capital" to Glen's inspired "high vocation,"[7] but the retrospective wisdom that accompanies and checks it from inception makes her sound less like the Brontëan genius of myth and celebrity and more like a young girl who had read Romantic poetry—like Marianne Dashwood had she riveted her energies on writing instead of Willoughby. Glen briefly harbors "a settled conviction [that] she was getting on admirably, and would ere long be able to restore the shattered fortunes of the then Westley of Glenarva."[8]

Novel Writing for Life Management in *The Athelings*

The most significant creative difference between Agnes and Glen is that Agnes cannot account for why she writes. After the publication of her first book, Agnes is asked, "How did it come into your head to write that delightful book?"[9] and later, "What put *that* into your idle little brain?" On both occasions, Agnes answers, "I do not know."[10] Penny Boumelha, writing about female writers at the fin de siècle, explains that the "concept of innate genius . . . enables the representation of achievement without conscious ambition. . . . If the power of genius simply resides within, then it becomes only another form of destiny to which women must assent."[11] Agnes accepts her gifts as a fortuitous mystery, but also borrows from life. Her success in character delineation, for instance, is proportional to her familiarity with her real-life models. In her first novel, *Hope Hazelwood*, the heroine resembles Agnes's sister, Marian, and the mother character is "but a delicate, shy, half-conscious sketch of [her own] dearest mother."[12] In a later novel, the hero emulates an acquaintance whom she will later marry, and the tentativeness of his portrait signifies suspense for the romance plot that will emerge:

> About her hero Agnes was timid, presenting a grand vague outline out of him, and describing him in sublime general terms; for she was not at all an experienced young lady, though she was an author, but herself regarded her hero with a certain awe and respect and imperfect understanding, as young men and young women of poetic conditions are wont to regard each other. From this cause it resulted that you were not very clear about the Sir Charles Grandison[13] of the young novelist. . . . [He] lay half visible, sometimes shining out in a sudden gleam of somewhat tremulous light, but for the most part enveloped in shadow.[14]

Agnes's "half visible" (rather than half-conceived) hero will be fleshed out, the narrator implies, by her increasing familiarity with his real-life counterpart. Oliphant's narrator uses a fictional hero, Richardson's Sir Charles Grandison, to connote the fictional version of Agnes's future husband, who is, of course, also fictional. When Lucy Snowe and Nell LeStrange invoke fictional conventions as they write their stories, we become alert to the fictionality of *those* stories and, refractively, the novels in which *they* are the story. But in *The Athelings*, the narrator insists upon Agnes's inexperience; it is "you" the reader who was "not very clear" about her Sir Charles Grandison; Agnes regards her half-drawn hero with the "awe and respect" commanded by a real person, not the license of a fiction writer. Her removal from this representational game of mirrors diminishes its metafictional self-consciousness by excluding it from her own field of observation. Novel writing for Agnes anticipates, and makes possible, what she will eventually find in life, which tilts the artistic practice toward instrumentalism. The reader can identify metafiction in the story of a writer who is herself a writer, but Agnes's novel about her future husband and *The Athelings* ultimately occupy different ontological levels: the first "comes true" while the second maintains its fictiveness.

Another novelist-character in *The Athelings*, Agnes's brother-in-law Louis, also writes a book that has functional influence over his personal circumstances. The rightful heir of a contested estate, Louis decides to write a biography of the current owner in hopes of establishing his own tie to the property. His method of writing relies on discovery rather than creation: it was "a true story, of which he laboured to find out every episode." The narrator raves, "Perhaps a more remarkable manuscript than that of Louis never existed; . . . [he] pursued his tale with all the zest, and much more than the excitement, of a romancer." Louis "pursued his story with a concentration of purpose which the greatest poet in existence might have envied." He "was a great deal too much in earnest to think about the sentences in which he recorded what he learnt. The consequence was, that this memoir of Lord Winterbourne was a model of terse and pithy English—an unexampled piece of biography."[15] The narrator's bombast seems aimed at reifying Louis's book beyond the status of a mere book: conceived without special regard to its sentences, "a history" verified "in every particular," "pursued" and "recorded," Louis's achievement models "pithy English" itself. Insofar as it helps to establish his rightful title, the biography yields material change, and the narrator's description of Louis's biography as an "unexampled" metonym for English elects this highest praise for the book that exemplifies the national language.

While Louis pursues his biography, Agnes writes a fictional version of the same story, which she calls *The Heir*. As she writes *The Heir*, it "passed out of her controlling hands . . . and began to exercise over her the sway which a real created thing always exercises over the mind even of its author. . . . It told its story."[16] Agnes "did not write [*The Heir*] carefully, but she did write it with fervour, and the haste of a mind concerned and in earnest."[17] In another example of her ease in publishing, *The Heir* seemingly avoids an editorial process, even though "it was not very much of a story, neither was it written with that full perfection of style which comes by experience and the progress of years; but it had something in its faulty grace, and earnestness, and simplicity, which was perhaps more attractive than the matured perfectness of a style which had been carefully formed."[18] The purity and appeal of Agnes's writing strengthen her relationship with the Rector, the "hero" whom she struggled to describe and will later marry. When the Rector reads *The Heir*, he "forgot all about the story, thinking of the writer of it; he became indifferent to what she had to tell, but dwelt and lingered—not like a critic—like something very different—upon the cadence of her voice."[19] Louis's biography evokes English, Agnes's novel evokes Agnes, and the books themselves fade away. By establishing Louis's inheritance and leading Agnes to her future husband, these books have tactical, not artistic, power. Moreover, the gender of the authors corresponds to what their books make happen: not to build a professional profile or artistic clout but to facilitate inheritance and marriage, respectively.

The narrator's appreciation of *The Heir* and Louis's biography for their *elision* of literary signs helps to explain why *The Athelings*, despite its many references to literature and even to novel writing, does not evince the metafictional techniques I am attributing to Riddell and the other novelists in this book. Oliphant's portrayal of writing in *The Athelings* consistently obscures its conscious invention. When Louis's sister, Rachel, praises him by saying that she "never read of any one, even in a book, like Louis. I think he ought to be a king,"[20] her words *should* ironize the existence of Louis in Oliphant's book, but they do not—they stay confined to the observations of a fond sister who invokes books as a detached metric of assessment. Oliphant's characters are the products of a narrator who conceals their fictiveness and so obscures how the characters work as artistic constructions.

Again, Agnes's writing matters not for her critical or public repute but for its efficacy in fulfilling her personal destiny—marriage to the Rector, Lionel Rivers. After the publication of *The Heir*, Rivers suffers a crisis of faith and leaves for an extended journey abroad. Here, the narrator's discussion of Agnes's writing changes from a summary of her novels' plots to a description of her vocation, which sounds more religious than professional: "The voice of the woman who dwelt at home went out over the world; it charmed multitudes who thought of nothing but the story it told, delighted some more who recognised that sweet faulty grace of youth, that generous young directness and simplicity which made the fable truth."[21] Far from the cozy scribbling around the fireplace that once entertained her family, Agnes's gift has become more profound and less distinct. This passage appears to be describing a biblical parable in its oracular characterization of Agnes reaching "multitudes" with her true "fables."

In one of very few critical studies of *The Athelings*, Brenda R. Weber describes Oliphant's representation of Agnes's writing as a negotiation between feminine decorum and respectable professionalism.[22] The image of Agnes reaching "multitudes" certainly implies professional reach, but Oliphant's substitution of the worldly business of editors, publishers, reviewers, and readers in the beginning of *The Athelings* for the parabolic power of writing that may convert an unbeliever at the end is hard to see as a way to negotiate professionalism. To the end of *The Athelings*, Agnes remains ignorant of or removed from the business of publishing: she never faces unscrupulous editors or damning reviews, or wrangles over copyright or payment. She manages to be successful without being indoctrinated into or implicated by publishing's philistine business practices. In the last scene of the novel, Agnes sits at her writing desk when Rivers suddenly appears after a long absence abroad. She asks where his travels have led him, and he lapses into a melodramatic conversion narrative:

> "You gave me a talisman, Agnes. . . . I have carried it all over the world. . . . I went to try your spell—I who trusted nothing—at the moment when everything had failed me. . . . I put yonder sublime Friend of yours to the experiment—I dared to do it! I took his name to the sorrowful, as you bade me. I cast out devils with his name, as the sorcerers tried to do. . . . I have found a cave in a wild mining district among a race of giants. I am Vicar of Bottallach, among the Cornish men—have been for four-and-twenty hours—that is the end."[23]

They join hands, and Rivers continues: "The end, but the beginning too. . . . Agnes, hear me still—I have something to more to say." But the narrator leaves this "something more" unsaid, suspending Agnes and Rivers in a realm of pure possibility that narrated language would transform to signification, and so embed with its own set of contingencies. Agnes "did not answer a word; she lifted her eyes to his face with one hurried, agitated momentary glance. Something more! but the whole tale was in the look. *They* did not know very well what words followed, and neither do we."[24] To its end, *The Athelings* consummates its greatest accomplishments off the page. The best books transcend their literary status: Louis's biography distills the essence of English; when Rivers reads *The Heir*, he "forgot all about the story" and thought only of its writer; in this final scene, a look embodies the "whole tale" for the characters, the narrator, and the readers. The narrator's ontological solidarity with characters and readers dispels the illusion of her control, projecting realism by eliminating the signs of textual invention. Agnes's writing career, successful though it has been, moves her toward romantic closure and away from her contribution to literature or women's professional advancement.

Mastering Ambition in *A Struggle for Fame*

Where Agnes's hopes of authorship portend quick success, Glen's aspirations collide with the realities of the London publishing world: "She began her life-task in utter ignorance of how to set about it. She did not know how books were printed or published. She had never met an author."[25] By a stroke of luck, a publisher's reader spots promise in her manuscript and introduces her to Mr. Vassett, who will be her first publisher. Mr. Vasset takes Glen's total ignorance of the business of literature in stride: "'Literature,' he began, speaking [to her] in a general and delicate manner, 'is, so far as I am aware, the only profession in which persons imagine they can embark without the smallest training or preparation, or the remotest idea of the labour involved in producing an even moderately successful work.'"[26] His remarks recall Eliot's wry observation in "Silly Novels by Lady Novelists" (1856) that "there is no species of art which is so free from rigid requirements" as fiction.[27] Glen discovers that a writer's success depends on market conditions, not talent. Mr. Vassett's kindly reader explains to her that if "Charlotte Brontë, or even Miss Martineau herself, were to offer [Mr. Vassett] a manuscript at the present moment . . . he would say its appearance must be deferred, otherwise he should reluctantly be obliged to decline it."[28] These circumstances adjust Glen's ambitions, and after many failed attempts to place her manuscript, she "lost heart altogether. She did not now believe in herself or her fitness to become an author"[29]:

> She was fairly educated, but she did not know enough to teach; and if she had, would rather have swept a crossing. She played well, but was nothing of a musician; her drawing was of the usual commonplace character; for languages she had no more aptitude than for arithmetic. . . . Such gifts as she possessed—and they were not many—did not lie in the direction of money-making.
>
> "I am fit for nothing," she thought one night.[30]

Glen's increasingly commodified understanding of success informs the way she develops her writing. While "plots and characters" came to her "almost unbidden," "her difficulty was to mould them into shape, to fit the different pieces of her puzzle together, so as to form an intelligible whole."[31] The task is to learn how to make a novel like an artisan instead of receiving one artlessly, like Agnes.

The repetition in these passages of the formal challenges Glen faces in translating ideas into a "mould" or "shape" exposes a feminine isolation in her early writing, which Riddell posits as an obstacle to her professional and critical success. Glen lives in "narrow lodgings in an unfashionable part of London" with her ailing father,[32] while her counterpart from Ireland, Barney Kelly, traverses the city and appropriates its stimulating scenes in writing. One of his early ventures into print is a "graphic . . . pen-and-ink sketch" of the bustling Hoxton market and its "stalls, the flaring naphtha, the eager sellers, the anxious buyers."[33] Kelly's "sketch" descriptively captures a vivid, physical space at a time when Glen's unfamiliarity with "the sights and sounds and customs of a foreign city" cast its subjects "outside her" and she suffers a crippling "absence of ideas."[34]

Unable to engage with London as a subject, Glen writes a manuscript drawn from her life in Ireland. She sells the novel to a publisher, but when a childhood friend unmasks her identity behind the pseudonym, the book "could not now be published." Unflattering portraits of friends and family members "told a story she never would have ventured to have put on paper had she not felt secure under the shelter of an assumed name"; "all comfort and security and freedom in writing was over."[35] Riddell's narrator regrets the censorship but understands it as a consequence of a woman's tenuous relationship to public life. "There are some women," she writes, "for whom even one leaf of the laurel crown proves too heavy a burden," and "it might have been better for Glen and those nearest and dearest to her if she had never written another line."[36] The invocation of not only Glen's but her family's reputation reflects the high stakes a woman writer, at mid-century, risked in attaching herself to professional life and any publicity that extended from it.

When Glen does finally publish a novel, the experience so disheartens her that once again she doubts her chosen path. The critical offensive against her novel offers an inventory of the biases faced by artistically ambitious women novelists: "The papers had not a good word to say for it; the critics were beautifully unanimous in making merry over her finest passages—in exposing the absurdity of her plot, the faults in her grammar, the solecisms of which she was guilty, the meagerness of her ideas, the poverty of her invention, the tallness of her talk, and the impossibility of many things which were literal facts ever having happened."[37] These flaws encapsulate a Victorian woman novelist's cultural exclusion from serious realism, and the contradiction inherent in her positioning herself as an authoritative literary voice. The absence of such critiques directed at Agnes's novels minimizes their impact, but Glen's ambitions are exposed cruelly by the critics' "merry" objections. Her plot is absurd, her grammar faulty, her ideas flimsy and exaggerated—all defects stemming from her peripheral relationship to the educated, experience-driven, objective standards that intellectual masculinity naturalizes. The "lonely girl" who grows up accompanied by the "phantom presence[s]" of her imagination, in aristocratic seclusion from the world of concrete facts and knowledge, inhabits unrealism as a birthright, much like Rhoda Broughton's Nell. The structural instability of her voice finds a narratological equivalent in metafiction's self-consciousness of its own design. The critics' disbelief in "many things which were literal facts" in Glen's novel epitomizes the impossibility of her situation relative to credibility: what is true is disbelieved, and what is not true is ridiculed. The insistence on reading women's novels as personal expressions makes their entry into the public and professional sphere an ontological contradiction.

But the next novel that Glen writes transforms her from an unconfident and derivative writer to an artistic innovator. This novel pursues a representational challenge rather than a romantic or social relationship, which the narrator explains as "a very daring thing—[she had] taken a very doubtful course in making love merely occupy the same position in her story that it does apparently in the lives of most of those with whom we come in contact."[38] As with her earlier novels, Glen first struggles with the challenge of organizing beauty and sensation into the design of a story:

> She thought she had no plot on which to found a story. Vaguely the lonely wolds, the solitary farmhouse, kept recurring to her memory; but she did not see her way to raise any superstructure upon such meager foundations, till one evening, when her husband and a friend of his were talking about the rich deep permanent colors to be seen in old church windows, which modern art sought in vain to reproduce, she looked across the table to her husband, and said: "I shall write a novel about stained glass."
>
> They all laughed at the idea. "Not a very likely subject," remarked the visitor.[39]

The book that Glen writes forgoes love as its central plot, and along with it the mass audience of novel readers—especially women, "who are," the narrator observes, "the public for whom a novelist has to cater."[40] Despite the sacrifice of popularity, the narrator elevates Glen's status as a writer through a telling comparison. Where "George Eliot counted her thousands, the *Family Herald* counts its tens of thousands!"[41] Evoking Eliot is a bold move in the middle of a novel that has thus far leveraged serious doubt about Glen's writing career.

The plot of the book about stained glass, *Ashtree Manor,* parabolically explains Glen's own artistic elevation. The novel features a young man whose rapt appreciation of the "painted window" in his church develops into "an overmastering ambition . . . to discover the secret of colour, which seemed to have died out with the monks of old." He dedicates his mission to the woman he loves, whom he treats as a muse: "for her sake he desired to emulate the blues, and the yellows, and the greens, and the reds." He elects to move to London, where "he felt certain he should be able to reduce many theories to practice, and find the colours modern humanity had so long wished for, and wished in vain." But in London, his romantic quest is eclipsed by a generic redirection in which Glen

> wove into the narrative the trials, the sorrows, the self-denials, the successes of trade—explained processes of manufacture unknown utterly to the reading public—took the outside world due east in London, and asked it to walk into dreadful little manufactories, and listen to 'shop' talk, and take an interest in the doings and sayings of men who had probably never been to a dinner-party in their lives . . . and were not acquainted with lords or baronets: but who were yet some of them gentlemen and some of them cads, following the nature of their kind.[42]

Glen has lived in London for several years, which dates the writing of this novel in *A Struggle for Fame* to the later 1850s or early 1860s. Riddell, writing in the early 1880s, thus places Glen's esoteric attention to the manufacture and "'shop' talk" of the glass industry on the early side of the granular urban realism that would rise in the 1880s with novelists such as Gissing and Zola. Eliot, already invoked as an artistic model for a select readership, however, could inspire Glen's attention to working life for its own sake. Eliot's publications in the late 1850s help to contextualize Glen's novel and the artistic development that the narrator attributes to her. In 1856 Eliot published "Silly Novels by Lady Novelists" in the *Westminster Review,* which retrospectively looks like a preview of the soberly intellectual novel-writing career she would begin the next year with *Scenes of Clerical Life* (1857). *Adam Bede*, published in 1859, shuns the silly and improbable in a thwarted love story of a carpenter at the turn of the nineteenth century; Eliot would next write about a miller and linen weaver in *The Mill on the Floss* (1860) and *Silas Marner* (1861). *Adam Bede*'s narrator defends such unglamorous subject matter by urging artists to "give the loving pains of a life to the faithful representing of commonplace things" to cultivate understanding of "fellow-mortals, every one . . . as they are."[43] In this same vein, as "faintly the beauty of simplicity was dawning on her,"[44] *Ashtree Manor*'s superiority to Glen's earlier books catapults her into a higher artistic echelon.

The narrator's reticence about the end of Glen's novel sustains the metafictional comparison between it and *A Struggle for Fame*, which we come to recognize as the precedent for the modal innovations praised in *Ashtree Manor*, especially the displacement of love for a more mundane study of work. "It is not necessary to tell how [*Ashtree Manor*] ended," the narrator explains; "how the author worked it out is all which concerns this tale. Painfully, surely, slowly, she gathered all her parts together."[45] (In contrast, the unwritten end of *The Athelings*—the "agitated" look exchanged between the Rector and Agnes that embodies their "whole story"—declares the marriage-plot ending, so prosaic a formal device that it does not draw our attention to the book at hand.) Glen's thoughtful crafting of *Ashtree Manor*, like its hero's pursuit of the lost technologies of colored glass and the unrecorded ("not necessary to tell") ending, trounces the conceit of genius and instills artistic value in process and method. Early in *A Struggle for Fame*, Riddell's narrator similarly refutes a narrative of progress when she reconstructs the events and desires that stimulate Glen to become a writer: "All thought is but the offspring of some previous thought; all invention only the outcome of a former plan. As the flower is contained in the seed, an apparently sudden project has been growing in silence to maturity. . . . When we see the result we are apt to forget there must of necessity have been a long time of growth."[46] Because this meditation on causality accompanies what young Glen experiences as an impassioned revelation by moonlight—"I will write"[47]—it modulates what she understands as a divine message, or perhaps what we can recognize as the Brontëan myth of genius. Only later does the adult Glen catch up to a view of art as *practice* in the pattern of Eliot's experimental realism, which *Ashtree Manor* celebrates in its hero's industrious quest for a transformative technology, regardless of its outcome. But Glen's cultivation of her art remains beyond the comprehension of the public and even her husband.

When the publicity-mad authoress Lady Hilda Hicks acknowledges Glen at the height of *Ashtree Manor*'s success, she tells Glen's husband that he "must be very proud . . . of what [Glen] has done." He answers that he is "more proud of what she is,"[48] tactically (and myopically) electing inner virtue over artfulness as the source of Glen's success.

"The Difference between Authors and Their Books"

Riddell's meticulous attention to the transformations in the mid-century publishing world reveals a rapidly changing and corporatizing field, but these shifts do not present any obvious advantages for women authors. Glen's new publisher, the enterprising but unethical Lance Felton, encourages her to circulate in society and so take advantage of her success, but doing so did her "no good, morally, physically, or intellectually. . . . At the end of a year . . . she had brought no single great thought, or original idea . . . out of the turmoil."[49] As Glen's old rival Barney Kelly scoffs, "She ought to stop at home and write her books and mind her house, and see her husband's slippers are warmed, instead of going about to parties and listening to foolish compliments, and frittering away such talents as God has given her in small-talk and company babble." But to Barney's wife, Glen's socializing makes sense: "Still she is a woman, and it is only natural, poor thing, she should like to visit, and hear people praising her books.'" Barney continues his critique of the rise of the "celebrity author," but turns from Glen to authors in general:

> "All this modern business of society making lions of authors, and authoresses rushing frantically into society, is a complete mistake. Not so did the great men, whose names will live as long as the English language is spoken, conduct themselves. Routs, and balls, and dinners three hours long, and garden-parties, knew them not. To the outside public they were only known by their works. Now the outside public is so constantly given the opportunity of seeing men who are thought great, at play, that it will soon begin to doubt if they ever do any work at all."[50]

Barney's nostalgia for an era when "great men" were "known for their works" did not extend to women authors, as we see in the early years of *A Struggle for Fame*, when the passing mention of a woman novelist's bid for anonymity confirms the risks of associating with authorship, and as already discussed in the case of Charlotte Brontë's skeptical public in chapter 1. "My name is

Yarlow—*Miss* Yarlow," says a woman Glen encounters at Mr. Pierson's editorial office. "('As if,' thought Mr. Pierson, 'any human being could imagine you were a married woman!')." Miss Yarlow continues, "But as I do not wish it to be published, I attached a *nom de plume* to the manuscript."[51] Barred from actual recognition by their *noms de plume*, the Miss Yarlows of London publishing have no chance of being "known by their works."

Even in the modernizing industry, Glen struggles against the public disbelief that a woman could have written as respected a novel as *Ashtree Manor.*

> "Who is the author?" everyone asked, and many people answered, "Oh! I know him very well indeed;" and then he was drawn respectively as a barrister, a gambler, a man who had neglected his wife, a man whose wife had run away from him, a man who was about town, a man who had been about town, but who now represented her Majesty as consul somewhere at the world's end; and, lastly, he was represented to Glen's husband, by a chatty individual who professed to know everyone, as "a devilish good fellow, sir—and clever too!"[52]

The public sooner attaches authorship to a wide diversity of male types than considers a female author. Even so, Lance Felton's operation entirely hinges on name recognition of the author: "We can't be bothered with reading manuscripts here . . . but bring us anything with a good name at top, and it goes straight to the printers."[53] When Glen first presents herself at Lance's firm, his assistant exposes the speciousness attached to her name: "Lance," cries his assistant, "here's 'Ashtree Manor.'"[54] Peterson cites an almost identical scene recalled in Riddell's publisher William Tinsley's *Random Recollections of an Old Publisher* (1900). Tinsley describes Riddell's first visit to the firm: "'Bill!' [his brother Edward] bawled to [Tinsley] in the back sanctum: 'here's *Too Much Alone!* By God! I have been wanting to find her.'"[55] Substituting the novel for the novelist confirms the interests of the publishing firm, which measures its business by book sales, but Lance proves to be no more discerning about Glen's authorship than the general public. He tells Glen that he did "everything but advertise for you in the *Times*. . . . Besides, you know, we thought you were a man."[56] He tells Glen, "I have often heard of the difference between authors and their books, but the difference between you and your books is something almost incredible. I said to myself when I read *Ashtree Manor*, 'This is written by some fellow who has knocked about the world and knows a thing or two. . . .' And now it turns out that the author is a woman, who talks more foolishly than I ever heard any woman, even my own wife."⁵⁷ The assumption that the author of *Ashtree Manor* is a man because the novel resists romance and superficiality not only capitulates to a reductive account of gender, but also treats fiction as a straightforward replica of its author.

If Glen's public remains unconvinced that she was responsible for her success, Agnes's loss of renown in *The Athelings* extends from an opposite expectation. Agnes's readers expect her personality and conversation to be contiguous with her novels, and so find her company disappointing: "Agnes's 'reputation' had died away, and left very little trace behind it. . . . The people who had been dying to know the author of *Hope Hazlewood*, had all found out that the shy young genius did not talk in character—had no gift of conversation, and, indeed, did nothing at all to keep up her fame; and if Agnes chanced to feel a momentary mortification at the prompt desertion of all her admirers, she wisely kept the pang to herself, and said nothing about it."⁵⁸ If women's art is not self-portraiture, which Agnes's readers expect it to be, then her relationship to inspiration is one of passive reception, or what Oliphant calls "genius." Agnes and Glen's readers are not in fact very different from each other, as none of them can connect the unassuming writer with her successful novels.

To accept that Glen has written novels with no obvious precedent in her life would be to replace a method of copying with one of imagining, which brings us to the heart of Glen's, and Riddell's, conception of realism. *A Struggle for Fame* illustrates two types of realism in the works conceived by its many writers. The first artistically reproduces real people, events, and places, which includes Glen's thwarted novel set in Ireland, Barney Kelly's sketches of London life and its neighborhoods, and the daring "novels" of a popular writer, Lady Hilda Hicks, who, like Glen, eventually leaves Mr. Vassett's firm for Lance's more profitable one. Mr. Vassett scrupulously edits Lady Hicks's novels, which are based upon real members of her London set—or at least he tries to, in an effort to avoid libel. Lance's permissive approach comes to reflect the increasingly commercial standards of publishing after the mid-century, when sales are justified at any cost and only helped by scandal. Lady Hicks wants money "so cruelly"⁵⁹ that she moves firms without qualms. *Ashtree Manor* exemplifies the exceptional and more serious type of realism that Riddell outlines in her novel. The mode of writing that this novel ushers in, along with its telling comparison to Eliot, is experimental, idea driven, and lifelike in its conscious deviation from the conventions associated with fiction: Glen strives to "make her people lifelike, to show them doing simple things in a simple manner, and talking as men and women do talk in real life, and not as they so often talk in books."⁶⁰ Her studious attention to the process of writing directs our attention to Riddell's choices: as the fictional novelist learns to write in the unconventional style of Eliot, with realism as an experimental principle instead of a completed replica, the novelist who explains this process—Riddell—is its refractive, working example. (In contrast Agnes, rather than straining to make her characters convincing, simply models them on her friends and family.)

The degree to which the innovations in Glen's later novels are tacitly identifiable in *A Struggle for Fame* might appear to sustain an argument that Riddell's novel resolutely denies: that a woman writer's imaginative scope is necessarily self-referential. The metafictional resonance of Glen's novels relative to Riddell's, however, can be seen as a tactic of disambiguation rather than replication. Another way of pitching this argument is to resist the tendency to see Glen as Riddell's autobiographical substitute. No matter how many similarities there are between Riddell's professional experience and Glen's—and several critics have established these[61]—Riddell's choice to write about the fictive identity of a novelist-heroine in the third person indicates a strategic artistic detachment. In turn, this detachment signifies exactly the *dis*embodiment that (imaginary) readers like Lance or (real) critics like Elizabeth Rigby and her charges of "immorality" against Brontë's *Jane Eyre* overlook: the conception that a woman's intellectual and imaginative reach exceeds her personal experience or represents a point of view she does not herself share. This projection of a woman's personal register even delimits her critical capacity. When, for instance, Glen writes a review that praises a "sweet heroine" of Barney Kelly's, he contemptuously concludes that she thinks he based his character on her.[62] Elsewhere, as he fields questions about Glen, even he poses the question, "Do you think she is the author?"[63] To Lady Hicks, he declines to give any details about Glen: "I don't think there is much to say about her. . . . She certainly doesn't look clever, or like a person capable of writing a successful book."[64] Glen's "struggle for fame" can be understood according to less obvious meanings than reverence and celebrity: the concept of repute, in its most basic sense of *being recognized* as an author, remains outside her grasp. The literary marketplace, especially as it becomes more commercialized, offers even once-successful authors no loyalty, and a few years after her success, Glen is surprised to find herself virtually unknown to readers and publishers. At the height of her powers, "Glenarva Lacere, then able almost to command her own prices, could not foretell that evil days were coming when she should be able to command no price at all."[65] And yet even at the height of her powers, success did not consolidate her writing with her identity: "No, not even then did any friend, or relation, or stranger realise it was really Glenarva who had won success, and not some quite independent power associated with her in an unaccountable and uncanny sort of alliance."[66]

A story about a serious novelist who never receives her due acclaim may read cynically, but *A Struggle for Fame* has a metafictional efficacy that surpasses Glen's experience. Riddell's third-person narrative teaches the reader through Glen's example how women writers can be underestimated. She makes Glen's ability to create characters and events beyond her small, feminine purview an explicit lesson in the novel from its beginning. Early on, Mr. Vassett's incomprehension of imaginative fiction sets up the terms of Glen's—and Riddell's—achievement in their respective novels:

> [Mr. Vassett] believed, if he believed in anything as regards authors, in plodding. Compilations, reminiscences, biographies, travels, historical romances, and such like, he looked upon with a certain favour; he could understand how they were done, and why; he was able to trace the progress of the busy shuttle, and predicate the result which would be produced by any practised hand. But to make something out of nothing, to write a book, not from observation, but from pure imagination, to create characters, and then make them move and speak and act like men and women;—it was "very odd," Mr. Vassett considered, "very odd indeed!"[67]

Glen's slow and careful cultivation of the realist techniques associated with Eliot constantly reflect upon *A Struggle for Fame*, so that *its* like accomplishments are both demonstrated and self-consciously framed. Where Riddell's descriptions of Glen's novels find a metafictional echo in *A Struggle for Fame*, a straightforward autobiography could not objectively make the same case—could not extol its own triumphs and provide convincing material evidence of them at the same time. When Riddell assumes the doubled position of a novelist writing a novel about a novelist, she delineates her own struggles with third-person objectivity and so orients them dispassionately as literature that reckons with a social category, the woman writer, and not just her personal experience *as* a woman writer. What looks like a semi-autobiographical novel is, or is also, a bid for autonomous art.

4

PSEUDONYMITY AS METAFICTION

One of the more curious and durable literary arguments to emerge in the later twentieth century was the attestation of novels by Victorian women as proof of their historical silence. This argument rests on a fundamental disconnect between what women wrote and published, and what they were projected to actually think, feel, or believe. The case for silent-but-published women often invoked Victorian women writers' use of male pseudonyms, which became a particularly resonant example of the way that the intellectual and social bias against women artists denied not only their professional expertise but also their very selfhood. The same small pool of pseudonym users—Mary Ann Evans (George Eliot) and Charlotte, Emily, and Anne Brontë (Currer, Ellis, and Acton Bell)—was often cited to represent this publishing tradition.[1] An oft-quoted reference to the tension between a male pseudonym and a woman novelist's "true" identity appears in Elizabeth Gaskell's *The Life of Charlotte Brontë* (1857), where Gaskell writes that Brontë "divided [her life] into two parallel currents—her life as Currer Bell, the author; her life as Charlotte Brontë, the woman."[2] As Catherine A. Judd explains, Brontë's "division between the public and the domestic, the masculine and the feminine, also be[came] aligned with a division between false and authentic selves"—"the 'artificial' male identity" and the "woman writer's 'real' (feminine and domestic) self."[3] Accordingly, these dual selves signified an identity crisis that could be problematized as broadly female—even if it yielded exceptional art—and as a problem for more liberated generations to resolve by freeing the "authentic" feminine voice from masculine trappings (including a male pseudonym) adopted in deference to socio-historical pressures. In this way, a historically situated female subject and contemporary feminist politics converge through the assumptions that artistic achievement, for women of either moment, turns upon personal recognition.

But why might a novel be expected to testify to its author's true self in the first place? The desire for it to do so can reveal a scholarly agenda that interprets a novel through the knowable traces of its author. As a compensatory exegesis, interest in women hemmed in by a patriarchal culture and publishing industry can be easier for contemporary scholars to engage with than novels that figure, for example, meditations on stereotypes we stridently oppose today: the strength or intellectual superiority of men, the tacit or explicit passivity of women. In the late 1970s, Sandra M. Gilbert and Susan Gubar's seminal study *The Madwoman in the Attic* (1979) exemplified how ostensibly deferential behaviors (Jane Eyre as Rochester's tamed helpmeet; Dorothea Brooke's sacrifice of public ambition for private duty) could be transformed into time capsules for twentieth-century feminists to open, an operation that located "real" meaning in the subtext of a woman's novel. The same logic applied to women's use of male pseudonyms, which dismissed the explicit masculine identification as a reluctant but expedient cover for the authentic woman whose book could not bear her name. Without question, Victorian women faced intellectual and artistic prejudice as novelists and the use of a male pseudonym could quite logically counteract or at least diffuse that bias. But if we move our critical lens from the reasons why women adopted male pseudonyms in the first place and consider how doing so affected their texts and not just their lives and careers, the use of a pseudonym like "George Eliot" or "Currer Bell" slips into a metafictional register that reconceptualizes its textual effect. It still tells a story about the experience of the Victorian woman writer, but the narratological evidence of that story takes precedence over its biographical significance. Following this objective, in the first half of this chapter I examine biographical explanations for a woman writer's use of a male pseudonym and compare the conclusions from that approach to those that a metafictional interpretation can yield through two brief analyses of Julia Frankau, who published novels under the name Frank Danby, and Margaret Harkness, who did so as John Law. Critics of both provocative novelists have determined the value and intent of their novels through biographical lenses.

The second half of the chapter turns to Eliza Lynn Linton's novel *The Autobiography of Christopher Kirkland* (1885). While the novel is often examined as a key to Linton's own complex life and character, my analysis follows the lead of contemporary metafictional criticism and interprets it through its fictional presentation and specifically its attention to the divergence of fiction from life. The avant-garde innovations of this novel, which anticipate a set of narratological possibilities familiar in postmodern novels, have been obscured by the biographical focus on its author as a tortured or stifled subject.

Pseudonymous and Implied Authors

Following a narratological argument instead of a quest to discern the author's true self, Wayne C. Booth's *The Rhetoric of Fiction* (1961) offers a different set of tools for analyzing the Victorian woman's use of a male pseudonym. The pseudonym (and not only that used by Victorian women) can be compared to one of Booth's most prominent narratological concepts, the implied author. For Booth, the act of identifying the implied author severs it from the "real" author, and in so doing erases whatever historical and social information that identity evokes. As we read, then, we formulate the voice and perspective that cumulatively forms our idea of the implied author; understanding the implied author is correlative to (and dependent on) understanding *the novel* attributed to it. This is a reversal of the signification process that begins with an author's historical identity and interprets the text accordingly. Booth's implied author, furthermore, never strays beyond the level of text. A critic examining the implied author in *Vanity Fair*, for instance, would not do so to float theories about Thackeray's personal insights and motivations; she would try to draw a curtain between them and the perspective(s) developed in the novel. Peter Lamarque describes the implied author, "or dramatic speaker," as "a set of attitudes informing a work that might or might not be shared with the real author"; an implied author is "just one fictional character among others in a work."[4] For Booth,

> in this distinction between author and implied author we find a middle position between the technical irrelevance of talk about the artist's objectivity and the harmful error of pretending that an author can allow direct intrusions of his own immediate problems and desires. The great defenders of objectivity were working on an important matter and they knew it. Flaubert is right in saying that Shakespeare does not barge clumsily into his works. . . . And he is surely right when he forces the hero of the [1845] version of *Sentimental Education* . . . to choose between the merely confessional statement and the truly rendered work of art.[5]

By using a nineteenth-century realist to exemplify an implied author's "truly rendered work of art" as opposed to an actual author's self-reflective one, Booth instantiates a process that Flaubert achieves by will ("he forces the hero . . . to choose"). In line with Booth, I interpret the implied author as a persona that the historical author creates but with which he or she does not necessarily identify. Similarly, Susan Lanser suggests that we forgo the effort to identify definitively the implied author and, instead, embrace the concept as mobile and text specific. Her description of "the implied author not as a body but as the clothes the body wears—clothes that can be altered, discarded, tried on, changed before or behind our eyes" accords with my approach, as it acknowledges the fictional dimension of the implied author as intentionally distinct from the author him- or herself.[6]

On a literal level, writers using pseudonyms disaffiliate from personal history by fronting their novels with a fiction. "Currer Bell," though usually examined as Charlotte Brontë's alter ego, compares ontologically with Brontë's other fictional authors Jane Eyre and Lucy Snowe. As one fiction that begets another by erasing the hand of the real author, "Currer Bell" is a metafictional announcement. This argument differs from Sharon Marcus's reading of "Currer Bell" as an expedient, professional front for Brontë: "The name Currer Bell enabled Brontë to materialize her professional self in abstract form, to put herself forward while simultaneously receding from view."[7] Scholars consistently treat "George Eliot," too, as Mary Ann Evans's strategic (though not secret) disguise—a point proven by the absolute replacement of her name with her pseudonym. To Lanser, Eliot adopts the role of the "man of maxims," a figure of expertise she mocks in *The Mill on the Floss* (1860) but also imitates, especially in her later novels.[8] Lanser argues that "the rhetoric of Eliot's fiction arrogates authority in a project designed precisely to construct a narrative hegemony."[9] Eliot adopted the rhetorical norms of hegemonic authority, but when we remember her as "George Eliot," this claim becomes dubious: can a fictional author imitate, or is that claim redundant? We do not write about David Copperfield imitating a particular authorial stance because he does not have a "real" one in the first place. We do write about Thackeray imitating the discourse of the sage or the satirist because we maintain the idea that the *real* Thackeray conceived these voices performatively and self-consciously. "George Eliot" is a simulation of a male novelist, and even when "he" becomes a revered "man of letters," there is a transference in place in which the public was complicit. When Colin MacCabe writes that Eliot's novels exemplify the "classic realist text" because they validate a dominant discourse of closed and indisputable meanings, he undermines his case for hegemonic realism by attaching it to a fictional persona.[10] As Michal Peled Ginsburg reminds us, "George Eliot did not create *Scenes of Clerical Life;* he did not exist before having written fiction."[11] Acknowledging the fictionality of a pseudonym changes its interpretation by freeing it from questions about its reflection of the real author, whether aspirational or confessional.

Returning to Foucault's conception of an "author function" as distinct from historical authorship further explicates what happens when we disentangle a pseudonym from its author's identity. Lamarque's argument that "Foucault's author function is not a construct specific to individual works but may bind together a whole oeuvre" by broadly determining "the very nature of the work itself"[12] alters the significance of Brontë's and Eliot's continued use of their pseudonyms after their real identities were known. Instead of exposing the specific woman writer's ambivalent occupation of professional authorship, this decision, following Lamarque's argument, could suggest that Brontë and Eliot committed their novels to the marketplace as an artistic oeuvre, not as expressions of individual women. In a telling analogy, Marcus writes that by using a pseudonym to write *Jane Eyre,* "Brontë engaged in a process of self-construction deemed a crucial aspect of professionalism";[13] but in the novel, Jane fosters authority by addressing her readers impersonally.[14] While Jane the literary character can choose a discursive mode that enlarges and so de-individuates her experience, Brontë's creation of this perspective via her pseudonym reflects "self-construction." But why wouldn't the pseudonym do the opposite—and have the same effect as Jane's de-corporealized (because written) engagement with a public world? Had Marcus written that Brontë's use of the pseudonym "engaged in a process of construction" instead of one of "self-construction," she would have shifted the developmental account from Brontë's personal stakes to the literary contribution of her novel. On its own merits this is a minor point, but it underlines feminist criticism's frequent emphasis on the story of the woman novelist before the reception and influence of her novel.

Even today, the understanding of a woman writer's identity continues to influence the interpretation of her novels, often as an investigative challenge that competes with or overshadows the novels. A brief review of two late-Victorian women writers who published under male pseudonyms can characterize how criticism rooted in biography still shapes interpretation. The novelists Julia Frankau and Margaret Harkness, who published under the names Frank Danby and John Law, respectively, have inspired criticism that eradicates the distance effected by the male names and seeks to know the "real" women behind them: for Frankau, this inspires speculation about her identification with Judaism, and for Harkness, efforts to unravel her cryptic political loyalties.

Frank Danby's Idylls in Maida Vale and Bohemia

The Jewish novelist Julia Frankau (1859–1916) is best known for two anti-Semitic novels she wrote in the late 1880s: *Dr. Phillips: A Maida Vale Idyll* (1887) and *A Babe in Bohemia* (1889). In the first novel, a craven "lady's doctor" of Maida Vale, Benjamin Phillips, murders his wife by staging a fatal ovariotomy in order to marry his Christian mistress, Mary Cameron, also the mother of his young daughter. But Mary throws him over for a Christian squire, their daughter dies, and Phillips is ostracized by his insular Jewish society. Rather than figure his repentance, however, the novel closes with an ominous nod to his rising surgical influence. *A Babe in Bohemia* arguably surpasses *Dr. Phillips* in offensiveness. Banned by Mudie's and largely condemned by the periodical press, it tells the story of Lucilla Lewisham, illegitimate daughter of a Bohemian reprobate. At seventeen, Lucilla loses her "idiot" twin brother to epilepsy, a disease known to be passed to the offspring of a syphilitic parent—by deduction, the twins' (absent) prostitute mother. Lucilla falls in love with a married journalist, Mordaunt Rivers, who leaves his alcoholic wife for her, but the mounting specter of her own inherited epilepsy leads finally to her grisly suicide. Both novels exaggerate the contemporaneous logic advanced by the French novelist Émile Zola. In his 1879 essay "The Experimental Novel," Zola proposes that the novelist should proceed in his dissection of character as precisely as the surgeon;[15] his argument for a dispassionate approach to the literary subject is one of the founding texts of naturalism. Zola describes the novelist's art as a procedural interest in nature over conscience[16] that helps to contextualize the increasingly detached mode of fiction that arose in the 1880s. Frankau's subordination of morality to medical power (*Dr. Phillips*) and congenital disease (*A Babe in Bohemia*) reads like a hyperbole of the naturalist mode. Furthermore, Frankau wrote her novels under a male, Christian pseudonym, Frank Danby—a name more immediately suggestive of anti-Semitism than her own.

Nevertheless, Frankau is often discussed, in the Victorian age and today, in literal terms: a self-hating Jew, a crude chronicler of urban life, a vulgar provocateur. Linda Hunt straightforwardly calls *Dr. Phillips* "a demonizing fable which belongs in the long tradition of anti-Semitic writing."[17] For Michael Galchinsky, the choice of the pseudonym constitutes a straightforward indication of Frankau's self-hatred.[18] More provocatively, Nadia Valman refers to *Dr. Phillips* as a "satire" but does not elaborate on the significance of the term. She reads the novel along with works by Amy Levy, Cecily Sidgwick, and Leonard Merrick as evidence of assimilated Anglo-Jewry's hostility to orthodox sects. Such novels, she writes, "cannot simply be dismissed as 'Jewish self-hatred[,]' . . . [for] creating fictions about [particular types of] Jews was indispensable to their construction of distinctive political and literary identities,"[19] among which I include the self-consciously gentile Frank Danby. In attending to the *constructedness* of anti-Semitic novels by Jewish writers, Valman acknowledges what many others do not: novels are works of the imagination, not historical records. Frankau made no effort to conceal her real identity behind her pseudonym, and biographical accounts refer to her unconventionality and wit. Reading her novels as sincere representations of her self-hatred or desire to identify with the majority culture overlooks the possibility of her clever exploitation of sensational tropes and generic expectations. While she is not describing Frankau in particular, Linda C. Dowling captures this point precisely: the "self-parodic or consciously ironic tones in fin-de-siècle literature have been muted by a heavily biographical emphasis in most discussions of the period."[20] If Frankau ventriloquized the perspective of an imaginary gentile racist in order to satirize *that* subject position, our critical attention to her own tortured identity has only extended the joke on us. Read from the point of view of a fictional character who articulates "the unspeakable" as a takedown of realism and satire of anti-Semitism, *Dr. Phillips* and *A Babe in Bohemia* epitomize the contingency of authorship.

Commanding the Authority of John Law

Margaret Harkness (1854–1923) was a late-century journalist and novelist best known for her string of "slum novels" in the late 1880s and early 1890s: *A City Girl* (1887), *Out of Work* (1888), *Captain Lobe: A Story of the Salvation Army* (1889; reissued in 1891 as *In Darkest London*), and *A Manchester Shirtmaker: A Realistic Story of Today* (1890). Friedrich Engels famously praised *A City Girl* as "a little work of art" but also regretted that Harkness portrayed the London poor "as a passive mass."[21] Victorian scholars have rediscovered Harkness and returned much of her work to print, but a survey of the recent scholarship on Harkness reveals how much our interest in her is dedicated to the historical woman, often bypassing her novels or using them as keys to her own character and political loyalties.

Harkness wrote all her novels and much of her journalism under the name John Law, sometimes with this name in quotation marks. The pseudonym did not conceal her real identity very long, if it was ever meant to conceal it at all, and the argument that it enabled her to write from a more radical perspective jars against a series of acerbic articles she wrote under her own name for the socialist weekly *Justice*. More intriguing is the fact that Harkness wrote about her personal experiences through the filter of the John Law alter ego in the distinctly biographical "A Year of My Life" (*New Review*, 1891), which considers the state of socialism on the Continent, and "The Cardinal as I knew Him" (*Pall Mall Gazette*, 1892), which eulogized Cardinal Manning, with whom Harkness worked during the London Dock Strike of 1889. Both articles refer to her own experiences reimagined through the persona of a man, and her masculine identification changes the experiences she narrates significantly. Critics have speculated about the choice of the name "John Law," and Joyce M. Bellamy and Beate Kaspar note that *Out of Work* was dedicated to John Law of Lauriston (1671–1729), "a director of finance in France" who "although unsuccessful was regarded by some French historians as the precursor of modern State Socialism."[22] We cannot know definitively Harkness's motives for choosing the name, nor did she provide this biographical reference when she used it. But pursuing the signage prompted by "John Law" means pushing into the background the experiences of the Margaret Harkness who lived in Whitechapel for a time, wrote critical journalism about slum life, had tempestuous relationships with individuals and organizations and an especially vexed connection to socialism. It means accepting that this self-erasure is what Harkness was setting in motion by using "John Law" beyond a point when the pseudonym could have had any efficacy of concealment. "John Law" must be important for exactly that neutrality, with the objective reason then almost invariably attached to maleness and a Scottish name, one that carries in it the very definition of jurisprudence.

Harkness's identification as Law can be seen as an extension of the depersonalization that was a trademark of this era's naturalist fiction and progressive, materialistic thought more generally. While her novels are not uncomplicated visions of a naturalist universe (they do not, for instance, illustrate the power of degeneration or heredity in any detail), the detachment associated with naturalism is unaccommodating to a biocritical mediation of the novels through Harkness's own life.[23] A comparison to a male writer can bring this point into relief. Criticism of Zola's twenty-novel cycle of a family beset by hereditary disease, *Les Rougon-Macquart*, for instance, rarely directs interpretation of the novels to the influences we see in Harkness criticism: Zola's personal relationships, the shifting nature of his politics, his neurosis.[24] In other words, we grant Zola the credulity of fiction while we hold women writers like Harkness and Frankau to interpretation filtered through personal history. This emphasis may be driven by sensitivity to the difficulty a woman writer faced in becoming a published author, which for most nineteenth-century women did constitute a narrative worthy of fiction: an unlikely ambition, social and personal obstacles, hard-won successes. But one of the unintended consequences of these narratives of progress can be biographical interpretations that detract attention from narratological patterns, effects, and achievements cultivated by the women writers in their novels.

Eliza Lynn Linton's Fictional Autobiography

Readers and critics of Eliza Lynn Linton (1822–1898) have worked hard to attribute the various identities that populate her nonfiction and fiction to their author, especially because so many of them are at odds with each other. Linton was a journalist and novelist notorious for her anti-feminism, which rankled against her own record of proto-feminist achievement. As a young woman she moved alone to London and earned her living as a writer, becoming the first woman to hold a salaried position at a daily newspaper, the *Morning Chronicle*.[25] She married the engraver and political radical W. J. Linton in 1858, but the marriage ended in divorce, and she was self-supporting for the rest of her life. As well as writing for numerous journals and newspapers, she was the author of over twenty novels, including *Lizzie Lorton of Greyrigg: A Novel* (1866), *Patricia Kemball* (1875), and *The Rebel of the Family* (1880). Pinning down Linton's personal beliefs meets a particular challenge in her 1885 novel, *The Autobiography of Christopher Kirkland*. Alternately described as Linton's autobiography from the point of view of a man and as a novel, this text has generated a range of critical interpretations of its eponymous narrator. To Vineta

Colby, the character Christopher Kirkland represents Linton's "transvestitism and unconscious masculinity."[26] The biographer Nancy Fix Anderson situates Linton's transformation into Christopher within a larger identity confusion, exemplified by the contradiction between Linton's attacks on professional and progressive women in her journalism, such as her scathing takedown of "The Girl of the Period" (*Saturday Review*, 1868), and her own career success and independence.[27] Lee Anne Bache offers a nuanced explanation for the inconsistency between Linton's success and the ideological values expressed in her journalism. The apparent contradiction between her proto-feminist achievements and her defense of traditional womanliness, Bache argues, creates "distance between public and private selves," and in the case of *Christopher Kirkland,* Linton assigns her life story to "the creative property of E. Lynn Linton, the author" instead of attaching it to "the lived experience of the private individual, Mrs. Lynn Linton."[28] This explanation recalls Gaskell's invocation of separate identities in Charlotte Brontë "the woman" and Currer Bell "the author." But it still revolves around a question of *whom* the text represents: the identity construct of a single author establishes the bottom line of interpretation. Lanser's challenge to this identity-based exegesis—the assumption that "a text has a singular, coherent implied author"[29]—provides a useful model for reading *Christopher Kirkland.* Lanser's redirection of the debate over the definite identity of the implied author into the more accommodating and variable question about the *purpose* an authorial signature serves in any given text moves the analysis from Linton's complex identity politics to the text of *Christopher Kirkland.* That is, while *Christopher Kirkland* is narrated from the point of view of an individual subject, its fictionality does not demand that our interpretation be adapted to a particular version of Linton or even an anthropomorphic construct. "Christopher Kirkland" can embody Linton's thoughts and experiences and wholly imaginary ones on equal footing and without prompting their assimilation into a coherent self. An early reviewer of the book for the *Athenaeum* came to a very different assumption about the relationship between author and titular character: "Mrs. Lynn Linton's new book is a puzzle. . . . Christopher Kirkland sometimes stands for the writer herself . . . but at other times he serves only as a conduit pipe for the author's views."[30] But these two positions are not in fact very far apart. In the first, Linton recasts herself as a man, and in the second, her male character embodies her "views." The primary distinction between these choices seems to be the degree of historical reenactment, with a shared ideological and psychological base.

Reading *Christopher Kirkland* through the Techniques of Postmodern Metafiction

The dissociation between author and fictional character—even one who is writing an autobiography—is commonplace in criticism of contemporary novels. As a fictional autobiography that makes identifiable references to Linton's life, *Christopher Kirkland* exemplifies the genre that Linda Hutcheon calls historiographic metafiction:[31] "historiographic" because such fiction demonstrates a self-awareness of the constructive act of writing history, and "metafiction" because it draws attention to the conditions and possibilities of its own representation. Historiographic metafiction is not restricted to postmodern or post-postmodern fiction (Daniel Defoe's *Robinson Crusoe* [1719], for instance, allegedly describes the experience of a real castaway, Thomas Selkirk), but the genre is dominantly correlated with the late twentieth and twenty-first centuries. Contemporary examples include Don DeLillo's *Libra* (1988), which reconstructs the assassination of John F. Kennedy by imagining that Lee Harvey Oswald was a pawn in a CIA scheme to spark a war with Cuba, and Margaret Atwood's *Alias Grace* (1996), which fabricates the motives behind an actual double murder committed in nineteenth-century Ontario, for which a young woman was imprisoned for life and her purported accomplice hanged. Critics and readers take for granted that the narrators of these works are unreliable and unauthoritative, and the task of narrating a "true story" is foreclosed by a postmodern disenchantment with realistic representation that does not require explanation. Gérard Genette explains this norm when he writes that the contemporary novel "does not hesitate to establish between narrator and character(s) a variable or floating relationship, a pronominal vertigo in tune with a freer logic and a more complex conception of "personality.""[32]

Contemporary and especially postmodern fiction often features its characters as vacated selves that respond haplessly to the impersonal will of the state. Linton's Christopher anticipates postmodern impotence in his consistent description of life events happening *to* him, without the agency that autobiographical subjects traditionally claim. This passivity originates in his unhappy childhood, which was shaped by his mother's death while he was an infant, and by the erratic choices of his father. Most egregiously, Christopher's father denies him a formal education. The arbitrariness of his self-education recalls Nell LeStrange's in *Cometh Up as a Flower*; like Nell, Christopher never learns to harness knowledge effectively: "This want of early training explains all my persistent intellectual deficiencies—my want of dialectical skill, my want of scientific accuracy, and how it is that I know nothing analytically, from the foundations upward, but only synthetically, concretely, as it stands. This must needs be, seeing that I have never built up any study brick by brick, nor chamber by chamber, but have only entered on the results of other men's work—inhabiting where they have created."[33] Christopher's inability to think causally, "from the foundations upward," subjects him to external influences, and without anyone to guide his reading choices, learning "was only a means to an end,"[34] a way to satisfy shifting curiosities. He attributes his lack of faith in the medium of textual language to his superficial education and his early reading habits: "As I learnt only to read and was not phenomenally laborious, I scamped the grammar and devoted myself to translation—that is, I neglected rules and learnt only words. This is the reason why, when I could read with ease and translate aloud rapidly while I read, French, Italian, German, Spanish, with a little Latin and less Greek, I could neither parse any of these languages correctly nor speak one fluently. I learnt without method, and I have never been able to disentangle my mind from the false order of the start."[35]

Attention to the surface level of a language, the memorization of words and pronunciations, gives Christopher a technical fluency without deep understanding. In another description of his assimilation of language, he explains that his acquisition of foreign languages was purely expedient:

> For instance, I learnt French out of curiosity to read an old illustrated "Telemachus" that we had, and thus to understand what the pictures meant; Italian to know about Petrarch and Dante, whose conventional portraits in our encyclopaedia had fascinated me; German, for "Faust"; Latin, to understand those brown-leather folios in the study library; Spanish for "Don Quixote"; and Greek in the vain hope of following Homer in the original. . . . Never subjected to that severe mental discipline which is but another form of moral control, I grew up in absolute mental unrestraint; and I have never been able to put myself into harness since.[36]

Christopher wants to understand texts and images in their original forms, pursuing congruence between sign and signification. His failure to do so implies a kind of proto-postmodern exile from a world where words and things align. One of his most striking insights into the provisionality of texts focuses on the status of the Bible. While reading Ovid one day at his family home in the country, "there shot through [his] brain these words which seemed to run along the page in a line of light: 'What difference is there between any of these stories [by Ovid] and those like to them in the Bible?[']"[37] Christopher does not *have* a metaphysical breakthrough—he reads one that appears as "in a line of light." Narrative is the vehicle by which he recognizes the contingencies of all narratives, including the urtext of Christianity. The reader becomes part of this circular logic, receiving Christopher's deconstructive message in the medium that also authorizes it.

A similar example in which words simultaneously empower him and convince him of the tenuousness of meaning occurs in an exchange with a married woman he passionately falls in love with, Mrs. Dalrymple. Christopher poses a question to her:

> "Have I any power over you?" . . .
>
> "You see it," she answered simply.
>
> I cannot describe the curious sense of inversion which these words created. I, who had been the slave, the worshipper, the subordinate, to be suddenly invested with power—to be even so prepotent as to compel obedience from the one who had hitherto been supreme—it was a change of parts which for the moment overwhelmed me with a sense of universal instability; and to the end of my life I shall never forget the strange confusion of pride and pleasure, of pain in loss yet joy in the sensation of a newborn power which possessed me, as the goddess thus became a woman, and made of me, who had been her slave, her master and a man.[38]

This exchange alerts Christopher that his reality is subject to a simple sentence, which reminds his readers that his "reality" *is* that of sentences and not actual referents. He continues the metaphor of his awakening by way of narrative when he describes his feelings after the Dalrymples abruptly move away: "Thus then, began and ended the first love of my life; and in this manner the Great Book was opened and the page turned down—half-read but ineffaceable. And ever and ever a fragrance steals from that closed page which neither length of time nor deeper knowledge of life can destroy."[39]

Christopher's description of his first love as a partially read book has a jarring relationship to the discursive business of autobiography. At the same time, he uses the metaphor of a book, compromised though it is, to essentialize a defining love. Jean-François Lyotard's synopsis of postmodernism as "incredulity toward metanarratives" and toward a narrative function that is "losing its functors, its great hero, . . . its great voyages, its great goal" as they are "dispersed in clouds of narrative language"[40] recalls Christopher's effaced "Great Book" and the nostalgic traces it leaves behind. His despondent observation at the end of the book that his "own law of life has been . . . that of loneliness and loss"[41] and that he "stand[s] absolutely alone, both spiritually and personally"[42] anticipates the sense of purposelessness so common to contemporary and postmodern novels.

"Entirely Conditional" Sex Roles

One of Christopher's formative observations concerns his growing awareness of the conditionality of traits and characteristics that are, or have been, essentialized according to sex and age.

> What determines the very ground-work of society, and its moralities, but this material fact of sex, with its secondary modification, age? The courage of the man, the self-devotion of the woman; the shame of cowardice and lying—a form of cowardice—with him whose strength includes the salvation of others as well as of himself, and the easy condonation accorded to both with her whose weakness excuses fear; his freer license, her chaster modesties; his sense of justice, . . . her narrowed sympathies born of the restricted cares of maternity; his reason, her instinct; his philosophy, her religion; his aggressiveness, her compassion. . . . And these are the bases of society and morality. How then can things so entirely conditional be treated as absolute?[43]

Criticism that turns Christopher into (or "back" into) Linton overlooks his revelation that social or sexual categories are contextual, not natural. Asserting Linton's authorial influence over Christopher's characterization subverts manifest arguments like his above, and implicitly suggests that Linton's sex is more determining to her fiction than her creative imagination. One aspect of the novel that critics routinely connect to Linton is Christopher's neglected education, but this neglect has an entirely different meaning when it is assigned to a man versus when it is assigned to a woman. Furthermore, the reader's simultaneous awareness of the loss that Christopher's lack of education represents, and of the ordinariness that the same lack would mean for Linton as a woman, infuses the text with a double meaning, or with the sense that its meaning is wholly relative—as Christopher argues about gendered values above. He asks at one point how "individuality, which began and is bound up with material conditions, [could] exist free from [material] conditions."[44] The material conditions he refers to include his own situation—uneducated, sheltered by his family's wealth and position, and despised by his father—all traits that, if designated to Linton, take on a very different signification. His identity formation and confusion *as a man*, that is, informs the entire novel. Juliette Atkinson writes that feminist critics "have been keen to interpret representations of 'doubleness' in women's lives as a sign of constraint and repression,"[45] but interpreting Christopher as Linton's double also constrains insofar as it predicates autobiographical experience over creative invention. Linton may share many traits with Christopher and ascribe many of her life events to him, but these commonalities are her artistic choices, not the unconstrained intrusions of her psyche.

Christopher's susceptibility to passing belief systems also undermines the presumption of a stable character, let alone one that could transcend an artistic sex change. During the historical scope of his autobiography, he claims that people were becoming "less credulous,"[46] but his own experience with skepticism seems less like a dawning of rational thought and more like a doomed search for stability. Without an educational foundation, he had "no logical method; no reserve force; no critical discrimination of values,"[47] and so he traces a dizzying exchange of one belief system for another that reads like a gambol through Victorian enthusiasms. After discarding his father's high-handed Christianity, Christopher passes through Chartist radicalism, a "superstitious" and folkloric phase, hallucinations of Christly wisdom, agnosticism, materialism, and "passionate idealism."[48] Evolutionary science seems to ground him for a time[49] but does not preclude forays into the paranormal.[50] He lands, in middle age, on a moral relativism that seems stabilizing insofar as it provides a framework for his fickleness: "Thus it was that I first began to see the moral law as a question of evolution and social arrangement, void of extrinsic divine ordination."[51] If we decide that Christopher's search for a guiding philosophy conceals Linton's effort toward the same, then we impose what we know about her subjectivity on a discursive representation that compares these various "ologies" from the point of view of intellectual history. A question posed by Lamarque in *The Philosophy of Literature* illuminates the stakes of this analysis: "What are the grounds for postulating an impersonal conception of an author as distinct from a personal conception?"[52] For a Victorian weighing the relative merits and weaknesses of these ideologies impersonally, that ground (whether fictional or not) must be focalized from a masculine perspective. Once marked as feminine, an authorial identity defaults to the personal, and its status as art disintegrates in favor of a circumstantial, subjective expression. We see this in minor novels like *A Woman's Story*, discussed in my introduction, wherein the identification of author Helen Lyndsey nullifies the artistic stature of the work written under her pseudonym "H.L.," and in the biocritical focus on Julia Frankau and Margaret Harkness that takes precedence over their fictional inventions.

Yet criticism that seeks to identify the real Linton in her portrait of Christopher has inspired complex explanations of a divided subjectivity, repressed lesbianism, and an ideological conservatism designed to make her own professional success socially acceptable. To Bache, *The Autobiography of Christopher Kirkland* gives us insights into "Linton's perception of her career and the problems of literary reputation for a female author best known for her ideologically 'masculine' and rhetorically extreme journalism."[53] For Peaches Henry, Linton incorporates the individualistic pattern of male-identified, autobiographical selfhood in order to "show the self she wanted to expose to her audience,"[54] suggesting that Linton wanted her readers to identify her behind the masculine cover. But Linton's extremism was voluntary, and while many disagreed with her, she had a long and extremely successful career. The idea that she was covertly strategizing, through Christopher, a path toward acceptance collides with her success and her vehement opinions. In another interpretation of *Christopher Kirkland* more attentive to feminist critical interests than the evidence of the text, Henry refers to its paradoxically individualistic and relational models of selfhood, arguing that through "the incorporation of both identity paradigms, Linton demonstrated that as a nineteenth-century woman she was certainly limited by Victorian definitions of female selfhood but not so completely constricted by them that she could not manipulate them to her own advantage."[55] Linton, in this account, was at once frustrated by social norms and able to upset them, which is less an argument than a rapprochement between historical certainty ("Victorian women were socially subjugated") and popular feminism ("but they valiantly resisted"). The former claim is undeniable, and the latter focuses on Linton's political defiance. But neither claim deliberates upon the text of *Christopher Kirkland*: these arguments depend on the sociohistorical context of Victorian publishing and its challenges to women writers, without the evidence of the writing that distinguished one of those women in the first place. Underwriting all these arguments about the "real" Linton in the portrait of Christopher Kirkland, though, is the assumption that *The Autobiography* is more autobiography than novel. "When we consider nonfiction narratives, say a biography or a historical narrative," writes Jonathan Culler, "we don't claim that there must be a narrator separate from the author. We can distinguish different authorial attitudes or strategies" to attach to the author, but these modalities do not require the conception of separate selves.[56] In lieu of a tipping point where a text's nonfictionality cedes to artistic license, signs like the invention of a man named "Christopher Kirkland" can be taken at face value instead of as a covert indication of a woman writer's projected desires.

Further, the efforts to align Linton with Christopher can require far more complexity than the imaginative latitude synonymous with fiction, especially when his experiences epitomize masculine privilege. When he makes the "pure and simple" decision to become a writer, for instance, in quick succession he has a poem accepted, moves to London, finds a job at a magazine, and within a short period of time has "accomplished [his] purpose and written [his] novel,"[57] which receives laudatory reviews. Christopher's description of literature as a "waste-pipe of unspecialized powers, which no one thinks demands an apprenticeship, and wherein all believe that fame and success are to be caught like wild goats, at a bound!"[58] suggests naïveté, but in fact reflects his experience. In contrast, recognition for Glenarva in Charlotte Riddell's *A Struggle for Fame* (1883) takes about twenty years and is cruelly short-lived. In New Woman novels, as I show in the following chapter, it is more common to end a novel about a woman writer's apprenticeship when she is still hoping to make a name for herself.[59] But in Christopher, Linton evidently chooses to write about a man of many talents and frustrations, who despite success in the literary profession still struggles to define himself and satisfy his inchoate longings for human connection and a deeper purpose.

All of Linton's biographers, Deborah T. Meem writes, "assume that Christopher Kirkland is Eliza Lynn Linton," and the first of them, George Somes Layard, "even readjusted names and sexes to make them fit with the author's actual life (and presumed heterosexuality)." Meem remains "suspicious of swallowing *Christopher Kirkland* whole in this way." However, she continues, philosophical judgments surfaced in the text "[hold], either way," whether attributed to Christopher or Linton.[60] They hold either way if the bottom line of interpretation is a distinctive identity construct, in which case it doesn't matter if the view is attributed to Linton or to what Meem calls her "alter ego," Christopher.

But as I've argued, Christopher's attention to the separation between language and its references, and the social construction of gender and personality, signify a fictional rather than autobiographical ontology. If we assume that Linton wrote *Christopher Kirkland* as an autonomous piece of art and not a form of confession designed to make other things happen (finesse the reception of her controversial writing, unburden herself of secret lesbianism[61]), the novel could be a working hypothesis of Christopher's opinions about the social conditions of identity and the subjective variability of the autobiographical genre. The hypothesis would be that Linton takes many of her own experiences, relationships, and intellectual developments and applies them to a wholly fictional man. In effect, as Christopher so often tells us, the change of sex yields a new set of circumstances: his lack of education is tragic, not simply the leisured custom of the upper and middle classes. The story of Christopher's failed marriage—which bears many similarities to Linton's own—can be explained with an equanimity inconceivable to a divorcée. When Christopher decides to publish, his talent immediately garners respect and remuneration. These altered plots use fiction, then, to expose the hypocritical social and sexual norms that all women and men experience, not just Linton.

Indeed, the scope of *Christopher Kirkland*, with its historiographic attention to developments in intellectual and religious philosophy, science, ethical theory, and mid- to late- century political thought could hardly make a stronger case for *detachment* from the private life of an individual woman. It recalls the sage discourse of writers like Carlyle, Ruskin, and Arnold who, like Christopher, position themselves above the fray of society in order to declaim sweeping truths and prophecies. Writing as a man, Linton imitates this discourse with more impunity than she could as a woman. But if we read Christopher as the cover for the "real" Linton, then his celebration of scientific rationalism and personal liberty sounds at best aspirational and at worst ironic. Instead of turning the text into a tortured exercise that either consciously (Meem) or unconsciously (Anderson) hopes that canny readers will discern the truth behind the text, it is easier to read *Christopher Kirkland* as beholden to its own aesthetic and political principles—that is, as a novel. In a similar vein, Lanser identifies the devaluation of fiction *qua* fiction when she argues for an intervention against "the cathexis with characters as if they were "real" people": "It may take a narratological deconstruction of the sign systems that produce character," she writes, "to inhibit the more imitative and uncritical investments in literary character."[62]

The process of wresting the fictional character from her historical author was and remains challenging precisely because the urge to connect historical women writers to their literature has had a lasting impact and, evidently, use value. Past readers (in the Victorian age and earlier twentieth century) tended to read Victorian women's fiction as autobiographical because they underestimated a woman's imaginative power and artistic detachment. From the rise of second-wave feminism, autobiographical attention to women's writing had a recuperative purpose: it channeled sympathy for women's historic subjugation into a representation of the woman writer herself—her desires, thwarted ambitions, and unheralded achievements. But both versions of autobiographical criticism can elide the business and accomplishments of fiction in favor of historical determinism and political argument. Attention to the metafictional significance of a writer-heroine (or writer-hero) repositions the novel as self-evidence rather than a biographical cue. The following chapter finds a version of this argument in two New Woman novels in which the novelist-heroines resist reproducing the narrative scripts expected of them, and so make a distinction between their insights as novelists and their lives as women—a differentiation we are still making today.

5

NEO-VICTORIAN VICTORIAN NOVELS

The Writer-Heroine as a New Woman

This chapter focuses on two late Victorian novels that exemplify, almost a century before the term was coined, the formal conventions attributed to neo-Victorian novels. In their field-defining *Neo-Victorianism: The Victorians in the Twenty-First Century* (2010), Ann Heilmann and Mark Llewellyn attribute to the genre "metatextual and metahistorical conjunctions . . . [that] interact within the fields of exchange and adaptation between the Victorian and the contemporary. . . . To be part of the neo-Victorianism we discuss in this book, texts . . . must in some respect be *self-consciously engaged with the act of (re)interpretation, (re)discovery, and (re)vision concerning the Victorians*."[1] Grant Allen's (1848–1899) *The Type-Writer Girl* (1897), published under the pseudonym Olive Pratt Rayner, and Emily Morse Symonds's (1860–1936) *A Writer of Books* (1898), published under the pseudonym George Paston, share these features except for a comparison between "the Victorian and contemporary" and "(re)discovery." No matter how archly actual Victorians like Allen and Symonds wrote about contemporary life, they could not politicize that setting in the same way that contemporary neo-Victorian writers can, nor does the choice of the period carry the novelty that it does for neo-Victorian fiction, however popular it may be. But Allen's and Symonds's novels epitomize the metafictional and metahistorical features Heilmann and Llewellyn (as well as other theorists of neo-Victorian fiction) identify. *The Type-Writer Girl* is narrated in mock-heroic mode by Juliet Appleton, a young woman making a living as a "typewriter" (or copyist) in London while also writing fiction. Juliet parodies other literatures, questions historical authority and contemporary values, and calls attention to her narrative's liminal status between realism and romance. A *Writer of Books* also features an aspiring novelist, Cosima Chudleigh, whose immersion in literary worlds ill-prepares her for the London publishing market. Cosima's tendency to interpret her experiences through literary conventions and plots undermines the novel's realism, as she is at once the subject of Symonds's novel and its metafictional informant. These textual features correlate with "the presence of self-consciousness or metafiction" that Sudha Shastri attributes to neo-Victorian novels that "revitalize literature" through their intertextual license.[2] My purpose is not to challenge the generic definition of neo-Victorianism but to propose that the oddity of comparing actual Victorian novels to neo-Victorian ones reflects how periodization and historicization can conceal Victorian formal innovations. And while scholars including Sally Ledger, Ann Ardis, Jane Eldridge Miller, and Lyn Pykett have persuasively charted the proto-modern features of New Woman novels,[3] conventions encoded as postmodern and neo-Victorian have not received equivalent attention.

My approach to *The Type-Writer Girl* and *A Writer of Books* resembles that followed by neo-Victorian critics who focus on the subversion of Victorian literary techniques rather than historical realism.[4] Heilmann employs a similar tactic in *New Woman Strategies: Sarah Grand, Olive Schreiner, and Mona Caird* (2004) when she brings "a distinctly new conceptual methodology to the subject by privileging *textuality* over cultural-historical investigation." But where I compare formal techniques in Allen's and Symonds's novels to the postmodern, neo-Victorian novel, Heilmann reads them through French feminist theory, in which the "engagement with mimicry, femininity, self-reflexivity, subversion, libidinality, and performativity" emphasizes "the writerly acts of New Woman authors."[5] I agree with Heilmann's characterization of New Woman writing and the formal innovations at the center of French feminist theory, but my anachronistic pairing of late Victorian novels with neo-Victorian methods deemed postmodern deliberately echoes the temporal dislocations posited in *The Type-Writer Girl* and *A Writer of Books*. These novels self-consciously respond to stale "Victorian" definitions of realism and women's writing much like today's neo-Victorian critics do, although that latter group evokes a century or more in their comparison of the old and the new.

As Heilmann implies, most critics of New Woman novels prioritize connections between the novels and the socio-history of the 1880s and 1890s. Lyn Pykett's observation that "New Woman fiction was sometimes reviewed alongside sociological and other polemical works, as if it were part of a seamless discourse on the Woman Question"[6] references the fin de siècle but applies equally well to contemporary scholarship. New Woman novels engage with the political climate of the late century, but many of them also question the realism of that engagement, especially as it disadvantages or excludes the woman novelist. Ann Ardis's claim that "most recent critics isolate the novelty of the New Woman novel at the level of character, dismissing other forms of experimentation in this fiction"[7] makes a similar distinction between the thematic level of this genre and its understudied formal techniques.

Since the 1970s at least, critics have commented on the proliferation of writer and artist characters in New Woman novels. For Sally Ledger, "one of the striking features of many New Woman novels is that they are peopled with female writers of feminist fiction,"[8] and for Elaine Showalter, the figure of the woman writer often "plays a representative role as fictional spokeswoman for the feminist generation of the 1890s."[9] More recently, Beth Palmer has argued that the writer-heroine in New Woman novels "carries the political interest of these diverse narratives. Her frustrations, disappointments, and interrupted creativity comment on the difficulties the 'new woman' faced as she tried to express herself and to earn a living."[10] These critics suggest that the writer-heroine functions expediently as a mouthpiece for the New Woman's issues and concerns. Showalter complains about the didactic tendency of such topical narratives when she asserts that Olive Schreiner, Sarah Grand, and George Egerton "had but one story to tell, and exhaust themselves in its narration,"[11] a charge that recalls the woodenly instrumentalist political economists who populated Harriet Martineau's *Illustrations of Political Economy* (1832) over sixty years before.[12]

This chapter also focuses on the New Woman writer-heroine, but with an important distinction from the sociopolitical approach characterized above. While Juliet Appleton and Cosima Chudleigh live, work, and love in the specific environment created and championed by New Women, political commitments are not their defining features. In keeping with the previous chapter's discussion of pseudonymity and metafiction, Allen's and Symonds's gender-switching pseudonyms also preclude a biocritical reading of Juliet and Cosima. In the absence of a polemical championship of New Womanhood and an autobiographical subtext, these heroines' experiences as writers self-reflexively implicate the novels in which they appear. Juliet's and Cosima's formal innovations register a break with the editorial norms and advice they receive as women writers; they are aware that they are forging uncharted territory, but the novels, not the narrators, ultimately testify to their innovations through their own self-evidence.

The proleptic form and promise of Juliet's and Cosima's writing ambitions—and by metafictional reflection, Allen's and Symonds's—resemble a mode of agency identified in recent philosophical writing. Agnes Callard, a philosopher who studies aspiration, writes that self-transformation occurs when we invert "the traditional relation of authority between the creator and created self. On an aspirational account of self-creation, the creator does not determine, choose, or shape the created self; rather, she looks up to, imitates, and becomes the created self. The source of normativity lies at the end of the process rather than at the beginning."[13] David Velleman similarly proposes that "we emulate ideals by *pretending* to satisfy them," and in so doing transmogrify the ideal into practice.[14] These hypotheses translate to literary criticism through the value they ascribe to the imaginary. In contrast, Freudian psychoanalysis, and the Marxist view of history—the two most influential methodological approaches to literature in the twentieth century, and arguably also the twenty-first—reverse Callard's and Velleman's aspirational models. They discover the "latent" and thus more "real" determinants of fiction in the repressed sexual conflicts of early childhood and the socioeconomic determinants of the historical period.[15] As compelling and instructive as these methods are, they operate from a position that assumes fruition, using Freudian psychoanalysis and Marxist determinism as both prequel to the fictional representation and its inevitable symbolic or ideological denotation. Fiction's status as a working hypothesis can be foreclosed by the determining logic of these methodologies.

The literary intertexts that interrupt, redirect, overwrite, and embellish the novels by Allen and Symonds (and those purportedly written by their heroines) are more informative to my reading than Freudian or Marxist methods or topical connections to New Womanhood. Juliet has been educated at Girton College and Cosima largely self-taught, but both recall Broughton's Nell LeStrange in their wide-ranging references to other literature. As with Nell, the literary circuitry that inflects their writing and dialogue evokes immersion in the English canon as well as classical and Continental traditions, a subjective engrossment coextensive with their own thoughts, experiences, and literary endeavors. The writer-heroines, however, navigate their literary immersion in different ways. Juliet's imitations and reappropriations are self-conscious, ironic, and playful; her habit of filtering everyday life through fictional tropes and texts distracts her from the quotidian burdens of the "type-writer girl."

Cosima begins her writing career believing that her secondhand literary expertise cannot substitute for the "experience" that male novelists take for granted, and that she hopes to expose herself to in London. For both heroines, then, literature as a body of knowledge and a presumptive career contends against real life, or, in the ontology of the novels, against realism.

The Type-Writer Girl: More Awesome than Real

By the end of the century, the ambiguity of authorship attached to pseudonymous writing had a more literal analog: "typewriters." The typewriter was a new breed of worker trained to take shorthand dictation in offices and was almost always a woman. The heroine and narrator of *The Type-Writer Girl*, Juliet Appleton joins the "ten thousand type-writer girls [that] crowd London."[16] Hillel Schwartz writes that at the turn of the twentieth century, stenography (the transcription of shorthand onto a typewriter) was "thought a woman's job, the stenographer 'a safe, efficacious, labor-saving device.' Other 'merely mechanical' tasks—tabulating, typing, telegraphy—also fell to women."[17] Juliet enters these anonymous ranks with her own typewriter, an elite education from Girton College, and recent experience living in an East End settlement as one of another new breed of workers: middle-class women who lived in the slums as modestly paid wardens, armed with ideals of Christian and sometimes socialist charity. Despite her respectable background and credentials, Juliet, an orphan, begins her adventure with just "six and eleven-pence as available assets."[18]

But before she turns to her own experiences, Juliet advances a de facto hermeneutic key for the text that follows. She muses upon the differences between feminine and masculine writing and the influence of canonical literatures on the present, referring to Samuel Butler's "eccentric theory" that a woman wrote the *Odyssey*. The epic poem reveals "the vagueness, the elusiveness, the melting, hazy charm of feminine craft"; "without thinking it true," she writes, "I love to believe it": "it thrills with mystery, and woman is the mystic. Look at its glorious dimness.... From morning to night, in that enchanted poem, on and on we sail, past uncertain isles or dubious blue headlands, begirt with fantastic forms, and in perils of the sea more awesome than real."[19]

By contrast, the *Iliad*, more real than awesome, is "a masculine poem," "a saga of men's ideas, so sharp in its outlines, so historical, so definite."[20] Women's writing, not beholden to such strictures, can pursue "adventure" over verisimilitude.

"If only we could have lived in those days!" people say. I answer, "You *are* living in them." It is not the days, not the places, not the things that change, but we who see them otherwise. Consider, the Mediterranean is the same sea today as when the Ithacan lady who wrote the *Odyssey* looked out on its blue zones to behold it peopled with strange forms and wizard shadows. For that nameless Sappho, that prehistoric Charlotte Brontë, that inchoate Elizabeth Barrett Browning, the Ionian man swarmed alive with Gorgons and Harpies as Loch Fyne with herrings. . . . You may steam down the prosaic Adriatic today in an Austrian Lloyd steamer—a fearsome Behemoth, bellowing, snorting, flame-breathing—and identify those charmed shores of Hellenic fancy. . . . Adventures are to the adventurous. Go through the world in search of Calypso, and you will surely find her. Be modern, and you will find only Willesden Junction. That may suffice for you. I live in "those days" as all lovers of the mystical have always lived in them.[21]

Juliet's condensed and fanciful literary history depicts the female Homer as an alter ego of Sappho, Charlotte Brontë, and Elizabeth Barrett Browning. She has already established that the female Homer theory is not true, and by using this conceit as the origin point of a feminine writing tradition, she previews the equivocal status of women's authorship that *The Type-Writer Girl* proposes more generally. Yet despite her preference for the mystical past, Juliet lurches from one modern adventure to another. She finds work as a typewriter, briefly joins a commune of agrarian socialists, returns to London and secures another job, starts to write fiction, falls in love with her boss, follows him to Venice, and finally rejects him out of a loyalty to his devoted fiancée. She ends the novel alone, still a typewriter girl. Her consecutive choices make it difficult to agree with her claim that "it is not the days, the places, or the things that change" but "the people who observe them." The discrepancy between her philosophy of adventure and her straitened material circumstances, however, undermines the realism of the story she narrates. She passes over her "life of routine" as a typewriter, making "no apology for dealing with it here only in a few brief episodes." Those episodes are transposed into a narrative "with blanks between, which just serve conveniently to divide the chapters."[22] Life experience adapts to, rather than dictates, the logos of the book: this determining fiction propels Juliet's narration and ultimately becomes its self-evidence.

The preference for an interesting story over history or realism, moreover, sanctions Juliet's creative appropriation of other texts, and replication and remediation are logical narrative acts for a writer whose market value rests on her speed and accuracy in duplicating the texts of men. From her cheerful endorsement of the *Odyssey*'s female author, she establishes a pattern for the rest of the novel in which intertexts conflate, overlap, and are loosened from their origins. Many of the texts she cites are themselves imitations of earlier versions, including Shakespeare's *Romeo and Juliet* (ca. 1594–96, inspired by Arthur Brooke's 1562 poem "The Tragicall Historye of Romeus and Iuliet"), *As You Like It* (1623, modeled after Thomas Lodge's 1590 novel *Rosalynde*), and Georges Bizet's *Carmen* (an 1875 opera that retells Prosper Mérimée's 1845 novella). Her inclusion of earlier texts recalls Nell LeStrange's, but without Nell's sense of exclusion from the realms of institutional and masculine knowledge. Where Nell lacks the history to organize her freewheeling juxtapositions, Juliet uses anachronism to proclaim her freedom from tradition, fully aware she is flouting the canon. Later in the novel, Juliet's boss (and future lover) "Romeo" tells her that she is "an intrepid young lady" and doubts "if you quite realize always in what galleys you have embarked." Juliet's answer, "I think I do,"[23] inspires the reader to see a pun where Romeo doesn't: she is as intrepid as a sailor seeking adventure (or Ithaca), as she is a practitioner of printed columns.

A proto-postmodern meditation on authorship resonates with Juliet's incorporation of past literatures in her own work. In Jorge Luis Borges's short story of 1939, "Pierre Menard, Author of the *Quixote*," an unnamed narrator describes the career of a late writer and critic, Pierre Menard, whose most ambitious project was the attempt to "produce a few pages which would coincide—word for word and line for line—with those of Miguel de Cervantes."[24] Menard understands that the *Quixote* conceived by Cervantes was a product of seventeenth-century influences and impressions. The challenge he sets for himself is not to re-create that creative context, which would be impossible, but "to go on being Pierre Menard and reach the *Quixote* through the experiences of Pierre Menard."[25] Yet even if it were a word-for-word copy of Cervantes's original, Menard understands that his replication would have an entirely different meaning in the twentieth century from the one it had in the seventeenth. The narrator uses an excerpt from *Don Quixote* to exemplify this linguistic contingency: "'Truth, whose mother is history, rival of time, depository of deeds, witness of the past, exemplar and adviser to the present, and the future's counselor.'" To

Cervantes, this is "mere rhetorical praise of history"; but to Menard, explains the narrator, "history—the *mother* of truth: the idea is astounding. Menard, a contemporary of William James, defines history not as an inquiry into reality but as its origin."[26] Similarly, Juliet's insertion of herself into canonical texts and roles (Odysseus, Juliet Capulet, Carmen) does not transform her into those earlier contexts or figures so much as it revives them for her own purposes, which in turn actuate new possibilities and meanings in the familiar works. Her superimposition of herself on and in these texts recalls *The Autobiography of Christopher Kirkland* (1885), in which the meaning of a sentence or narrated experience changes drastically according to the writer's sex. Were Juliet, for instance, to reprise Cervantes's history, "the *mother* of truth" platitude that Menard tries out, the dissonance would exceed the historical anachronism that Borges's narrator finds so incongruous; neither a seventeenth-century nor a fin de siècle Juliet could invoke the masculine empowerment implicit in the truth as rival, witness, exemplar, advisor, and counselor. Likewise, her self-identification as Odysseus or Shakespeare's Juliet creates a dissonance both historical and gendered, not reprising the originals so much as reconfiguring them. Linda Hutcheon summarizes this effect when she writes that historical metafiction allows for "a consideration of the different and the heterogenous, the hybrid and the provisional" that is "not a rejection of the former values in favor of the latter," but rather "a rethinking of each in light of the others."[27]

Juliet's reconfigurations of other texts do not cohere into a unified commentary or political position, even within or relative to her own historical moment. When she invokes the quest narratives of Saint George and Odysseus, for instance, she vows to "set forth into the world, a Princess Cleodolind[28] of the nineteenth century, ready to face the dragons that, as I well know, abound in it, and full of faith in the St. George who will come to rescue me. I mean to sail away on my Odyssey, unabashed, touching at such shores as may chance to beckon, yet hopeful of reaching at last the realms of Alcinous."[29] Juliet identifies with Cleodolind in the Saint George myth but then reverses this gendered position by positing herself as Odysseus, not Penelope. The origin texts are simultaneously revived and subverted without any clear indication of what message—if any—Juliet transmits. Especially in the context of the New Woman heroines who can seem goal-oriented and dogmatic, Juliet's capriciousness challenges contemporary scholars' attempts to define the novel's political message. Leah Price writes about the "profound ambivalence of the novel's ethical agenda" relative to its treatment of women, automation, and creativity, and

Tara MacDonald agrees that "the feminist politics of this novel are difficult to ascertain."[30] Indeed, the novel's ostensible focus on its titular profession dissipates into a plot device to move Juliet in and out of professional settings with relative ease and a modest income stream. Allen, via Olive Pratt Rayner, via Juliet, situates *The Type-Writer Girl* amid concerns more ontological than sociological.

"Still a Type-Writer Girl," and Yet Much More

On the face of it, Juliet's spirited flights into adventure and romance are a logical escape from the rules governing high realism at this time, which Christoph Ehland and Cornelia Wächter describe as a gendered effort to ensure masculine exclusivity: "the 'masculine' avant-garde was increasingly under perceived threat by the ever-expanding market of the supposedly 'feminine' middlebrow."[31] Ledger argues that late-century male realists such as George Gissing, George Moore, and Jack London "had as their aim the creation of a 'new' realism (heavily influenced by the Zolaesque school of literary naturalism) which focused upon the harsh economic and sexual realities of life in the late nineteenth century," a style hostile to respectable femininity and "the ken of women writers, who supposedly specialized in the more confined domestic world of romance and marriage."[32] These gendered norms are easily detectable in Juliet's modest characterization of her writing as amateur and in her reception by male literary figures in the novel. In the most dramatic instance of this reception, the great novelist Sidney Trevelyan visits Romeo's office. After a condescending monologue in which he insults Romeo by way of references to Dante, Shelley, and the literary philistines he deplores, Trevelyan notices Juliet at her desk.

> Suddenly, he burst out in a quite different voice, snorting like a warhorse, "Send that young woman away!" he cried, executing a sort of ponderous rhinoceros-dance before me. "Send her away! I tell you I can't stand her. I won't have her scribbling there and making notes of all I say. She's a paragraphist—a paragraphist: the vilest spawn on God's earth, a paragraphist! What do you mean by setting spavined shorthand writers to report my *obiter dicta*?" . . . he cried, waving his hands at me as if I were a gadfly. "Go off! I won't be listened to and paragraphed! I could feel you paragraphing me. Away, young woman: away with you."[33]

Trevelyan is not well-informed enough to know that "paragraphist" is the wrong term for a typewriter, and his claim that he can "feel [her] paragraphing [him]" adds a vague lewdness on top of the professional insult. But this exchange effectively reverses the ridicule onto Trevelyan: by appearing to represent the scene ingenuously, Juliet has the last word. She may be ejected from his presence, but her text demotes the great novelist from approbation to the target of satire.

Juliet further exposes the literary establishment's condescension to women writers in her editorial exchanges with Romeo. He encourages her writing, appreciates her comments on his own poetry, but also has patronizing ideas about "woman's place in literature": "So many women, he said, wrote of life with a note of personality rare among men. They put more heart in it."[34] Though he writes dense poetry filled with classical references, in his advice to Juliet he recycles the old convention whereby women write about their immediate experiences. "He urged me," writes Juliet, "to try my hand at a short story of the modern girl who earns her own living in London—'for example, this little friend who uses your type-writer.'"[35] The "little friend" Romeo refers to is Elsie, a struggling typewriter whom Juliet befriends and supports with contract work. Juliet "was grateful" that he "divert[ed] the theme [of the typewriter girl] from [her] own personality,"[36] but this "diversion" is, of course, refuted by the text that expresses it. Still, Juliet maintains a deferential stance toward Romeo's expertise: "I promised to make an attempt . . . with one of my earliest East-End reminiscences, or else with a little vignette of the infant anarchists. . . . For a week or two I worked hard in my stray moments at this my poor little literary first-born. I put its phrases in curl-papers till I was sick of twisting them. When it was ripe for the birth, I confess I thought meanly of it. . . . I brought it to Romeo, trembling. He read it and was enthusiastic."[37]

Romeo offers to publish her story in the magazine he edits, but Juliet refuses: "I will not allow it to be printed where—where personal acquaintance and your recommendation may disturb the editor's calmer opinion." Romeo is "sorry to lose it" and remains "vexed" after it comes out in another magazine, insisting that "after all, you were *my* discovery."[38] Juliet's anxiety at soliciting Romeo's opinion, her principled avoidance of editorial bias, and his claim of "discovery" are entrenched signs of the masculine control of literary publishing. Far from being the amateur scribblings of a typewriter girl, Juliet's depiction of her writing and publishing experience attests to *The Type-Writer Girl*'s awareness of its own production. Lawrence Rainey agrees that Juliet "more than matches wits with her male counterparts," but argues that her unchanged status at the end of the novel ("I am still a type-writer girl—at another office"[39]) correlates her with the picaresque hero(ine) who "cannot assume the responsibilities of mature sexuality, or marriage, without ceasing to be [herself]."[40] Given the complexity of Juliet's authorship, which I discuss below, Rainey's character-driven interpretation of the novel differs from my emphasis on formal self-consciousness. Juliet may be in the same professional position at the close of her story, but by implicating Juliet's authorship, the published book we are reading invalidates her claim that nothing has changed.

Such metafictional agency contrasts to scenes in New Woman novels that portray "women's writing" as merely a symbolic placeholder for fame or personal ambition. As mentioned in the introduction, Mary Cholmondeley's *Red Pottage* (1899) features a New Woman novelist, Hester Gresley, whose tyrannically conservative brother, the Reverend Gresley, destroys her masterpiece while it is still in manuscript form. Beyond this central drama, however, *Red Pottage* engages in an extensive conversation about the place of women's art at the late century, with a cast of characters that articulates a full range of opinions on the subject.[41] One such character, the decadent Lady Newhaven, epitomizes the confidence available to those who never venture beyond a speculation of their talents.

> "It seems curious," said Lady Newhaven, after a pause, "how the books are mostly written by the people who know least of life. Now, the *Sonnets from the Portuguese*. People think so much of them. I was looking at them the other day. Why, they are nothing to what I have felt. I sometimes think if *I* wrote a book—I don't mean that I have any special talent—but if I really sat down and wrote a book with all the deep side of life in it, and one's own religious feelings, and described love and love's tragedy as they really are, what a sensation it would make! It would take the world by storm."[42]

Lady Newhaven's contemplation of the power of her unexpressed feelings satirizes the persistent link between women's writing and personal reflection, as well as the Victorian cliché that women wrote in hopes of fame and causing a "sensation." Meanwhile, later in the novel, when Hester explains that she loved her lost book "for itself—not for anything it was to bring me,"[43] she describes a dispassionate commitment to literature.

Geraldine Mitton's *A Bachelor Girl in London* (1898) tells the story of Judith Danville, a provincial New Woman who moves to London and becomes a typewriter and struggling journalist. Most of the novel concerns Judith's complex education in social class, which she navigates through a series of thwarted romantic relationships before the novel ends in her happy engagement. Judith's work as a typewriter, like Juliet's, requires her to economize strictly. In the middle of the novel, she returns home for a brief visit and has a revelation. "The journalistic instinct, which had been covered by the necessity for hard, mechanical work, leapt to the surface and flowed over all other feeling.... 'The secrets of utterance, of expression, of that through which along any intellectual or spiritual power within one can take effect upon others to overawe or charm them to one's side.' ... This [idea] had set alight her vitality and turned her blood to liquid energy. She would write, would be an agency in the world.... Now everything had become warm, prosperous, coherent. Her loneliness and desolation had flowed from the need of expression."[44]

Recalling Glenarva Westley's proclamation by moonlight in *A Struggle for Fame*, Judith's epiphany could be a turning point in Mitton's novel. She has been surrounded by successful novelists and journalists in London, including the brilliant man to whom she will later become engaged, so her sudden inspiration does have local precedent. But never again does the urge to write seize her emotions, and Mitton's narrator half-comically explains that "because one girl had had good food, complete rest, and change of scene for a fortnight; consequently from a typist in a London office she was transformed by imagination into one of the great goddesses in the literary sphere. Truly the world would be ridiculous were it not so pitiful!"[45] Judith's momentary ambition—unlike the manifest achievements of *The Type-Writer Girl* and, below, *A Writer of Books*—surfaces at an ontological remove from *A Bachelor Girl in London*. Mitton does not invite the reader to imagine that *her* novel is even implicitly the product of favorable material circumstances, or of the desire to "find means of making visible to others that which was vividly apparent, delightful, [and] of lively interest"[46] that Judith briefly felt.

The Writer's Writer

When Juliet begins *The Type-Writer Girl* by simultaneously proclaiming and refuting the existence of the female Homer, she foreshadows the conditions under which the rest of the book unfolds: its instability of authorship, the use and revision of other texts, and a critical climate elusive to (or suspicious of) women writers. The deconstruction of Allen's male authorship plays an important role in the reception of the novel as well as in the larger history of the woman writer's professional consolidation. The novel was published under the name Olive Pratt Rayner, which Grant Allen, the actual author, embellishes with a personal dedication:

> To
> Theodore Rayner
> and
> Oliver Wendell Pratt
> A Wife's Homage,
> A Sister's Love.

Allen promotes Olive Pratt Rayner's imaginary career by attaching her name to another novel, *Rosalba: The Story of Her Development* (1899), and expands on her identity in other texts as well. An October 1897 issue of the *Literary World*, for example, includes the following notice:

> The authoress of the "Typewriter Girl," the new novel, a review of which appears in our column this week, is an American lady, the daughter of Dr. Pratt, of Salem, Massachusetts. Dr. Pratt was a great admirer of his *confrère*, Dr. Oliver Wendell Holmes, after whom he called his son, Oliver Wendell Pratt, and also his daughter, Olive, the authoress of this story. She married, in 1896, Mr. Theodore Rayner, a British subject, who has vineyards near Verona, where the gifted lady now resides, making occasional winter trips to Venice and to Florence. She retains, however, her maiden name, in conjunction with her husband's, and prefers to be known as Olive Pratt Rayner.[47]

The review referred to in this notice calls *The Type-Writer Girl* "very well worth reading," "the breeziest and most lively book that we have had the pleasure of handling for a long time past." The reviewer continues:

> [*The Type-Writer Girl*] may not be absolutely fact all the way through, but internal evidence convinces us that Mrs. Rayner writes from personal experience, or from evidence obtained at first hand. . . . Miss Appleton is shrewd, sensible, and at times flippant, but she is a delightful little personage, and no one can follow her experiences without admiring the qualities which bring her safely through trials that are laughable only in her reception of them.[48]

The title of this review, "A Lively Autobiography," and the paratextual reinforcement of the novel's autobiographical (or at least feminine) provenance suggests that women's novels are still identified, in 1898, with the women who wrote them. But more importantly, this identification capitalizes on the woman novelist as a professional type. Allen's composite of Olive Pratt Rayner (with her intellectual father, expatriate husband, Continental lifestyle, and particular feelings about the name she uses) authenticates the novel ("Mrs. Rayner writes from personal experience, or from evidence obtained at first hand"), which reflexively authenticates *her*. In pragmatic terms, the credible qualities of a woman novelist have disconnected from any *actual* woman novelist.

An impact of this useful fiction surfaces after Allen's death in 1899 when the issue of Olive Pratt Rayner's imprimatur surfaces in *The Writer*, an American literary magazine, in 1900. This notice opens by announcing that "since the death of Grant Allen the fact has been made known that he was the author of the novel, 'The Typewriter Girl' [sic], which was published several years ago as the production of Olive Pratt Rayner." The writer then excerpts the personal description of Olive Pratt Rayner quoted above in the *Literary World*, almost word-for-word, but attributes it to the *London Mail*.[49] What *The Writer*'s writer changes in the near-duplication is incidental: "making occasional winter trips to Florence and to Venice" instead of "Venice and Florence," and "after whom he named his son" instead of "after whom he called his son." The notice continues: "Considering the style of this circumstantial paragraph, it is fair to presume that it was inspired by the publisher of the story, or was sent out to editors as publishers' 'press notices' usually are. In that case the publisher must have known that he was lying, and that his deception of the public was gratuitous and entirely without excuse."[50]

The concern of *The Writer*'s writer for a deluded public seems overblown in the context of readers of fiction and the frequency with which Victorian novelists, male and female, adopted pseudonyms. Nevertheless, the fiction of *The Type-Writer Girl*'s authorship spins away from the novel (about a woman writer) into a frame narrative (about a different woman writer) and becomes a horseless carriage of a story that follows its own disorderly route. In true metafictional style, the discourse surrounding *The Type-Writer Girl* in the literary world repeats the muddled attributions, reappropriations, and gender politics that underwrite the novel. In her essay on *The Type-Writer Girl*, Price describes the typewriter as a "wedge" "between text and hand" that creates a "precondition for the modernist disjunction of writing from subjectivity,"[51] but I propose an earlier sequence of this disjunction. From the time that Lucy Snowe, accused of plagiarism, performs a live enactment of her writing skills to the biographical contortions that critics of *The Autobiography of Christopher Kirkland* (both Victorian and present day) have privileged over Eliza Lynn Linton's fictional imagination, the writer-heroines I trace dramatize the work of literary creation so that its female achievement becomes a disembodied subjective style, and so conceivable by men as well as women.

Talking Back with *A Writer of Books*

For many of its theorists, the neo-Victorian novel's frequent focus on a marginalized subject or social group constitutes a corrective political act. Peter Carey's *Jack Maggs* (1997), a reworking of *Great Expectations* in which the title character is based on Dickens's shadowy Magwitch, or Sarah Waters's *Tipping the Velvet* (1998), which conjures a rich lesbian community in Victorian London, are just two of many acclaimed neo-Victorian novels that explore subject positions rarely, if ever, examined in detail in actual Victorian fiction. As the critic Helen Davies explains in *Gender and Ventriloquism in Victorian and Neo-Victorian Fiction* (2012), "An association between 'voice' and social agency is clearly at work within such accounts of neo-Victorianism, and it is in this context that the notion of 'having a voice' has become one of the more compelling motifs of identity politics. . . . We see that the 'silenced' Victorians are granted a 'voice' by contemporary authors. . . . In this sense, then, neo-Victorian fiction might be interpreted as subversively 'talking back' to Victorians."[52] For Davies, neo-Victorian novels imagine undocumented subjects through the wisdom of hindsight. But as I have been arguing, novels including *The Type-Writer Girl* and *A Writer of Books* respond to hegemonic authority within the fin de siècle through formal tools identified with metafiction, including intertextual allusion and parody. Middle-class (if improvident) heroines like Juliet and Cosima are certainly not as alienated from Victorian society as Carey's Australian convict or Waters's scrappy urban lesbian, but their stories still identify and respond to oppressive politics. In Symonds's novel, overtly a third-person account of Cosima's development as a writer, the collusion of omniscience, Cosima's free indirect discourse, theories of the novel, and intertextual allusion dissolve any firm boundary between narrator and heroine, or fiction as a discursive subject and the book in hand. By exemplifying the representational techniques that Cosima slowly learns to articulate, *A Writer of Books* not only talks back to Victorian literary and social conventions but also manifestly updates them.

A Writer of Books follows the path of a *künstlerroman*. Motherless Cosima grows up in a provincial town with a librarian father negligent in every way but book provision: "thrown almost entirely upon books for companionship and amusement," "in time books became to her the realities of life, and human beings merely the shadows."⁵³ She enjoys the company of a friend, Tom Kingston, until he moves to the colonies, and they grow apart. "At twenty, after a voluntary apprenticeship of several years, [Cosima] formally adopted literature as a profession, and began to write a novel."⁵⁴ When her father dies, she and her novel move to London where she circulates the book among publishers, writes a second novel, and immerses herself in the British Library and the motley collection of people who live at her boardinghouse. Under financial pressure, she revises her novel to suit a popular readership and becomes increasingly discouraged about her literary prospects. When she reunites with Tom, she agrees to marry him in hopes that marital stability will allow her to write according to her own style. Tom's conventionality quickly convinces Cosima that the marriage was a mistake, however, and her writing suffers until she heeds the advice of the celebrated historian Quentin Mallory and his sister, Lucilla, also a writer. Their influence, and Cosima's passionate but unconsummated love for Mallory, help her find an authentic literary voice, and in a parallel plot, she defies social expectation and leaves her marriage.

A Multiplied Point of View

Starting with the novel's title, a conspiratorial interplay of literary history, irony, and social judgment allows the narrator of *A Writer of Books* to occupy several positions simultaneously. Many important eighteenth-century novels signal the story of a young woman's maturation and entrance into society in declarative but passive titles like *A Writer of Books*, such as *Clarissa, or The History of a Young Lady* (Samuel Richardson, 1748), *Evelina, or The History of a Young Lady's Entrance into the World* (Frances Burney, 1778), or even *The Fortunes and Misfortunes of Moll Flanders* (Daniel Defoe, 1722). Some Victorian novels adopt the didactic style of these titles but in a slyly parodic way, as in *The Portrait of a Lady* (Henry James, 1881), *The Romance of a Shop* (Amy Levy, 1888), *The Story of a Modern Woman* (Ella Hepworth Dixon, 1894), or *A Waif's Progress* (Rhoda Broughton, 1905). Like these, *A Writer of Books* appoints its titular subject the status of archetype, which we come to recognize as Cosima's—not the narrator's—perspective. For the narrator and the people Cosima meets in

London, her forthright claim to literature exposes her ignorance of the market. One publisher "knew plenty of girls who confessed to 'writing a little' or 'scribbling nonsense,' but he had never before met [a girl] who announced that she had adopted literature for her profession with as much assurance."[55]

Like Juliet and Nell LeStrange, Cosima identifies so strongly with literary characters that her thoughts and observations often import those characters' points of view, crowding her own consciousness with a moving field of fictional specters. When she first arrives in London, for instance, the impact of the scene so overwhelms her that the division between reality and fiction falters. She disembarks the train into Liverpool Street Station and

> for a few moments she stood apart, and watched the jostling crowds, finding it almost impossible to realise that this tired, lonely, frightened girl was really she, and not some heroine of romance, whose adventures she was reading by the light of the station lamps. She even began, half unconsciously, to look out for the appearance of the hero, the villain, or at least of the confidante. But her reverie was only interrupted by a porter, who inquired if she had any luggage. In a strange confusion between shadows and realities, Cosima replied:—
>
> "Yes, she must have got some luggage, and I suppose she will want a cab."[56]

Slipping into a third-person perspective, Cosima adopts the narrator's point of view but lacks the narrator's omniscience; this is not a representation of the real world seeping into the fictional one, but one in which the fictional world doubles its mediating remove. When Cosima reaches her boardinghouse, she recovers some equanimity, but by way of a literary precedent. Greeting the proprietor, Miss Durrant, Cosima explains that "'everything seems strange and bewildering at first. I feel like Lucy Snowe when she first arrived at Villette,' she added, in full confidence that the allusion would be understood."[57] The narrator exposes Cosima's naïveté in this last phrase, but at the same time the reference to Lucy Snowe illuminates the *reader's* picture of Cosima (assuming that the reader is familiar with Brontë's novel). An uneven field of reception distances Cosima from a bewildered Miss Durrant and heightens the reader's understanding of her at once.

The reader's contribution to this dynamic interpretative field increases with the novel's accumulating evidence that the kind of book Cosima attempts to write is the one describing her efforts. An early description of London as a closed book drifts toward literalism through the reader's cumulative interpretation of the novel: "Every day when [Cosima's] self-set literary tasks were over, she explored the sites of London, but she still felt impatiently that the great city lay like a clasped book before her, a book every page of which she longed to turn, while as yet she could only gaze upon the cover."[58]

As the reader assimilates Cosima's progressive familiarity with London, the city-as-book metaphor dissolves into metafiction. Other references to books that are simultaneously referential and self-identifying include Cosima's first impression of Quentin Mallory—"Cosima walked slowly home, feeling as if she had just passed through an entirely novel experience"[59]—and a description of her first novel: "One unfortunate trick she had caught from her eighteenth-century models, the tendency to pause from time to time to discourse to the reader, to take him into her confidence, to stray down the pleasant paths of digression, or to dwell with over-insistence upon the qualities, admirable or otherwise, of the offspring of her brain. Unhappily, the reflections and moralisings, dear to the hearts of readers of eight-volumed novels, in a largely-leisured age, find no favour with the public of the present day."[60]

The prolix first sentence of this quotation reproduces Cosima's stylistic quirk, obscuring the difference between her writing and its characterization. These signals of self-consciousness transmit the constructedness of writing, the choices a novelist makes, and the impact of those choices on the narrative. The ontological messiness that these metafictional observations alert us to can be read on a thematic level as the evidence of a young woman, so sheltered in life and familiar with books, that she experiences the world through a literary filter. This would not be wrong. But these instances also point to the novel's fundamental collapse of a distinction between the "real" and the "literary," effecting a phenomenological breach that, attached to a young female character, signals naïveté in place of formal experimentalism.

The Problem with Experiential Learning

Cosima's confident identification of herself as a writer slowly erodes as she learns what styles and genres women writers are expected to adopt. As in so many New Woman novels, *A Writer of Books* confronts the canonical values that differentiate great writers from hacks, which also means male novelists from female ones. At first, Cosima overlooks the degree to which her sex excludes her from canonical realism and tries to emulate the example of great writers. "Of one immense disqualification for her chosen profession Cosima was mournfully aware—her lack of experience and knowledge of the world. Thoughts of Balzac, Flaubert, the De Goncourts, the Daudets, came to depress her at her work. They had drunk deep in the cup of life, and wrote of that they did know; while she, a girl, recluse, bred in a library, had gained all her knowledge second-hand."[61]

What Cosima simplifies as her "lack of experience and knowledge of the world" reflects the more inflexible categories of sex and class. When she vows, for instance, "to learn something of all sides of life and all sorts and conditions of men,"[62] she appropriates the subject of Walter Besant's *All Sorts and Conditions of Men: An Impossible Story* (1882) without the masculine privilege that underwrites his fictional confrontation of poverty.[63] Her intention to write in the style of the novelists listed above recalls an ominous pattern in New Woman novels about women novelists who attempt fin de siècle realism or naturalism. Hester Gresley in *Red Pottage* has a nervous breakdown after her brother burns her unsparingly truthful second novel. Priscilla Momerie in Annie E. Holdsworth's *The Years That the Locust Hath Eaten* (1896) destroys her health writing what she calls her "Book of the Great City," a novel in which she aims to "make the wail of the city heard in the homes of the rich,"[64] and dies before she learns of its publication. These plots critique the literary establishment's method of industry gatekeeping: women writers are diminished by their exclusion from a side of public life that their engagement with reflexively punishes.

Cosima begins to realize how profoundly her sex determines her professional success and artistic profile when she makes contact with publishers, such as Mr. Carlton, a publisher who lives at her boardinghouse and who makes friendly overtures to her in spite of his "old-fashioned prejudice against literary ladies as a class."[65] His interest in her turns out to serve designs more lecherous than editorial, and his writing advice rehashes the tired dependence of a woman's novel on her personal experience. When Cosima explains that she tries to "write about life as I know it" but admits that she has never been in love, he recommends that she improve her potential to write great art by chasing romantic and personal disaster: "Pray, how do you expect to write a successful novel without the one indispensable experience? . . . What is the use of that without feeling—knowing? Shall I tell you what you want? You want to fall in love with the wrong man, to marry him, to have three or four children, to weary of him, to lose a child, to fall in love with the right man, to sacrifice everything for him, and finally to be deserted by him. Then when you were faded, and lonely, and disillusioned, and middle-aged, you might write a great novel."[66]

Mr. Carlton's recipe for literary greatness replays the trajectory of *The Years That the Locust Hath Eaten*, noted above. In that novel, Priscilla strays from Mr. Carlton's path only in minor ways: her one child dies as an infant, and she stays with her callous husband out of duty, forsaking romance with "the right man," whom she meets after her marriage. Faded, lonely, and disillusioned, Priscilla writes a great novel but dies at age twenty-four, well before middle age. Like that of Mr. Carlton's hypothetical woman novelist, Priscilla's art stems from her personal sacrifice; she is less the agent of her fiction than its martyr. The next publisher Cosima meets, Mr. Haddon, reverses Mr. Carlton's recommendation to become her own artistic subject by advising her to disavow any traces of originality. He accepts her novel on the condition that she "cut out all the dissertations and the dialogue that doesn't advance the action of the story" and make it "show how much [she] knew." Above all, the novel should end happily: "You must marry that young couple," he tells her, "instead of killing the girl. My public likes happy endings."[67] If Mr. Carlton suggests that she become her own tragic heroine, Mr. Haddon advises her to excise herself from her art altogether; to publish with him she must avoid "putting too much of her own personality into her work, of straying too far from the beaten paths of fiction."[68]

Reconciling Art and Gender Roles

As stark it is, even the publishers' choice between suffering for art or disappearing from it altogether recedes after Cosima and Tom marry, and she realizes that conventional marriage and her artistic ambition cannot coexist. In one of the novel's many analogies between artistic and maternal reproduction, Cosima finds herself unable to write during her marriage: her "once fertile brain seemed to become dull and barren, her imagination absolutely refused to work, and she began to fear that her marriage . . . had deadened or destroyed her literary faculty."[69] Her creative infertility becomes literalized when she gives birth to a stillborn child. Soon after, Cosima discovers that Tom, overtly an upstanding and entirely conventional husband, has been trying to seduce her friend, Bess. Cosima knows that a divorce would not be granted on the evidence of Tom's clandestine letters to Bess, but she chooses to "think no more of duty, since duty was only rewarded by deceit and betrayal."[70] While the earlier

Cosima sought external experience to substantiate her writing, she mingles art and life when she dissolves her marriage on its basis as a legal fiction: "I no longer have a husband," she announces to Bess, "I am free to follow my own inclinations. If the law doesn't allow me to dissolve my marriage, why then I'll be a law unto myself. No woman has ever had a voice in making the laws, and therefore no woman is bound to obey them."[71]

While Cosima was divided from Tom by the "unwritten social law which ordains that man shall live in a world of realities, and woman in a world of dreams,"[72] her relationship with Quentin teaches her to follow the example of his scholarship and transcend social and artistic gender barriers. Quentin's historical method explicitly revises history's traditional identification as a masculine field built upon facts and evidence. He proudly identifies himself as "a connoisseur in novels" and explains to Cosima how fiction informs his scholarship:

> You don't suppose that an historian reads history, do you? History, other people's history, is just what he is most anxious to avoid. Do you think that Macaulay could have painted the eighteenth century as well as he did, if he had wasted much time over its history? His cunning lay in the fact that he knew Fielding and Richardson and Smollett and Miss Burney pretty well by heart. Novels, plays, letters, and memoirs are the modern historian's bricks and mortar.... It is the life and thought and manners of a people that he desires to portray, the *vie intime* of a country and a period. If he cannot reproduce the spirit, the very atmosphere of the age, he has failed, and his work takes its place among the deadheads on the top shelves of the library.[73]

Quentin's *magnum opus*, a multivolume *History of National Character*, likewise translates the "thought and manners of a people" into rigorous scholarship. According to his sister, he "works upon old-fashioned lines," spending many years "reading, travelling, and forming his style." The first volume of his *History* took him "five years to write," as he "devotes so much time to the construction of each paragraph, the polishing of each sentence."[74] His approach to history as artful composition would satisfy Catherine Morland's ingenuously metafictional critique of history in *Northanger Abbey*: "I often think it odd that [history] should be so dull," she observes, "for a great deal of it must be invention. The speeches that are put into the heroes' mouths, their thoughts and designs the chief of all this must be invention, and invention is what delights me in other books."⁷⁵ Catherine's judgment anticipates Quentin's critique of the French naturalists, whom he faults for mistaking "observation [as] an effective substitute for real feeling."⁷⁶ His response to Cosima's second novel also prioritizes feeling over execution: "'It is a well-built book,' remarked Quentin, when Cosima begged for his candid opinion. 'But there is not enough of yourself in it. I should say that you had written it with one eye on the public, and the other on the publisher. The machinery is too apparent; one's attention is constantly distracted from the puppets to the strings. And the author makes gallant, though happily not always successful, efforts to appeal to the taste of the average reader.'"⁷⁷

Quentin's evaluation discards the sex of the novelist as a critical metric and replaces it with the novelist's character, a validation that emerges in *A Writer of Books* as a capacious alternative to the industry standards identified with canonical, masculine realism. Cosima attends to his advice and writes her next novel "to amuse myself. . . . It is the type of book that interests me, and that I believe in."⁷⁸ Her new autonomy as a writer accords with some of the New Woman novels' most independent women writers. In *Red Pottage*, Hester "'jars against the preconceived ideas'" that other people have about fiction and talks about the novel she is writing "as a young girl talks of her lover."⁷⁹ Mrs. Malcolmson, a minor novelist-character in Sarah Grand's *The Heavenly Twins*, admits "candidly" that she wrote her novel "for my own benefit, of course," which inspires particular anger and disapproval from her social circle when the novel is successful.⁸⁰

The end of her marriage to Tom should allow Cosima to be with Quentin, who has loved her from a respectful distance, but Quentin, conscientious expert on character, does not permit her to live beyond the law. "You are a proud woman and you would suffer; and I who would bear punishment and shame so joyfully for your sake, should be obliged to stand aside and see you made a scapegoat by an outraged world."⁸¹ Though devastated, Cosima agrees, and they vow never to meet again. This parting occurs at the end of the novel, and in the short scenes that follow Cosima quickly realizes "that all was not lost, that life was not over." Her new resolve comes with the anticipation of her next book: the "new work was going to be *the* book, the flawless masterpiece that every author is always going to write,"⁸² and on the last page, she goes to her writing table to begin. On the face of it, this ending reads like narrative convenience, a pat conversion from grief to optimism. But the narratological work it accomplishes far outpaces these rudiments of plot. Cosima, by the end of *A Writer of Books*, has tacitly revealed herself to have been its narrator all along. As one cannot write her own ending, her book ends with a scene of her writing, fusing her roles as heroine and writer into the same temporal frame. Gerard Genette names this technique "narrative metalepsis" or the "double temporality of the text that emerges just as two realms fully overlap . . . the world in which protagonist exists, and the world of which the narrator relays."[83] A more explicit and dramatic version of this narratorial self-disclosure happens at the end of Ian McEwan's *Atonement*, in which a mature Briony Tallis, the novel's heroine from age thirteen, breaches the intradiegetic conceit of the novel and reveals herself to have been its narrator all along. Upon this revelation, the novel's realistic scaffolding abruptly falls away and *Atonement* transforms into metafiction.

Narrative metalepsis is more subtle in *A Writer of Books*, but Cosima (in the guise of narrator) has prepared us for it throughout: in her disconcerting break into third-person form at the train station, in the free indirect interruptions that punctuate the narrator's perspective, and finally, in her mature formulation of novel writing. When Quentin asks her what type of novel she hopes to write, she narrates herself narrating a description of the book we are reading: "I would give you, if I could . . . the most precious and difficult thing of all—I would give the effect of growth, change, and development. A novel ought to be a biography, or part of a biography; it should show the development of a man or a woman, the shaping and moulding of heart, mind, and character by the slow-working influences of their environment."[84]

A novel so skeptical of realistic objectivity as *A Writer of Books* could not, after all, be couched in the voice of an omniscient narrator. Cosima's artful narratorial disguise answers, too, to Quentin's complaint that in her second novel the "machinery [was] too apparent" and "one's attention [was] constantly distracted from the puppets to the strings." Confirming the innocuous design achieved in *A Writer of Books*, one of the novel's reviewers interprets its narrator and Cosima as separate figures, but his language inadvertently attests to the single subject I am proposing. The reviewer critiques the narrator's attitude toward Cosima, writing, "We cannot share all the writer's sympathy for her at the close, but we are glad that she found something to take the place of love . . . and believe enough in her talents to think her cure for despair a very serviceable one."[85] The "writer's sympathy for her'" refers to the narrator and Cosima, respectively, but after this attribution the two subjects are interchangeable: syntax collapses them together even if the reviewer does not.

Once again, the metafictional achievement superficially attributed to the heroine-novelist has a complex textual history. Symonds published the novel under the pseudonym George Paston, as she had her earlier novels, and she executes this masculine front credibly: reviewers praise "the ease and excellence of the style,"[86] which they also call "cold,"[87] "intellectual rather than emotional,"[88] and "exceedingly clever."[89] Symonds's real identity, or at least her femininity, seems to have been common knowledge as all the reviews refer to George Paston with female pronouns. They readily accept, then, that the gender *identity* projected by the narrator may not accord with the actual sex of the novel's author. The admission that writing can be gendered as a stylistic choice or representational technique significantly advances the zero-sum diagnoses of the sex of the authors of *Villette* and *Cometh Up as a Flower* in 1853 and 1867, respectively. For those earlier critics, confirming the author's sex had to precede the assessment of her novel, as the standards for male and female novelists differed.[90]

In *A Writer of Books*, however, the metafictional signal "George Paston" interferes with any autobiographical chain of logic that Emily Morse Symonds's identity could set in motion, and stymies at least one reviewer's ability to pass judgment on the author's intentions. George Cary Eggleston, writing for the *Literary News*, reports that "'George Paston' is the pen-name of the latest English woman who writes novels. Why women who write novels take masculine pen-names . . . it is beyond masculine ingenuity to determine. But the facts remain."[91] The fact behind the pseudonym adoption, that is, remains unsolved, and the reviewer must turn instead to an interpretation of the novel. Unwittingly, Eggleston follows the interpretive order that the pseudonym activates whereby the story of the novel eclipses that of its indeterminate author.

For the purposes of my argument, the most illuminating review of *A Writer of Books* takes issue with the metafictional self-consciousness of the novel. Writing anonymously for *Outlook*, this reviewer argues,

> If the author's aim was primarily to produce a pure work of art, then she has undoubtedly handicapped herself by her very choice of material. The more overwhelming the illusion of life, the greater the success of the artist, and it is therefore necessary that the reader be taken away from the thoughts of pens, ink, and paper. We confess we found it rather a nuisance to have to be smelling the ink all the way through this book, and our appreciation of its better pages was seriously marred by

the "professional" character of the work. Now the interest of the book does not lie in the fact that it is the study of an author, but in the fact that it is the study of a human being—whose profession, though part of the character, was not so in the deepest analysis.[92]

The reviewer may prefer fiction that disguises its artifice over *A Writer of Books*' awareness of its own medium, but more to my point, the final sentence unintentionally testifies to the professional progress of the Victorian woman novelist. The reviewer does not mention gender when describing Cosima but refers to the novel's "study of an author" and "study of a human being," and the credibility of its female author goes unchallenged. By separating from any specific referent to a person or a sex, the "woman novelist" here enters the realm of abstract subjecthood.

CONCLUSION

The Victorian woman novelist's movement from dilettante to artist did not have starting and ending dates, but over the second half of the nineteenth century, "woman novelist" progressively became a social category dissociated from individual upstarts, eccentrics, or geniuses. Where critics hedged in evaluating *Jane Eyre* without knowing Currer Bell's gender, *A Writer of Books* generated criticism about that novel's portrayal of authorship, not female authorship. The novelists from Charlotte Brontë to Emily Morse Symonds examined in *Victorian Metafiction* use the figure of the woman writer to draw attention to the choices that underwrite narrative creation, and perhaps most consequentially, the novels that tell these stories become the tacit evidence of their plots about novel writing. In positioning Victorian metafiction as a transformative step in the representation of "woman novelist" as a serious, dispassionate artist, I am reversing the familiar chronology whereby the modernist novel triumphs by rejecting its Victorian predecessor. As described in the introduction, scholars have routinely concluded that modernists including Virginia Woolf, Gertrude Stein, Dorothy Richardson, Katherine Mansfield, Rebecca West, and Jean Rhys earned critical and elite status through superior self-awareness, the osmotic influence of a wiser and more cynical age, or, most galling, sheer talent. But modernists were writing in a period that could more readily accept the novel as an artistic object not wholly divisible to its author's gender and personal experience.

The critical oversight of Victorian metafiction may be attributed, perhaps more than to any other post-Victorian critic, to Virginia Woolf. Woolf leverages modernist innovations to characterize Victorian novels by women as autobiographical, superficial, and hostage to approved conventions. The "reading and criticism" of the current day, she writes in *A Room of One's Own* (1929), "have given [modernist women] a wider range, a greater subtlety. The impulse towards autobiography may be spent. [The woman writer] may be beginning to use writing as an art, not a method of self-expression."[1] But where Woolf attributes contemporary novelists' artistic distance to the field of "reading and criticism," she holds Victorian novelists like Charlotte Brontë accountable for their failure to achieve modernist disengagement. Her claims, however, often formulate the very problems to which she holds the earlier novelist accountable:

> I opened [*Jane Eyre*] at chapter twelve and my eye was caught by the phrase "Anybody may blame me who likes." What were they blaming Charlotte Brontë for, I wondered? And I read how Jane Eyre used to go up on to the roof when Mrs. Fairfax was making jellies and looked over the fields at the distant view. And then she longed—and it was for this that they blamed her—that "then I longed for a power of vision which might overpass that limit; which might reach the busy world, towns, regions full of life I had heard of but never seen: that then I desired more of practical experience than I possessed; more of intercourse with my kind, of acquaintance with variety of character than was here within my reach."[2]

Jane's provocation of blame becomes, in Woolf's summary, Brontë's, and in the evocative passage that follows an undifferentiated Jane Eyre/Charlotte Brontë scans the horizon for opportunities and experiences seemingly beyond her reach. In conflating Brontë with her heroine, Woolf forges an autobiographical link where Brontë created an imaginary character. Woolf thus overlooks *Jane Eyre* as the patent proof of Brontë's quite triumphant introduction to the "busy world."

Woolf's characterization of Brontë's suppressed rage, moreover, becomes a better example of that fury than the evidence furnished by Brontë's novels: "If one reads [her books] over and marks that jerk in them, that indignation, one sees that [Brontë] will never get her genius expressed whole and entire. Her books will be deformed and twisted. She will write in a rage when she should write calmly. She will write foolishly where she should write wisely. She will write of herself where she should write of her characters. She is at war with her lot. How could she help but die young, cramped and thwarted?"[3] Without knowing why Woolf so determinedly collapses Brontë into her characters, we can observe how this indictment reinforces her chronology of the woman's novel as it moves from personal complaint to objectified art. Elsewhere, Woolf accounts for this transformation only vaguely, implicating the invisible hand of history rather than any actual fictional technique: "The change which has turned the English woman from a nondescript influence, fluctuating and vague, to a voter, a wage-earner, a responsible citizen, has given her both in her life and in her art a turn towards the impersonal."[4] Where did this beneficent change come from? Woolf refers to a "lifting of some aspects of gender oppression" that "allowed women writers to extend their range from their own suffering to the lives of women in general," which in turn inspired fiction "far more genuine and far more interesting today than it was a hundred or even fifty years ago."[5]

But transformations of the novel do not happen through the judgments and renunciations of powerful critics: they happen in novels that cumulatively and collectively change their own medium. Transformations in the history of the novel, in fact, resemble metafiction in their illusion of textual self-determination. One of the great feminist metafictions of the late twentieth century, Margaret Atwood's *The Handmaid's Tale* (1985), parodies the idea that a writer could embody the privileged distance of her future readers. In the novel's epilogue, set two hundred years in the future, Professor Piexoto critiques Offred's journals at an academic symposium. So many details are left out, he complains. "Some of them could have been filled in by our anonymous author, had she a different turn of mind. She could have told us much about the inner workings of the Gileadean empire, had she the instincts of a reporter or spy".[6] By regretting Offred's inability to see past her carceral state and enlighten future readers, Piexoto's speech satirizes academic historical presentism that intervenes into history—which includes milder and fully compassionate efforts to adapt Victorian narratives to today's standards of self-actualization and representation.

I am not suggesting that Woolf's strident dissociation from the Victorians ushered in a gender-neutral critical domain. Great interwar and mid-century novelists like Elizabeth Taylor, Rosamond Lehmann, Elizabeth Bowen, and Mollie Panter-Downes may have evaded the belittling title of "woman novelist," but their relegation to the "middlebrow" carries its own twentieth-century gender biases.[7] Still, by the mid-twentieth century, the stereotypes attached to Victorian women's writing that I have examined in this book are distant enough to inspire parody. In Elizabeth Taylor's brilliant novel *Angel* (1957), the titular heroine is born in 1885 and becomes a commercially successful novelist in the early Edwardian era. Famously modeled on Marie Corelli, Taylor's Angelica Deverell transports herself from humble beginnings to the heights of celebrity, only to fall out of favor with a twentieth-century readership increasingly hostile to florid melodrama.[8] Along the way, Angel unwittingly confirms the worst clichés attached to Victorian "lady" novelists:

> *Miss Brontë's sense of humour was feeble.* (Leslie Stephen, "Charlotte Brontë," Dictionary of Literary Biography)[9]
> "No one is to laugh at *me.*" [Angel's] green eyes blazed at him.
> "Who would dare?" he said lightly. "For you would never laugh at yourself. But perhaps a sense of humour is a drawback in a novelist," he mused.
> "I shan't be writing funny books."
> "No, of course not," he said gravely, and thought: I wonder.[10]

> *Agnes Atheling was not wise; she had no particular gift for conversation, and none whatever for logic; no accomplishments, and not a very great deal of information.* (Margaret Oliphant, The Athelings)[11]
> "What is the theme of the new book?"
> "It is about an actress."
> "Are you interested in the theatre, Miss Deverell?"
> "I have never been to one."
> "Then you are a great reader, perhaps?"
> "No, I don't read much. I haven't got any books, and nowadays I am always writing."
> "But even so, most authors take some interest in the works of others. Is there no Public Library you could join?"
> A little colour came into her cheeks and she said, "I don't think I should want to."[12]

> *The critics were beautifully unanimous in making merry over [Glen's] finest passages—in exposing the absurdity of her plot, the faults in her grammar, the solecisms of which she was guilty; the meagerness of her ideas, the poverty of her invention, the tallness of her talk.* (Charlotte Riddell, A Struggle for Fame)[13]
> [Angel's] vanity had been stunned by the way in which her book had been received. No trumpets had come thrusting out from behind clouds, proclaiming "genius" and "masterpiece." For a long time nothing at all

had happened, and then, slowly, the abuse and sarcasm had begun. The very passages of which she had been most proud, had been printed as if they were richly humorous; her dialogue, her syntax, her view of life, her descriptions of society were all seen to be part of some new and quite delicious joke."[14]

Would it be wrong to say that a woman's heroine is always a glorified version of herself? (W. L. Courtney, *The Feminine Note in Fiction* [1904])[15]

When the sun poured too strongly into her bedroom, she wiped her forehead with the sheet—without disturbing the cats—and went on writing. She remembered that in this way she had written so much of her first novel, translating herself, as its heroine, to the Paradise House of her imagination. Now she was a famous writer, living in Paradise House itself.[16]

With its deadpan delivery and caustic plot, this novel about a novelist never insinuates a metafictional connection to its author. As Taylor's friend Robert Liddell observed, *Angel* was "an odd book; even for Mrs. Taylor it is a considerable achievement, but it hardly feels like *her* achievement—there is an anonymity about it, while most of her work is clearly signed."[17] Most of the Victorian novelists I have explored confirm their artistic autonomy through fictional figures that implicate them ontologically, but Taylor's *Angel* stays firmly embedded in the textual episteme.

A century earlier, such dissociation between a novelist and her novel-writing heroine was impossible. "You are a poet shackled to a woman," wrote Flaubert to Louise Colet, his friend and sometimes lover in 1853, the same year that Brontë published *Villette*. "Do not imagine you can exorcise what oppresses you in life by giving vent to it in art," he continued.[18] Flaubert does not account for interpretive norms beyond Colet's—or Brontë's—control, even though his metaphor of shackling transmits these norms: the woman side of the poet-woman or novelist-woman equation was, for most of the reading public, an announcement of the primacy of the personal.

The argument of this book collides with an interpretive tradition that from the eighteenth century through the present day evaluates women's fiction by looking for its reflection of its author. In the more extreme forms of this critical tradition, women are said to write novels as a form of personal catharsis—a desire to be "heard"—so that self-revelation, whether explicit or encoded, confers a measure of truth curiously valued in the fictional medium. A different book might ask why this interpretive method has been so persistent, surviving revolutions in marital, sexual, reproductive, and political rights, and transcending the structuralist and post-structuralist logic that replaces any transhistorical feminine traits with those particular to a certain class, race, and society. Indeed, the rhetoric of critical feminism is so informed by the importance of a woman's self-expression that proposing an alternative way to read women's novels can feel like heresy. Still, we might ask: What has approximately fifty years of privileging personal feelings actually accomplished for a feminist literature? Testimony is invaluable when it makes someone feel better, but when we evaluate women's fiction primarily through the lenses of projected empathy and personal expression, we are not redressing the reasons that make these lenses so easy to identify with in the first place. "Giving a voice" to personal experience may not be the most effective way to confront social, economic, and political inequities; attention to the personal as an interpretive method, after all, is a discretionary activity. This book has been more concerned with documenting an important fictional phenomenon specific to Victorian novels: the metafictional creation of women's novels as autonomous objects of art in (and often against) a conservative literary marketplace.

NOTES

INTRODUCTION

1. Freedgood, *Worlds Enough*, 32.
2. Neumann and Nünning, "Metanarration and Metafiction."
3. See, for instance, Fludernik, *"Natural" Narratology*; Peters, *Feminist Metafiction*; Lanser and Warhol, *Narrative Theory Unbound*.
4. McKeon, "Writer as Hero," 18.
5. Callard, *Aspiration*, 5–6.
6. Barrett Browning, *Aurora Leigh*, 329.
7. Barrett Browning, *Aurora Leigh*, 328.
8. Barrett Browning, *Aurora Leigh*, 239.
9. Charles LaPorte also examines *Aurora Leigh*'s proleptic and "audacious" influence on its own reception but locates this "peculiarity" in a narrative pattern. See "*Aurora Leigh*," 832, 833.
10. Shaw, *Narrating Reality*; Levine, *Realistic Imagination* and *Dying to Know*; Jaffe, *Victorian Novel Dreams*; and Armstrong, *How Novels Think*.
11. Jaffe, *Victorian Novel Dreams*, 3.
12. Kornbluh, "Present Tense Futures," 100.
13. Bonaparte, *Poetics of Poesis*, 14.
14. Bonaparte, *Poetics of Poesis*, 223.
15. Bonaparte, *Poetics of Poesis*, 3.
16. Sadleir, *Things Past*, 107.
17. Barrett Browning, *Aurora Leigh*, 157.
18. Kristeva, *Kristeva Reader*, 42.
19. Hutcheon, "Historiographic Metafiction."
20. Paston, *Writer of Books*, 207.
21. Gass, *Fiction and Figures*; Scholes, "Metafiction."
22. Alter, *Partial Magic*; Boyd, *Reflexive Novel*; Federman, *Surfiction*; and Hutcheon, *Poetics of Postmodernism*.
23. Currie, *Metafiction*, 2–4.
24. See, for instance: Alter, *Partial Magic*; Christensen, *Meaning of Metafiction*; Currie, *Metafiction*; Hutcheon, *Narcissistic Narrative*; McCaffery, *Metafictional*

Muse; Scholes, *Fabulation and Metafiction*; Stonehill, *Self-Conscious Novel*; and Waugh, *Metafiction*.
25. The critics who refer to *Don Quixote* are Hutcheon, Stonehill, and Christensen. Those who refer to *Tristram Shandy* are Alter, Hutcheon, Stonehill, Christensen, Currie, and Waugh. Scholes refers to Sterne.
26. Hutcheon, *Narcissistic Narrative*, xii, 4. A further study of critical books on postmodern novels shows that these terms are often conflated, as shown in definitions that could also stand in for metafiction, such as in Acheson's declaration that "postmodern novels present the world as a place that is endlessly complex and uncertain, often mirroring it by way of their self-conscious arbitrations and constructedness" ("*French Lieutenant's Woman*," 399).
27. Waugh, *Metafiction*, 14, 6–7.
28. Currie, *Metafiction*, 5.
29. Stonehill, *Self-Conscious Novel*, 37.
30. McCaffery, *Metafictional Muse*, 10.
31. Hutcheon, *Narcissistic Narrative*, 5.
32. Alter, *Partial Magic*, 93, 101, 87. This historical generalization excludes all nineteenth-century novels that question the stable identity of society or the accuracy of its description, which to my mind describes all of them that stray from the certain convictions of the didactic form, including almost all that we are likely to know and read today.
33. Waugh, *Metafiction*, 2, 11. See also Ronald Sukenick, *In Form: Digressions on the Act of Fiction* (Carbondale: Southern Illinois University Press), 1985, in which Sukenick similarly argues that the late twentieth-century world is too complex to be accommodated by fictional convention. Earlier forms of the novel were simpler, he contends, because the world was easier to define.
34. Craik, *John Halifax*, 59.
35. Waugh, *Metafiction*, 6–7.
36. I know this because I once had a class of advanced undergraduates purchase their own copies of *John Halifax, Gentleman* on the internet. They paid as little as five cents for a variety of editions, many of which contained inscriptions that referred to the novel's celebration of Christian values or its inspirational power. More than one of our (Canadian) class's editions was inscribed as a prize from the Boy Scouts of America.
37. Stonehill, *Self-Conscious Novel*, 38.
38. Jaffe, *Victorian Novel Dreams*, 2.
39. Siegle, *Politics of Reflexivity*, 8.
40. Alter, *Partial Magic*, 88.
41. Warhol, *Gendered Interventions*, 17–18.
42. Currie, *Metafiction*, 213.

43. McCaffery, *Metafictional Muse*, 10.
44. Waugh, *Metafiction*, 6–7.
45. Lanser, *Fictions of Authority*, 88.
46. Carlyle, *On Heroes*, 27.
47. Mill, "Subjection of Women," 555.
48. See, for example, *Victorian Autobiography: The Tradition of Self-Interpretation* (1986) and *Traditions of Victorian Women's Autobiography: The Poetics and Politics of Life Writing* (1999).
49. See, for instance, Waugh, "Postmodern Fiction," 72: "By the 1970s, the theoretical assault on metalinguistic foundations was developed into the postmodern insistence that objects of knowledge are not so much entities on which language reflects as artifacts actually constructed through and within language. . . . Fiction . . . inevitably takes a turn towards philosophical self-interrogation of its own epistemological and ontological status."
50. Levine, *Realistic Imagination*, 15 (my italics).
51. Clayton, "Genealogy of Postmodernism," 181.
52. Clayton, "Genealogy of Postmodernism," 187.
53. Friedman and Fuchs, *Breaking the Sequence*, 3.
54. Irigaray, *Ce sexe qui n'en est pas un*, 78.
55. Heilmann, *New Woman Strategies*, 3.
56. DuPlessis, *Writing beyond the Ending*, 4.
57. Friedman and Fuchs, *Breaking the Sequence*, 3.
58. Gilbert and Gubar, *War of the Words*, 193.
59. Gray, *Language Unbound*, 16.
60. Gardiner, "On Female Identity," 185, 187.
61. Marcus, "Feminist Aesthetics," 12.
62. Friedman and Fuchs, *Breaking the Sequence*, 7.
63. See "Woman of Maxims: George Eliot and the Realist Imperative," in Lanser, *Fictions of Authority*, 81–101.
64. Thompson, "Lost Horizons," 68–69.
65. Zakreski, *Female Artistic Labour*, 70.
66. Easley, *First-Person Anonymous*, 3.
67. Zakreski, *Female Artistic Labour*, 98.
68. Nehamas, "Writer, Text," 272.
69. Nehamas, "Writer, Text," 272.
70. Nehamas, "Writer, Text," 273.
71. Judd, "Male Pseudonyms," 253.
72. From an unsigned review in *North British Review* 267 (1857): 443–62, quoted in Gaillet, "Reception," 118.
73. Trollope, "Mary Gresley," 60.

74. Trollope, "Mary Gresley," 53.
75. Trollope, "Mary Gresley," 97.
76. Trollope, "Mary Gresley," 52.
77. Trollope, "Mary Gresley," 67.
78. Trollope, "Mary Gresley," 74.
79. Trollope, "Mary Gresley," 84.
80. Trollope, "Mary Gresley," 94.
81. Trollope, "Mary Gresley," 96–97.
82. Trollope, "Mary Gresley," 84.
83. Trollope, "Mary Gresley," 85.
84. For further discussion of Southey's letter, see chap. 1, note 32.
85. Blackburne, *Molly Carew*, 1:44.
86. Blackburne, *Molly Carew*, 3:3.
87. Aguilar, "Authoress," 219.
88. Meteyard, *Struggles for Fame*, 3:367.
89. Aikin-Kortright, *Anne Sherwood*, viii.
90. Aikin-Kortright, *Anne Sherwood*, vii (original italics).
91. Oliphant, *Athelings*, 1:22, 1:21.
92. Trollope, *Way We Live Now*, 15.
93. Tabor, *Diary of a Novelist*, 4.
94. Harraden, *Ships That Pass*, 148–49.
95. Harraden, *Ships That Pass*, 229.
96. Walker, introduction to *Ruth Hall*, 12.
97. Walker, introduction to *Ruth Hall*, 14.
98. Willis, *Ruth Hall*, iii-iv.
99. Willis, *Ruth Hall*, 255.
100. Willis, *Ruth Hall*, 268.
101. Willis, *Ruth Hall*, 255.
102. Willis, *Ruth Hall*, 333.
103. Hall, *Woman's Story*, 1:188, 1:168.
104. Hall, *Woman's Story*, 2:100–101 (original italics).
105. Hall, *Woman's Story*, 3:302 (original italics).
106. Hall, *Woman's Story*, 3:315 (original italics).
107. Hall, *Woman's Story*, 3:315.
108. Hall, *Woman's Story*, 3:318 (original emphasis).
109. Hall, *Woman's Story*, 1:241, 1:261, 1:100.
110. Fanny Burney quoted in Milnes and Sinanan, introduction to *Romanticism*, 15.
111. Wilford, *Nigel Bartram's Ideal*, 41 (original italics).
112. See chap. 1, section "Charlotte Brontë, Currer Bell, and the Specter of Autobiography."

113. Wilford, *Nigel Bartram's Ideal*, 49.
114. Wilford, *Woman's Story*, 233.
115. Wilford, *Woman's Story*, 66 (original italics).
116. Wilford, *Woman's Story*, 66–67.
117. Wilford, *Woman's Story*, 73, 245.
118. Wilford, *Woman's Story*, 344.
119. Wilford, *Woman's Story*, 209.
120. Wilford, *Woman's Story*, 221 (original italics).
121. Wilford, *Woman's Story*, 209.
122. Wilford, *Woman's Story*, 267–68.
123. Wilford, *Woman's Story*, 270.
124. Wilford, *Woman's Story*, 306.
125. Cholmondeley, *Red Pottage*, 93.
126. Cholmondeley, *Red Pottage*, 89–90.
127. Cholmondeley, *Red Pottage*, 72.
128. Cholmondeley, *Red Pottage*, 55.
129. Cholmondeley, *Red Pottage*, 55.
130. Cholmondeley, *Red Pottage*, 183.
131. Cholmondeley, *Red Pottage*, 102–3 (original italics).
132. Works that have compared *Red Pottage* to *Middlemarch* or George Eliot's oeuvre include Peterson's *Traditions of Victorian Women's Autobiography*, Oulton's introduction to *Red Pottage*, Vineta Colby's "'Devoted Amateur': Mary Cholmondeley and *Red Pottage*," and Showalter's introduction to *Red Pottage*.
133. Cholmondeley, *Red Pottage*, 243.

1. METAFICTION IN "NOVEL GUISE"

1. Lanser, *Narrative Act*, 23.
2. Backscheider, "Literary Culture," 514.
3. Gallagher, *Nobody's Story*, xviii.
4. See Wells, "Henry Austen's Authorship.'" Wells points out the lack of evidence that Henry Austen is the definitive author of the "Biographical Notice."
5. Henry Austen, "Biographical Notice," 5.
6. W. R. Greg, "False Morality of Lady Novelists," *National Review* 8 (1859): 148.
7. R. H. Hutton, "Novels by the Authoress of 'John Halifax,'" *North British Review*, 1858, in Helsinger, Sheets, and Veeder, *Woman Question*, 3:52–53.
8. Leslie Stephen, *Cornhill Magazine*, December 1877, quoted in Allott, *Brontës*, 415.
9. W. L. Courtney, *The Feminine Note in Fiction* (London: Chapman & Hall, 1904), quoted in Miles, *Female Form*, 11.
10. Watt, *Rise of the Novel*, 298.

11. Henry James, *Partial Portraits* (New York: Macmillan, 1894), 101.
12. Gilbert and Gubar, *Madwoman in the Attic*; Showalter, *Literature of Their Own*; Moers, *Literary Women*; and Spacks, *Female Imagination*.
13. Jacobus, review of *Madwoman in the Attic*, 520 (original italics).
14. Parkin-Gounelas, *Fictions of the Female Self*, 2.
15. Parkin-Gounelas, 6–7.
16. "For centuries, women have been ashamed of writing about themselves, and yet have longed to recount the experiences that have shaped their lives" (Sanders, "'Fathers' Daughters,'" 153).
17. A. W. Fonblanque, from an unsigned review, *The Examiner*, November 27, 1847, in Allott, *Brontës*, 77.
18. G. H. Lewes, from an unsigned review, *Fraser's Magazine* 36 (December 1847), in Allott, *Brontës*, 84.
19. From an unsigned review, *Era*, November 14, 1847, in Allott, *Brontës*, 79.
20. Elizabeth Rigby, from an unsigned review, *Quarterly Review* 84 (December 1848), in Allott, *Brontës*, 111.
21. From an unsigned review, *Christian Remembrancer* 15 (April 1848), in Allott, *Brontës*, 89.
22. G. H. Lewes, unsigned notice, *Westminster Review* 48 (January 1848), in Allott, *Brontës*, 87.
23. Edwin Percy Whipple, "Novels of the Season," *North America Review* 141 (October 1848), in Allott, 98.
24. Lewes, unsigned notice, in Allott, *Brontës*, 87.
25. Unsigned review, *Christian Remembrancer*, in Allott, *Brontës*, 89.
26. Unsigned review, *Athenaeum*, December 25, 1847, in Allott, *Brontës*, 218.
27. Anne Brontë, *Tenant of Wildfell Hall*, xxxix.
28. Charlotte Brontë to W. S. Williams, April 20, 1848, in Charlotte Brontë, *Letters*, 2:51.
29. Charlotte Brontë, "Biographical Notice of Ellis and Acton Bell," in Emily Brontë, *Wuthering Heights*, 436.
30. Brontë, "Biographical Notice," 438.
31. Kreilkamp, *Voice and Victorian Storyteller*, 126.
32. Robert Southey, in his famous letter to a young Brontë requesting his advice, suspected that her writing might be motivated by "a view to celebrity" (Southey to Charlotte Brontë, March 12, 1837, in Brontë, *Letters*, 1:167).
33. Brontë, *Shirley*, 7.
34. Charlotte Brontë to James Taylor, November 6, 1849, in Brontë, *Letters*, 2:280.
35. Carlisle, "Face in the Mirror," 262.
36. Olsen, "Biography in Literary Criticism," 442.

37. See Nehamas, "Writer, Text, Work, Author."
38. LaPorte, "*Aurora Leigh*," 839.
39. Gaskell, *Life of Charlotte Brontë*, 215.
40. Johnson, "Desire (to Write)," 174.
41. Carlyle, *Sartor Resartus*, Gutenberg.
42. Barros, *Autobiography*, 23.
43. Barros, *Autobiography*, 23.
44. Brontë, *Villette*, 60–61.
45. Brontë, *Jane Eyre*, 98.
46. Carlyle, *Sartor Resartus*, Gutenberg.
47. Gibson, "Charlotte Brontë's First Person," 204.
48. Carlyle, *Sartor Resartus*, Gutenberg.
49. Carlyle, *Sartor Resartus*. Gutenberg.
50. Pennington, *Creating Identity*, 142.
51. Pennington, *Creating Identity*, 154, 140.
52. Freeman, "Cordons of Protection," 651.
53. Carlyle, *Sartor Resartus*, Gutenberg.
54. Brontë, *Villette*, 369.
55. Brontë, *Villette*, 373.
56. Brontë, *Villette*, 373.
57. Brontë, *Villette*, 284.
58. Brontë, *Villette*, 109.
59. Brontë, *Villette*, 580–81 (original italics).
60. Brontë, *Villette*, 581.
61. Charlotte Brontë to W. S. Williams, January 28, 1848, in Brontë, *Letters*, 2:23.
62. Brontë, *Villette*, 582.
63. Brontë, *Villette*, 582–83 (my italics).
64. Brontë, *Villette*, 581.
65. Brontë, *Villette*, 581.
66. Brontë, *Villette*, 582.
67. See also Ann Heilmann and Mark Llewellyn, eds., *Metafiction and Metahistory in Contemporary Women's Writing* (London: Palgrave, 2007).
68. The four novels that mark the emergence of feminist metafiction for Greene are Drabble's *The Waterfall* (1969), Lessing's *The Golden Notebook* (1962), Laurence's *The Diviners* (1974), and Atwood's *The Edible Woman* (1969).
69. Greene, *Changing the Story*, 2.
70. Drabble, *Waterfall*, 52–53.
71. Shields, *Swann*, 24.
72. Culler, *On Deconstruction*, 64.
73. Case, *Plotting Women*, 106.

74. Brontë, *Villette*, 713.
75. Brontë, *Villette*, 326–27 (original emphasis).
76. Brontë, *Villette*, 716.
77. Brontë, *Villette*, 716.
78. Carlyle, *Sartor Resartus*, Gutenberg (original emphasis). Oliver Yorke was the pseudonym of William Maginn (1794–1841), cofounder and editor of *Fraser's Magazine*. That the Editor invokes Maginn's fictional persona here contributes to the text's attempts to obscure the relationship between the world of thought and material reality.

2. RHODA BROUGHTON'S *COMETH UP AS A FLOWER*

1. Broughton, *Cometh Up*, 38.
2. Broughton, *Cometh Up*, 39.
3. Defoe, *Robinson Crusoe*, 1.
4. Dickens, *David Copperfield*, 1.
5. Peterson, *Victorian Autobiography*, 183.
6. Broughton, *Cometh Up*, 40.
7. Broughton, *Cometh Up*, 59.
8. Broughton, *Cometh Up*, 65.
9. Broughton, *Cometh Up*, 78.
10. Broughton, *Cometh Up*, 96.
11. See, for example, Mascuch, *Origins*, 22–23.
12. Löschnigg, "Postclassical Narratology," 256.
13. Löschnigg, "Postclassical Narratology," 259.
14. Broughton, *Cometh Up*, 36.
15. Broughton, *Cometh Up*, 301, 330.
16. Broughton, *Cometh Up*, 230.
17. Broughton, *Cometh Up*, 253.
18. Brontë, *Jane Eyre*, 98.
19. Broughton, *Cometh Up*, 236 (original italics).
20. Eliot, *Adam Bede*, 166.
21. Broughton, *Cometh Up*, 41.
22. Broughton, *Cometh Up*, 239.
23. Broughton, *Cometh Up*, 75.
24. Broughton, *Cometh Up*, 259.
25. Broughton, *Cometh Up*, 313–14.
26. An exception to this generic norm is Carlyle's frequent use of historical present in *The French Revolution: A History* (1837). My thanks to Herbert Tucker for this point.

27. More, *Female Education*, 202–3.
28. Broughton, *Cometh Up*, 48.
29. Broughton, *Cometh Up*, 154.
30. Broughton, *Cometh Up*, 115.
31. Broughton, *Cometh Up*, 153.
32. Broughton, *Cometh Up*, 154.
33. Broughton, *Cometh Up*, 274.
34. Pamela Gilbert, editor of the 2010 Broadview edition of *Cometh Up as a Flower*, notes that this poem refers to the death of Anne Boleyn and that Tamar Heller, editor of the 2004 Pickering & Chatto edition, identifies the lines as Ainsworth's (Broughton, *Cometh Up*, 274).
35. Baisnée-Keay, introduction to *Women's Life Writing*, 5.
36. Flint, *Woman Reader*, 257.
37. Hutcheon, *Poetics of Postmodernism*, 5.
38. Broughton, *Cometh Up*, 296.
39. Broughton, *Cometh Up*, 296.
40. Broughton, *Cometh Up*, 232.
41. Alcott, *Little Women*, 302.
42. Broughton, *Cometh Up*, 254.
43. Broughton, *Cometh Up*, 112.
44. Broughton, *Cometh Up*, 51.
45. Broughton, *Cometh Up*, 279.
46. Broughton, *Cometh Up*, 263 (original italics).
47. Broughton, *Cometh Up*, 263–64.
48. Broughton, *Cometh Up*, 282.
49. Broughton, *Cometh Up*, 272.
50. Broughton, *Cometh Up*, 336.
51. Broughton, *Cometh Up*, 337.
52. Broughton, *Cometh Up*, 39.
53. Broughton, *Cometh Up*, 106.
54. Broughton, *Cometh Up*, 333 (original italics).
55. Broughton, *Cometh Up*, 332.
56. Broughton, *Cometh Up*, 333.
57. From an unsigned review, *London Review*, March 16, 1867, in Broughton, *Cometh Up*, 339.
58. Broughton, *Cometh Up*, 334.
59. From an unsigned review, *London Review*, March 16, 1867, in Broughton, *Cometh Up*, 339.
60. From an unsigned review, *Athenaeum*, April 20, 1867, in Broughton, *Cometh Up*, 340.

61. Sadleir, *Things Past*, 107.
62. From an unsigned review, *Athenaeum*, April 20, 1867, in Broughton, 339.
63. From an unsigned review, *Spectator*, October 19, 1867, in Broughton, 342.
64. Black, *Notable Women Authors*, 42.
65. Black, *Notable Women Authors*, 41.
66. Black, *Notable Women Authors*, 42.
67. From an unsigned review, *The Times*, October 19, 1867, in Broughton, *Cometh Up*, 342.
68. See Golban, *Victorian Fiction*, 166, for a discussion of the critical tendency to interpret the "I-narrator" as the biographical author.
69. Heller, "Disposing of the Body," 140
70. Broughton, *Fool in Her Folly*, 9–10.
71. Broughton, *Fool in Her Folly*, 11.
72. Broughton, *Fool in Her Folly*, 24.
73. Broughton, *Fool in Her Folly*, 30.
74. Broughton, *Fool in Her Folly*, 85.
75. Broughton, *Fool in Her Folly*, 104 (original italics).
76. Broughton, *Fool in Her Folly*, 60.
77. Broughton, *Fool in Her Folly*, 61–62 (original italics).
78. Broughton, *Fool in Her Folly*, 62.
79. Broughton, *Fool in Her Folly*, 62.
80. Broughton, *Fool in Her Folly*, 63.
81. Faber, "One Sister's Surrender," 158.
82. Black, *Notable Woman Authors*, 41.
83. Sadleir, *Things Past*, 91.

3. "THE DIFFERENCE BETWEEN AUTHORS AND THEIR BOOKS"

1. Oliphant, *Athelings*, 1:21.
2. Oliphant published review essays in the 1860s that were critical of the sensation genre's provocation of emotions and suspense. See Oliphant, "Sensation Novels," *Blackwood's Edinburgh Magazine* 91 (1862): 564–84, and "Novels," *Blackwood's Edinburgh Magazine* 94 (1867): 257–80.
3. Peterson, *Woman of Letters*, 100.
4. Riddell, *Struggle for Fame*, 88.
5. Riddell, *Struggle for Fame*, 89.
6. Riddell, *Struggle for Fame*, 89.
7. Peterson, *Woman of Letters*, 160.
8. Riddell, *Struggle for Fame*, 90.
9. Oliphant, *Athelings*, 1:45.

10. Oliphant, *Athelings*, 1:185; 3:167–68 (original italics).
11. Boumelha, "Woman of Genius," 172.
12. Oliphant, *Athelings*, 1:56.
13. The idealistic and noble hero of Samuel Richardson's 1754 epistolary novel of the same name.
14. Oliphant, *Athelings*, 3:127–28.
15. Oliphant, *Athelings*, 3:97–98.
16. Oliphant, *Athelings*, 3:118.
17. Oliphant, *Athelings*, 3:127.
18. Oliphant, *Athelings*, 3:128.
19. Oliphant, *Athelings*, 3:136–37.
20. Oliphant, *Athelings*, 2:149.
21. Oliphant, *Athelings*, 3:247–48.
22. Weber, *Women and Literary Celebrity*, 127.
23. Oliphant, *Athelings*, 3:253–54.
24. Oliphant, *Athelings*, 3:254 (original italics).
25. Riddell, *Struggle for Fame*, 91.
26. Riddell, *Struggle for Fame*, 49.
27. Eliot, "Silly Novels," 144.
28. Riddell, *Struggle for Fame*, 162–63.
29. Riddell, *Struggle for Fame*, 184.
30. Riddell, *Struggle for Fame*, 239.
31. Riddell, *Struggle for Fame*, 225.
32. Riddell, *Struggle for Fame*, 122.
33. Riddell, *Struggle for Fame*, 210.
34. Riddell, *Struggle for Fame*, 200.
35. Riddell, *Struggle for Fame*, 232.
36. Riddell, *Struggle for Fame*, 236.
37. Riddell, *Struggle for Fame*, 239.
38. Riddell, *A Struggle for Fame*, 289.
39. Riddell, *Struggle for Fame*, 287.
40. Riddell, *Struggle for Fame*, 289.
41. Riddell, *Struggle for Fame*, 289.
42. Riddell, *Struggle for Fame*, 290.
43. Eliot, *Adam Bede*, 197.
44. Riddell, *Struggle for Fame*, 286.
45. Riddell, *Struggle for Fame*, 290.
46. Riddell, *Struggle for Fame*, 89.
47. Riddell, *Struggle for Fame*, 89.
48. Riddell, *Struggle for Fame*, 353.

49. Riddell, *Struggle for Fame*, 365.
50. Riddell, *Struggle for Fame*, 361.
51. Riddell, *Struggle for Fame*, 159.
52. Riddell, *Struggle for Fame*, 290–91.
53. Riddell, *Struggle for Fame*, 311.
54. Riddell, *Struggle for Fame*, 323.
55. Tinsley quoted in Peterson, *Woman of Letters*, 164.
56. Riddell, *Struggle for Fame*, 337–38.
57. Riddell, *Struggle for Fame*, 339.
58. Oliphant, *Athelings*, 47.
59. Riddell, *Struggle for Fame*, 174.
60. Riddell, *Struggle for Fame*, 225.
61. See, for instance, Peterson, *Woman of Letters*, 151; Murphy, *Irish Novelists*, 6; and Kelleher, "Representing Ireland," 91.
62. Riddell, *Struggle for Fame*, 360.
63. Riddell, *Struggle for Fame*, 341.
64. Riddell, *Struggle for Fame*, 344.
65. Riddell, *Struggle for Fame*, 366.
66. Riddell, *Struggle for Fame*, 185.
67. Riddell, *Struggle for Fame*, 46.

4. PSEUDONYMITY AS METAFICTION

1. See this argument in Tuchman and Fortin, *Edging Women Out*.
2. Gaskell, *Life of Charlotte Brontë*, 2:40.
3. Judd, "Male Pseudonyms," 258.
4. Lamarque, *Philosophy of Literature*, 109. Lamarque nevertheless distinguishes between an implied author and Foucault's author function: the latter is less literary character and more strategic conceptualizer of the work itself.
5. Booth, *Rhetoric of Fiction*, 75–76.
6. Lanser, "(Im)plying the Author," 158.
7. Marcus, "Profession of the Author," 215.
8. See Lanser's chapter "Woman of Maxims: George Eliot and the Realist Imperative" in *Fictions of Authority*, 81–101.
9. Lanser, *Fictions of Authority*, 83.
10. MacCabe, *Revolution of the Word*, 15–16.
11. Ginsburg, "Pseudonym," 543.
12. Lamarque, *Philosophy of Literature*, 109.
13. Marcus, "Profession of the Author," 215.
14. Marcus, "Profession of the Author," 211.

15. Zola, "Le roman expérimental," 70–71.
16. Zola, "Le roman expérimental," 96.
17. Hunt, "'Jewish Novel,'" 237.
18. Galchinsky, "'Permanently Blacked,'" 180.
19. Valman, *Jewess*, 175.
20. Dowling, "*Venus and Tannhäuser*," 27.
21. Friedrich Engels to Margaret Harkness, April 1888, in Harkness, *City Girl*, ed. Sparks, 132, 133.
22. Bellamy and Kaspar, "Harkness, Margaret Elise," 105.
23. Harkness's novels can benefit from the interpretive optics of naturalism from the perspective of an objective narrator, but they are not encompassed by this category textually: as Rob Breton has deftly shown, the novels rely on a sentimental rhetoric to appeal to their potentially indifferent, middle-class readers. See Breton, "Sentimental Socialism."
24. I discuss Harkness's construction of "John Law" in reference to her style of fictional characterization in "Absent Character: from Margaret Harkness to John Law."
25. Anderson, *Woman against Women*, 52, 62.
26. Colby, *Singular Anomaly*, 23.
27. Anderson credits Linton, who worked for the *Morning Chronicle* from August 1848 to April 1851, as the first woman to draw a regular salary—twenty guineas a month—writing for a daily newspaper. Anderson, *Woman against Women*, 52, 62.
28. Bache, "More than a Name," 31.
29. Lanser, "(Im)plying the Author," 157.
30. "The Autobiography of Christopher Kirkland," *Athenaeum*, July 25, 1885, in Linton, *The Autobiography of Christopher Kirkland*, ed. Meem and Holterhoff, 389.
31. Hutcheon, "Historiographic Metafiction."
32. Genette, *Narrative Discourse*, 246.
33. Genette, *Narrative Discourse*, 235–36.
34. Linton, *Christopher Kirkland*, 52.
35. Linton, *Christopher Kirkland*, 52.
36. Linton, *Christopher Kirkland*, 52–53.
37. Linton, *Christopher Kirkland*, 78.
38. Linton, *Christopher Kirkland*, 104.
39. Linton, *Christopher Kirkland*, 105–6.
40. Lyotard, *Postmodern Condition*, xxiv.
41. Linton, *Christopher Kirkland*, 379.
42. Linton, *Christopher Kirkland*, 380.

43. Linton, *Christopher Kirkland*, 326.
44. Linton, *Christopher Kirkland*, 327. Compare to the following quote from Broughton, *Cometh Up as a Flower*, 95–96: "Is it possible that one is through the whole course of one's life the same individual being? Is one possessed of but one individual soul? Does it not rather seem that each man or woman is in himself or herself a succession of individual beings, possessing, one after another, several successive souls? . . . Our estimate of things and people, our habits, tastes, dispositions, at certain periods of our life are so radically different from, and totally antagonistic to, what they are at other such periods, that I think it is hardly possible that their variations should be accounted for by any of the alterations that it is within the province of time, sorrow, or any change of inner or outer life to effect."
45. Atkinson, *Victorian Biography*, 160.
46. Linton, *Christopher Kirkland*, 70.
47. Linton, *Christopher Kirkland*, 85.
48. Linton, *Christopher Kirkland*, 62, 75, 80, 83, 87, 97.
49. Linton, *Christopher Kirkland*, 115.
50. Linton, *Christopher Kirkland*, 148.
51. Linton, *Christopher Kirkland*, 158.
52. Lamarque, *Philosophy*, 108.
53. Bache, "Making More," 29.
54. Henry, "Revised Approach," 32.
55. Henry, "Revised Approach," 33–34.
56. Culler, "Narrators," 42.
57. Linton, *Christopher Kirkland*, 109.
58. Linton, *Christopher Kirkland*, 109.
59. See, for instance, Olive Pratt Rayner's *The Type-Writer Girl*, Ella Hepworth Dixon's *The Story of a Modern Woman*, and Emily Morse Symonds's *A Writer of Books*.
60. Meem, "Lesbian Consciousness," 541–42, n. 21.
61. Meem argues this in "Lesbian Consciousness."
62. Lanser, "More (Feminist) Narratology," 38.

5. NEO-VICTORIAN VICTORIAN NOVELS

1. Heilmann and Llewellyn, *Neo-Victorianism*, 4 (original italics).
2. Shastri, *Intertextuality and Victorian Studies*, 53, 55.
3. Ledger, *New Woman*; Ardis, *New Women*; Miller, *Rebel Women*; Pykett, *"Improper" Feminine*.

4. See, for instance, Kate Mitchell, *History and Cultural Memory in Neo-Victorian Fiction: Victorian Afterimages* (NY: Palgrave Macmillan, 2010), and Christian Gutleben, *Nostalgic Postmodernism: The Victorian Tradition and the Contemporary British Novel* (Brill, 2001).
5. Heilmann, *New Woman Strategies*, 3 (original italics).
6. Pykett, *"Improper" Feminine*, 7.
7. Ardis, "'Retreat with Honour,'" 334.
8. Ledger, *New Woman*, 27.
9. Showalter, introduction to *Literature*, viii. See also Bryony Randall, "'Everything Depend[s] on the Fashion of Narration': Women Writing Women Writers in Short Stories of the Fin de Siècle," in *Cross-Gendered Literary Voices: Appropriating, Resisting, Embracing*, edited by Kim Rina and Claire Westall (New York: Palgrave Macmillan, 2012), 36–53.
10. Palmer, *Women's Authorship*, 166.
11. Showalter, *Literature*, 175.
12. Martineau's nine-volume *Illustrations of Political Economy* explained principles of political economy through didactic stories about industrial effects such as population growth and labor strikes.
13. Callard, *Aspiration*, 13.
14. David Velleman, "Brandt's Definition of Good," *Philosophical Review* 97 (1998): 100–101, quoted in Callard, *Aspiration*, 83 (original italics).
15. Clayton, "Olive Schreiner," 32.
16. Allen, *Type-Writer Girl*, 73–74.
17. Schwartz, *Culture of the Copy*, 187.
18. Allen, *Type-Writer Girl*, 28.
19. Allen, *Type-Writer Girl*, 23–24.
20. Allen, *Type-Writer Girl*, 24.
21. Allen, *Type-Writer Girl*, 25.
22. Allen, *Type-Writer Girl*, 85.
23. Allen, *Type-Writer Girl*, 99.
24. Borges, "Pierre Menard," 39.
25. Borges, "Pierre Menard," 40.
26. Borges, "Pierre Menard," 43 (original italics).
27. Hutcheon, *Poetics of Postmodernism*, 42. Llewellyn offers a similar definition of neo-Victorian fiction in "What Is Neo-Victorian Studies," 168: "What the neo-Victorian represents . . . is a different way into the Victorians—for students and faculty alike. This is not contemporary literature as a substitute for the nineteenth century but as a mediator into the experience of reading the 'real' thing."

28. Cleodolind is the mythical princess whom Saint George rescues from the dragon.
29. Allen, *Type-Writer Girl*, 26–27.
30. Price, "Impersonal Secretaries," 132; MacDonald, "'Heroine,'" 123.
31. Ehland and Wächter, introduction to *Middlebrow and Gender*, 2.
32. Ledger, *New Woman*, 179.
33. Allen, *Type-Writer Girl*, 91 (original italics).
34. Allen, *Type-Writer Girl*, 97.
35. Allen, *Type-Writer Girl*, 99.
36. Allen, *Type-Writer Girl*, 99.
37. Allen, *Type-Writer Girl*, 100.
38. Allen, *Type-Writer Girl*, 100–101.
39. Allen, *Type-Writer Girl*, 139.
40. Rainey, "Secretarial Fiction," 312.
41. For an extensive discussion of the status of women's writing in *Red Pottage*, see Heilmann, *New Woman Strategies*; Ardis, "'Retreat with Honour,'"; and Oulton's introduction to *Red Pottage*.
42. Cholmondeley, *Red Pottage*, 111.
43. Cholmondeley, *Red Pottage*, 261.
44. Mitton, *Bachelor Girl*, 172.
45. Mitton, *Bachelor Girl*, 173.
46. Mitton, *Bachelor Girl*, 171.
47. "Table Talk," 236.
48. "Lively Autobiography," 228.
49. *London Mail* was a newspaper traceable to the mid-century, but not, by my efforts, to the 1890s.
50. *The Writer*, 7. The complete excerpt of "the *London Mail*" in *The Writer* follows: "That smart, witty, and amusing novel, 'The Typewriter Girl' [*sic*] appears to be 'catching on.' Its author is an American lady, the daughter of Dr. Pratt, of Salem, Massachusetts. Dr. Pratt was a friend and admirer of Dr. Oliver Wendell Holmes, after whom he named his son, Oliver Wendell Pratt, and also his daughter, Olive, the author of this story. Eighteen months ago Miss Pratt married Mr. Theodore Rayner, a British subject, who has vineyards near Verona, where the accomplished lady now resides, making occasional winter trips to Florence and to the Venice which she so well describes in the concluding chapters of 'The Typewriter Girl' [*sic*]. Olive Pratt Rayner is a pretty little brunette, who affects mannish manners. She is now writing another novel."
51. Price, "Impersonal Secretaries," 130.
52. Davies, *Gender and Ventriloquism*, 3.
53. Paston, *Writer of Books*, 4, 5.

54. Paston, *Writer of Books*, 10.
55. Paston, *Writer of Books*, 23.
56. Paston, *Writer of Books*, 13.
57. Paston, *Writer of Books*, 15.
58. Paston, *Writer of Books*, 37.
59. Paston, *Writer of Books*, 124.
60. Paston, *Writer of Books*, 32.
61. Paston, *Writer of Books*, 32.
62. Paston, *Writer of Books*, 45.
63. In Besant's *All Sorts and Conditions of Men*, two idealistic philanthropists move to the East End in hopes of alleviating despair.
64. Holdsworth, *Years*, 256.
65. Paston, *Writer of Books*, 24.
66. Paston, *Writer of Books*, 54, 55.
67. Paston, *Writer of Books*, 78, 79.
68. Paston, *Writer of Books*, 94.
69. Paston, *Writer of Books*, 142.
70. Paston, *Writer of Books*, 242.
71. Paston, *Writer of Books*, 242.
72. Paston, *Writer of Books*, 183.
73. Paston, *Writer of Books*, 123–24 (original italics).
74. Paston, *Writer of Books*, 88.
75. Austen, *Northanger Abbey*, 122.
76. Paston, *Writer of Books*, 128.
77. Paston, *Writer of Books*, 143.
78. Paston, *Writer of Books*, 207.
79. Cholmondeley, *Red Pottage*, 71, 65.
80. Grand, *Heavenly Twins*, 334.
81. Paston, *Writer of Books*, 247.
82. Paston, *Writer of Books*, 258 (original italics).
83. Genette, *Narrative Discourse*, 235–36.
84. Paston, *Writer of Books*, 207–8.
85. From an unsigned review, *Bookman*, November 1898, 56.
86. From an unsigned review, *Spectator*, October 15, 1898, 530.
87. From an unsigned review, *Academy*, December 24, 1898, 520
88. From an unsigned review, *Academy*, November 12, 1898, 246. Anita Miller identifies this reviewer as novelist Arnold Bennett, a close friend of Symonds and her family (afterword to *Writer of Books*, 262).
89. George Cary Eggleston, from an unsigned review, *Literary News*, May 1899, 142.

90. As discussed in chapter 1, the link between the author's sex and the literary value of his or her novel constitutes the plot of Florence Wilford's 1869 *Nigel Bartram's Ideal*. Nigel Bartram thinks highly of the sensation novel *Mark's Dream* until Marian, his future wife and the novel's secret author, convinces him that it is the work of a woman's pen, at which point his review of the novel transforms from admiring to scathing. Wilford's narrator confirms the artistic hypocrisy of his judgment but resolves the novel with another double standard: Nigel permits Marian to publish a second novel only when his health prevents him from supporting them.
91. Eggleston, from an unsigned review, *Literary News*, May 1899, 142.
92. Anon., *The Outlook*, Jan. 28, 1899, 825.

CONCLUSION

1. Woolf, *Room*, 79–80.
2. Woolf, *Room*, 68.
3. Woolf, *Room*, 69–70.
4. Woolf, "Women and Fiction," 50.
5. Woolf, "Women and Fiction," 48.
6. Atwood, *Handmaid's Tale*, 393.
7. See Humble, *Feminine Middlebrow*, and Ehland and Wächter, introduction to *Middlebrow and Gender*.
8. Stewart, "Woman Writer," 22, 34.
9. Stephen, "Charlotte Brontë," *Dictionary of Literary Biography*, vol. 6 (1886).
10. Taylor, *Angel*, 33.
11. Oliphant, *Athelings*, 21 (my italics).
12. Taylor, *Angel*, 54.
13. Riddell, *Struggle for Fame*, 239 (my italics).
14. Taylor, *Angel*, 69.
15. W. L. Courtney, *The Feminine Note* (London: Chapman & Hall, 1904), quoted in Miles, *Female Form*, 11 (my italics).
16. Taylor, *Angel*, 185.
17. Robert Liddell, "The Novels of Elizabeth Taylor," *Review of English Literature* 1, no. 2 (1960): 56, quoted in Stewart, "Woman Writer," 28.
18. Flaubert, *Letters*, 201.

BIBLIOGRAPHY

PRIMARY SOURCES

Aguilar, Grace. "The Authoress." In *Home Scenes and Heart Studies*, 227–44. London: D. Appleton, 1853.

Aikin-Kortright, Fanny. *Anne Sherwood, or The Social Institutions of England*. 3 vols. London: Richard Bentley, 1857.

Alcott, Louisa May. *Little Women*. Minneapolis: Lerner Publishing Group, 2014.

Allen, Grant [Olive Pratt Rayner, pseud.]. *The Type-Writer Girl*. Edited by Clarissa J. Suranyi. Peterborough, ON: Broadview Press, 2004. Originally published 1897.

Allott, Miriam Farris, ed. *The Brontës, the Critical Heritage*. London: Routledge & Kegan Paul, 1974.

Atwood, Margaret. *The Handmaid's Tale*. New York: Fawcett, 1987.

Austen, Henry. "Biographical Notice of the Author." In *"Northanger Abbey" and "Persuasion,"* edited by R. W. Chapman, 3–9. Vol. 5 of *The Novels of Jane Austen*. 3rd ed. Oxford: Clarendon Press, 1933. Notice originally published in 1817.

Austen, Jane. *Northanger Abbey*. Edited by Claire Grogan. 2nd ed. Peterborough, ON: Broadview Press, 2002.

Besant, Walter. *All Sorts and Conditions of Men*. Edited with an introduction and notes by Kevin Morrison. London: Victorian Secrets, 2012. Originally published in 1882.

Barret Browning, Elizabeth. *Aurora Leigh*. Edited with an introduction and notes by Kerry McSweeney. New York: Oxford University Press, 2008.

Black, Helen C. *Notable Women Authors of the Day*. London: Maclaren, 1906. Originally published in 1893.

Blackburne, E. Owens. *Molly Carew: An Autobiography*. 3 vols. London: J. Masters, 1884.

Borges, J. L. "Pierre Menard, Author of the *Quixote*." In *Labyrinths*, 36–44. New Directions: New York, 1962. https://stacks.stanford.edu/file/druid:yk975pg2189/yk975pg2189.pdf.

Bowles, Caroline. "Fanny Fairfield." *Blackwood's Magazine*, February–April 1836. http://orlando.cambridge.org.proxy3.library.mcgill.ca/protected/svPeople?people_tab=2&crumbtrail=on&formname=r&heading=h&person_id=bowlca&subform=1#FannyFairfield.

Brontë, Anne. *Agnes Grey*. Edited by Angeline Goreau. New York: Penguin Random House, 1989. Originally published in 1847.

———. *The Tenant of Wildfell Hall*. Edited by Herbert Rosengarten. Oxford: Clarendon Press, 1992. Originally published in 1848.

Brontë, Charlotte. *Jane Eyre*. Edited by Jane Jack and Margaret Smith. Oxford: Clarendon Press, 1969. Originally published in 1847.

———. *The Letters of Charlotte Brontë*. Edited by Margaret Smith. 3 vols. Oxford: Clarendon Press, 1995–2004.

———. *The Professor*. Edited by Margaret Smith and Herbert Rosengarten. Oxford: Clarendon Press, 1987. Originally published in 1857.

———. *Shirley*. Edited by Herbert Rosengarten and Margaret Smith. Oxford: Clarendon Press, 1979. Originally published in 1849.

———. *Villette*. Edited by Herbert Rosengarten and Margaret Smith. Oxford: Clarendon Press, 1984. Originally published in 1853.

Brontë, Emily. *Wuthering Heights*. Edited by Hilda Marsden and Ian Jack. Oxford: Clarendon Press, 1976. Originally published in 1847.

Broughton, Rhoda. *Cometh Up as a Flower*. Edited by Patricia K. Gilbert. Peterborough, ON: Broadview Press, 2010. Originally published in 1867.

———. *Cometh Up as a Flower*. Edited by Tamar Heller. Vol. 4 of *Varieties of Women's Sensation Fiction: 1855–1890*, edited by Andrew Maunder, 213–452, 471–506. Abingdon: Routledge, 2004. Originally published in 1867.

———. *A Fool in Her Folly*. With a foreword by Belloc Lowndes. London: Odhams Press, 1920.

———. *A Waif's Progress*. London: Macmillan, 1909. Originally published in 1905.

Burney, Frances. *Evelina, or The History of a Young Lady's Entrance into the World*. Garfield Heights, Ohio: Duke Classics, 2012. Originally published in 1778.

Carlyle, Thomas. *On Heroes, Hero-Worship, and the Heroic in History*. Edited by David R. Sorensen and Brent E. Kinser. New Haven, CT: Yale University Press, 2013. Originally published in 1840.

———. *Sartor Resartus*. https://www.gutenberg.org/files/1051/1051-h/1051-h.htm. Originally published in 1836.

Carey, Peter. *Jack Maggs*. London: Faber & Faber, 1997.

Cholmondeley, Mary. *Red Pottage*. With an introduction by Carolyn W. de la L. Oulton. Vol. 9 of *New Woman Fiction, 1881–1899*. London: Routledge, 2016. Originally published in 1899.

———. *Red Pottage*. With an introduction by Elaine Showalter. London: Virago, 1985. Originally published in 1899.

Craik, Dinah Mulock. *John Halifax, Gentleman*. Edited by Lynn M. Alexander. Peterborough, ON: Broadview Press, 2005. Originally published in 1856.

Defoe, Daniel. *The Fortunes and Misfortunes of the Famous Moll Flanders*. Minneapolis, MN: Lerner Publishing Group, 2014. Originally published in 1722.

———. *Robinson Crusoe*. Edited by Thomas Keymer. Oxford: Oxford University Press, 2007. Originally published in 1719.

Dickens, Charles. *David Copperfield*. Edited by Nina Burgis. Oxford: Clarendon Press, 1981. Originally published in 1850.

Dixon, Ella Hepworth. *The Story of a Modern Woman*. Edited by Steve Farmer. Peterborough, ON: Broadview Press, 2004. Originally published in 1894.

Drabble, Margaret. *Waterfall*. London: Penguin, 1971.

Eliot, George. *Adam Bede*. Edited by Carol A. Martin. Oxford: Oxford University Press, 2001. Originally published in 1859.

———. "Silly Novels by Lady Novelists." In *The Victorian Art of Fiction: Nineteenth-Century Essays on the Novel*, edited by Rohan Amanda Maitzen, 127–44. Peterborough, ON: Broadview Press, 2009.

Fern, Fanny. *See* Willis, Sara Payson.

Fowles, John. *The French Lieutenant's Woman*. London: Jonathan Cape, 1969.

Frankau, Julia. *A Babe in Bohemia*. London: Spencer Blackett, 1889.

———. *Dr. Phillips: A Maida Vale Idyll*. London: Keynes Press, 1989. Originally published in 1887.

Gaskell, Elizabeth. *The Life of Charlotte Brontë, Author of "Jane Eyre," "Shirley," "Villette," &c*. Vol. 2. New York: D. Appleton, 1892. Originally published in 1857.

———. *Mary Barton*. London: Penguin, 1997. Originally published in 1848.

———. *North and South*. London: Penguin, 1996. Originally published in 1854.

Grand, Sarah. *The Beth Book*. Toronto, ON: G. N. Morang, 1897.

———. *The Heavenly Twins*. New York: Street & Smith, 1901. Originally published in 1893.

Greg, W. R. "False Morality of Lady Novelists." *National Review* 8 (1859): 144–67.

Hall, Anna Maria. *A Woman's Story*. 6 vols. London: Hurst & Blackett, 1857.

Harkness, Margaret. *A City Girl: A Realistic Story*. Edited by Tabitha Sparks. Peterborough, ON: Broadview Press, 2017. Originally published in 1887.

Harraden, Beatrice. *Ships That Pass in the Night*. London: Lawrence & Bullen, 1893.

Holdsworth, Annie E. [Max Beresford, pseud.]. *The Years the Locust Hath Eaten*. New York: Macmillan, 1895.

James, Henry. *The Portrait of a Lady*. Edited by Michael Anesko. Cambridge: Cambridge University Press, 2016. Originally published in 1881.

Lessing, Doris. *The Golden Notebook*. London: Michael Joseph, 1962.

Levy, Amy. *The Romance of a Shop*. Edited by Susan David Bernstein. Peterborough, ON: Broadview Press, 2006. Originally published in 1888.

Linton, Eliza Lynn. *The Autobiography of Christopher Kirkland.* Edited by Deborah T. Meem and Kate Holterhoff. Brighton, UK: Victorian Secrets, 2011. Originally published in 1885.

Martineau, Harriet. *Illustrations of Political Economy.* 9 vols. London: Charles Fox, 1832–34.

McEwan, Ian. *Atonement.* London: Jonathan Cape, 2001.

Meteyard, Eliza. *Struggles for Fame.* 3 vols. London: T. C. Newby, 1845.

Mill, John Stuart. "The Subjection of Women." In *On Liberty and Other Essays,* edited and with an introduction by John Gray, 469–582, 591–92. Oxford: Oxford University Press, 2008. Originally published in 1869.

Mitton, Geraldine. *A Bachelor Girl in London.* London: Hutchinson, 1898.

More, Hannah. *Strictures on the Modern System of Female Education.* Vol. 3 of *The Works of Hannah More.* London: Henry G. Bohn, 1853. Originally published in 1799.

Oliphant, Margaret. *The Athelings, or The Three Gifts.* 3 vols. Edinburgh: W. Blackwood, 1857.

———. "Novels." *Blackwood's Edinburgh Magazine* 94 (1867): 257–80.

———. "Sensation Novels." *Blackwood's Edinburgh Magazine* 91 (1862): 564–84.

Paston, George [Emily Morse Symonds]. *A Writer of Books.* With an afterword by Anita Miller. London: Chapman & Hall, 1898.

Rayner, Olive Pratt. *See* Allen, Grant.

Reid, T. Wemyss. *Charlotte Brontë.* New York: Scribner, Armstrong, 1877.

Richardson, Samuel. *Clarissa: or, the History of a Young Lady: Comprehending the Most Important Concerns of Private Life. And Particularly Shewing, the Distresses that May Attend the Misconduct Both of Parents and Children, in Relation to Marriage.* 8 vols. London, 1748.

Riddell, Charlotte. *A Struggle for Fame.* N.p.: Tramp Press, 2014. Originally published in 1883.

Sartre, Jean-Paul. *La nausée.* Paris: Gallimard, 1972. Originally published in 1938.

Shelley, Mary. Introduction to *Frankenstein,* 169–70. Edited by J. Paul Hunter. New York: W. W. Horton, 1996. Originally published in 1818.

Shields, Carol. *Swann: A Mystery.* Toronto: Stoddart, 1987.

Stephen, Leslie. "Charlotte Brontë." In *Dictionary of Literary Biography,* vol. 6, edited by Leslie Stephen. London: Smith, Elder, 1886.

Sterne, Laurence. *The Life and Opinions of Tristram Shandy, Gentleman.* Edited by Graham Petrie. With an introduction by Christopher Ricks. Harmondsworth: Penguin Books, 1967. Originally published 1759–67.

Symonds, Emily Morse. *See* Paston, George.

Tabor, Eliza. *The Diary of a Novelist.* London: Hurst & Blackett, 1880.

Taylor, Elizabeth. *Angel.* Introduction by Hilary Mantel. London: Virago, 1957.

Tennyson, Alfred. "Mariana." In *The Major Works,* edited by Adam Roberts, 11–13. Oxford: Oxford University Press, 2009. Originally published in 1830.
Trollope, Anthony. "Mary Gresley." In *An Editor's Tales,* 49–97. London: Strahan, 1870.
———. *The Way We Live Now.* New York: Broadview Press, 2005.
Vonnegut, Kurt. *Slaughterhouse-Five.* New York: Dell, 1969.
Waters, Sarah. *Tipping the Velvet.* London: Virago, 1991.
Wilford, Florence. *Nigel Bartram's Ideal.* London: Frederick Warne, n.d.
Willis, Sara Payson [Fanny Fern, pseud.]. *Ruth Hall: A Domestic Tale of the Present Time.* https://www.gutenberg.org/files/40814/40814-h/40814-h.htm. Originally published in 1855.
Wollstonecraft, Mary. *"Mary, A Fiction" and "The Wrongs of Woman, or Maria."* Edited by Michelle Faubert. Peterborough, ON: Broadview Press, 2012. Originally published in 1788 and 1798, respectively.
The Writer 11, no. 1. January 1900. https://archive.org/stream/writer01goog/writer01goog_djvu.txt.
Zola, Émile. "Le roman expérimental." In *Le roman expérimental,* edited by Aimé Guedj, 59–97. Paris: Garnier-Flammarion, 1971. Originally published in 1879.

SECONDARY SOURCES

Acheson, James. "John Fowles's *The French Lieutenant's Woman.*" In *A Companion to the British and Irish Novel, 1945–2000,* edited by Brian W. Shaffer, 398–408. Malden, MA: Blackwell, 2005.
Alter, Robert. *Partial Magic: The Novel as a Self-Conscious Genre.* Berkeley: University of California Press, 1975.
Altick, Richard D. *The English Common Reader: A Social History of the Mass Reading Public, 1800–1900.* Chicago: University of Chicago Press, 1957.
Anderson, Nancy Fix. *Woman against Women in Victorian England: A Life of Eliza Lynn Linton.* Bloomington: Indiana University Press, 1987.
Ardis, Ann. *New Women, New Novels: Feminism and Early Modernism.* New Brunswick, NJ: Rutgers University Press, 1990.
———. "'Retreat with Honour': Mary Cholmondeley's Presentation of the New Woman Artist in *Red Pottage.*" In *Writing the Woman Artist: Essays on Poetics, Politics, and Portraiture,* edited by Suzanne W. Jones, 333–50. Philadelphia: University of Pennsylvania Press, 1991.
Armstrong, Nancy. *How Novels Think: The Limits of Individualism from 1719–1900.* New York: Columbia University Press, 2006.
Atkinson, Juliette. *Victorian Biography Reconsidered: A Study of Nineteenth-Century "Hidden" Lives.* Oxford: Oxford University Press, 2010.

Auerbach, Erich. *Mimesis: The Representation of Reality in Western Literature*. Translated by Willard R. Trask. With a new introduction by Edward W. Said. Princeton, NJ: Princeton University Press, 2013. Originally published in 1946.

Bache, Lee Anne. "Making More than a Name: Eliza Lynn Linton and the Commodification of the Woman Journalist at the Fin de Siècle." In *Women in Journalism at the Fin de Siècle: Making a Name for Herself*, edited by F. Elizabeth Gray, 21–36. New York: Palgrave Macmillan, 2012.

Backscheider, Paula R. "Literary Culture as Immediate Reality." In *A Companion to the Eighteenth-Century English Novel and Culture*, edited by Paula R. Backscheider and Catherine Ingrassia, 504–38. Malden, MA: Blackwell, 2005.

Baisnée-Keay, Valérie. Introduction to *Women's Life Writing and the Practice of Reading: She Reads to Write Herself*, edited by Valérie Baisnée-Keay, Corinne Bigot, Nicoleta Alexoae-Zagni, and Claire Bazin, 1–19. London: Palgrave Macmillan, 2018.

Barros, Carolyn A. *Autobiography: Narrative of Transformation*. Ann Arbor: University of Michigan Press, 1998.

Barthes, Roland. "The Death of the Author." In *Image, Music, Text*, 142–48. New York: Hill & Wang, 1977.

Beetham, Margaret. *A Magazine of Her Own? Domesticity and Desire in the Woman's Magazine, 1800–1914*. New York: Routledge, 1996.

Bellamy, Joyce M., and Beate Kaspar. "Harkness, Margaret Elise (1854–1923), Socialist Author and Journalist." In vol. 8 of *Dictionary of Labour Biography*, edited by Joyce M. Bellamy and John Saville, 103–12. London: Palgrave Macmillan, 1987.

Belsey, Catherine. *Critical Practice*. London: Methuen, 1980.

Bock, Carol A. "Authorship, the Brontës, and *Fraser's Magazine*: 'Coming Forward' as an Author in Early Victorian England." *Victorian Literature and Culture* 29, no. 2 (2001): 241–66.

Bonaparte, Felicia. *The Poetics of Poesis: The Making of Nineteenth-Century English Fiction*. Charlottesville: University of Virginia Press, 2016.

Booth, Wayne C. *The Rhetoric of Fiction*. Chicago: University of Chicago Press, 1961.

Boumelha, Penny. "The Woman Genius and the Woman of Grub Street: Figures of the Female Writer in British Fin-de-Siècle Fiction." *English Literature in Transition, 1880–1920* 40, no. 2 (1997): 164–80.

Boyd, Michael. *The Reflexive Novel: Fiction as Critique*. Lewisburg, PA: Bucknell University Press, 1983.

Braun, Gretchen. "'A Great Break in the Common Course of Confession': Narrating Loss in Charlotte Brontë's *Villette*." *ELH* 78, no. 1 (2011): 189–212.

Breton, Rob. "The Sentimental Socialism of Margaret Harkness." *English Language Notes* 48, no. 1 (2010): 27–39.

Callard, Agnes. *Aspiration: The Agency of Becoming*. New York: Oxford University Press, 2018.

Carlisle, Janice. "The Face in the Mirror: *Villette* and the Conventions of Autobiography." *ELH* 46, no. 2 (1979): 262–89.

Case, Alison A. *Plotting Women: Gender and Narration in the Eighteenth- and Nineteenth-Century British Novel*. Charlottesville: University Press of Virginia, 1999.

Christensen, Inger. *The Meaning of Metafiction: A Critical Study of the Selected Novels by Sterne, Nabokov, Barth and Beckett*. Bergen, Norway: Universitetsforlaget, 1981.

Clayton, Cherry. "Olive Schreiner: Life into Fiction." *English in Africa* 12, no. 1 (1985): 29–39.

Clayton, Jay. "Dickens and the Genealogy of Postmodernism." *Nineteenth-Century Literature* 46, no. 2 (1991): 181–95.

Colby, Vineta. *The Singular Anomaly: Women Novelists of the Nineteenth Century*. New York: New York University Press, 1970.

———. "'Devoted Amateur': Mary Cholmondeley and *Red Pottage*." *Essays in Criticism* 20, no. 2 (1970): 213–28.

Culler, Jonathan. *On Deconstruction*. Ithaca, NY: Cornell University Press, 1983.

———. "Some Problems Concerning Narrators of Novels and Speakers of Poems." In *Optional-Narrator Theory: Principles, Perspectives, Proposals*, edited by Sylvie Patron, 33–52. Lincoln: University of Nebraska Press, 2021.

Currie, Mark, ed. *Metafiction*. London: Longman, 1995.

Davies, Helen. *Gender and Ventriloquism in Victorian and Neo-Victorian Fiction: Passionate Puppets*. Basingstoke, Hampshire: Palgrave Macmillan, 2012.

Dowling, Linda C. "*Venus and Tannhäuser*: Beardsley's Satire of Decadence." *Journal of Narrative Technique* 8, no. 1 (1978): 26–41.

DuPlessis, Rachel Blau. *Writing beyond the Ending: Narrative Strategies of Twentieth-Century Women Writers*. Bloomington: Indiana University Press, 1985.

Eakin, Paul John. "Relational Selves, Relational Lives: The Story of the Story." In *True Relations: Essays on Autobiography and the Postmodern*, edited by G. Thomas Couser and Joseph Fichtelberg, 63–81. Westport, CT: Greenwood, 1998.

Easley, Alexis. *First-Person Anonymous: Women Writers and Victorian Print Media, 1830–1870*. New York: Routledge, 2004.

Ehland, Christoph, and Cornelia Wächter, eds. Introduction to *Middlebrow and Gender, 1890–1945*, 1–17. Leiden, The Netherlands: Brill | Rodopi, 2016.

Faber, Lindsey. "One Sister's Surrender: Rivalry and Resistance in Rhoda Broughton's *Cometh Up as a Flower*." In *Victorian Sensations: Essays on a Scandalous Genre*, edited by Kimberly Harrison and Richard Fantina, 149–59. Columbus: Ohio State University Press, 2006.

Federico, Annette R, ed. *Gilbert and Gubar's "The Madwoman in the Attic" after Thirty Years*, with a foreword by Sandra M. Gilbert. Columbia: University of Missouri Press, 2011.

Federman, Raymond. *Surfiction: Fiction Now and Tomorrow.* Chicago: Swallow Press, 1975.

Flaubert, Gustave. *The Letters of Gustave Flaubert, 1830–1857.* Edited by Francis Steegmuller. Cambridge, MA: Harvard University Press, 1980.

Flint, Kate. *The Woman Reader, 1837–1914.* 2nd ed. Oxford: Clarendon Press, 1995. Originally published in 1993.

———. "Women, Men and the Reading of *Vanity Fair*." In *The Practice and Representation of Reading in England*, edited by James Raven, Helen Small, and Naomi Tadmor, 246–62. Cambridge: Cambridge University Press, 1996.

Fludernik, Monika. *Towards a "Natural" Narratology.* New York: Routledge, 1996.

Fokkema, Aleid. "The Author: Postmodernism's Stock Character." In *The Author as Character: Representing Historical Writers in Western Literature*, edited by Paul Franssen and Ton Hoenselaars, 39–51. Madison, NJ: Fairleigh Dickinson University Press, 1999.

Foucault, Michel. "Qu'est qu'un auteur?" In vol. 1 of *Dits et écrits: 1954–1988*, edited by Daniel Defert and François Ewald, 789–821. Paris: Gallimard, 1994. Originally published in 1969.

Freedgood, Elaine. *Worlds Enough: The Invention of Realism in the Victorian Novel.* Princeton, NJ: Princeton University Press, 2020.

Freeman, Meghan. "Cordons of Protection: The Stage of Spectatorship in Charlotte Brontë's *Villette*." *Victorian Literature and Culture* 41, no. 4 (2013): 643–75.

Friedman, Ellen G., and Miriam Fuchs, eds. *Breaking the Sequence: Women's Experimental Fiction.* Princeton, NJ: Princeton University Press, 1989.

Gaillet, Lynee Lewis. "Reception of Elizabeth Barrett Browning's *Aurora Leigh*: An Insight into the Age's Turmoil over the Representation of Gender and Theories of Art." *Studies in Browning and His Circle* 20 (1992): 115–22.

Galchinsky, Michael. "'Permanently Blacked': Julia Frankau's Jewish Race." *Victorian Literature and Culture* 27, no. 1 (1999): 171–83.

Gallagher, Catherine. *Nobody's Story: The Vanishing Acts of Women Writers in the Marketplace, 1670–1820.* Oakland: University of California Press, 1995.

Gardiner, Judith Kegan. "On Female Identity and Writing by Women." In *Writing and Sexual Difference*, edited by Elizabeth Abel, 177–91. Brighton, Sussex: Harvester Press, 1982.

Gass, William H. *Fiction and the Figures of Life.* New York: Alfred A. Knopf, 1970.

Gibson, Anna. "Charlotte Brontë's First Person." *Narrative* 25, no. 2 (2017): 203–26.

Gilbert, Sandra M., and Susan Gubar. *The Madwoman in the Attic: The Woman Writer and the Nineteenth-Century Literary Imagination.* With an introduction by Lisa Appignanesi. 2nd ed. New Haven, CT: Yale University Press, 2000. Originally published in 1979.

———. *The War of the Words*. Vol. 1 of *No Man's Land: The Place of the Woman Writer in the Twentieth Century*. New Haven, CT: Yale University Press, 1988.

Ginsburg, Michal Peled. "Pseudonym, Epigraphs, and Narrative Voice: *Middlemarch* and the Problem of Authorship." *ELH* 47, no. 3 (1980): 542–58.

Golban, Petru. *Victorian Fiction as a Bildungsroman: Its Flourishing and Complexity*. Newcastle-upon-Tyne: Cambridge Scholars Publishing, 2019.

Gray, Nancy. *Language Unbound: On Experimental Writing by Women*. Champaign: University of Illinois Press, 1992.

Greene, Gayle. *Changing the Story: Feminist Fiction and the Tradition*. Bloomington: Indiana University Press, 1992.

Gusdorf, Georges. "Conditions and Limits of Autobiography." In *Autobiography: Essays Theoretical and Critical*, translated and edited by James Olney, 28–48. Princeton, NJ: Princeton University Press, 1980.

Haller, Elizabeth K. "Perception and the Suppression of Identity in *Villette*." *Brontë Studies* 35, no. 2 (2010): 149–59.

Haugom Olsen, Stein. "Biography in Literary Criticism." In *A Companion to the Philosophy of Literature*, edited by Garry L. Hagberg and Walter Jost, 436–52. Oxford: Blackwell, 2009.

Heilmann, Ann. *New Woman Strategies: Sarah Grand, Olive Schreiner, and Mona Caird*. Manchester: Manchester University Press, 2004.

Heilmann, Ann, and Mark Llewellyn. *Neo-Victorianism: The Victorians in the Twenty-First Century, 1999–2009*. Basingstoke, Hampshire: Palgrave Macmillan, 2010.

Heller, Tamar. "Disposing of the Body: Literary Authority, Female Desire and the Reverse Künstlerroman of Rhoda Broughton's *A Fool in her Folly*." In *New Women Writers, Authority and the Body*, edited by Melissa Purdue and Stacey Floyd, 139–58. Cambridge: Cambridge Scholar's Press, 2009.

———. Introduction to *Cometh Up as a Flower*. In *Sensation with a Purpose: Felicia Skene, "Hidden Depths" (1866); Erotic Sensationalism: Rhoda Broughton, "Cometh Up as a Flower" (1867)*, edited by Lillian Nayder and Tamar Heller. Vol. 4 of *Varieties of Women's Sensation Fiction: 1855–1890*, edited by Andrew Maunder. Abingdon: Taylor & Francis, 2004.

———. "Rhoda Broughton." In *A Companion to Sensation Fiction*, edited by Pamela K. Gilbert, 281–92. Malden, MA: Wiley-Blackwell, 2011.

Helsinger, Elizabeth K., Robin Lauterbach Sheets, and William Veeder. *Literary Issues*. Vol. 3 of *The Woman Question: Society and Literature in Britain and America, 1837–1883*. Chicago: University of Chicago Press, 1989. Originally published in 1983.

Henry, Peaches. "A Revised Approach to Relationality in Women's Autobiography: The Case of Eliza Linton's *The Autobiography of Christopher Kirkland.*" *a/b: Auto/Biography Studies* 20, no. 1 (2005): 18–37.

Holmes, Frederick M. "The Novel, Illusion, and Reality: The Paradox of Omniscience in *The French Lieutenant's Woman.*" In *Metafiction*, edited by Mark Currie, 206–20. London: Longman, 1995.

Humble, Nicola. *The Feminine Middlebrow, 1920s to 1950s: Class, Domesticity, and Bohemianism.* Oxford: Oxford University Press, 2004.

Hunt, Linda. "Amy Levy and the 'Jewish Novel': Representing Jewish Life in the Victorian Period." *Studies in the Novel* 26, no. 3 (1994): 235–53.

Hutcheon, Linda. "Historiographic Metafiction: Parody and the Intertextuality of History." In *Intertextuality and Contemporary American Fiction*, edited by Patrick O'Donnell and Robert Con Davis, 3–32. Baltimore: John Hopkins University Press, 1989.

———. *Narcissistic Narrative: The Metafictional Paradox.* 2nd ed. London: Methuen, 1984. Originally published in 1980.

———. *A Poetics of Postmodernism: History, Theory, Fiction.* New York: Routledge, 1988.

Huyssen, Andreas. "Mass Culture as Woman: Modernism's Other." In *Studies in Entertainment: Critical Approaches to Mass Culture*, edited by Tania Modleski, 188–207. Bloomington: Indiana University Press, 1986.

Irigaray, Luce. *Ce sexe qui n'en est pas un.* Translated by Mackenzie Bleho. Paris: Éditions de Minuit, 1977.

Jacobus, Mary. Review of *The Madwoman in the Attic: The Woman Writer and the Nineteenth-Century Imagination*, by Sandra M. Gilbert and Susan Gubar, and *Shakespeare's Sisters: Feminist Essays on Women Poets*, edited by Sandra M. Gilbert and Susan Gubar. *Signs* 6, no. 3 (1981): 517–23.

Jaffe, Audrey. *The Victorian Novel Dreams of the Real: Conventions and Ideology.* New York: Oxford University Press, 2016.

James, Louis. *English Popular Literature, 1819–1851.* New York: Columbia University Press, 1976.

Jameson, Fredric. "*The Shining*." *Social Text*, no. 4 (1981): 114–25.

Johnson, Patricia E. "Charlotte Brontë and Desire (to Write): Pleasure and Prohibition." In *Anxious Power: Reading, Writing, and Ambivalence in Narrative by Women*, edited by Carol J. Singley and Susan Elizabeth Sweeney, 173–84. Albany: State University of New York Press, 1993.

Judd, Catherine A. "Male Pseudonyms and Female Authority in Victorian England." In *Literature in the Marketplace: Nineteenth-Century British Publishing and Reading Practices*, edited by John O. Jordan and Robert L. Patten, 250–68. Cambridge: Cambridge University Press, 2003. Originally published in 1995.

Kanwit, John Paul M. *Victorian Art Criticism and the Woman Writer.* Columbus: Ohio State University Press, 2013.

Kelleher, Margaret. "Representing Ireland." In vol. 6 of *The History of British Women's Writing, 1830–1880*, edited by Lucy Hartley, 91–106: London, Palgrave Macmillan, 2018.

Konstantinou, Lee. *Cool Characters: Irony and American Fiction.* Cambridge, MA: Harvard University Press, 2016.

Kornbluh, Anna. "Present Tense Futures of the Past." *Victorian Studies* 59, no. 1 (2016): 98–101.

Kreilkamp, Ivan. *Voice and the Victorian Storyteller.* Cambridge: Cambridge University Press, 2005.

Kristeva, Julia. *The Kristeva Reader,* edited by Toril Moi. New York: Columbia University Press, 1986.

Laporte, Charles. "*Aurora Leigh, A Life-Drama,* and Victorian Poetic Autobiography." *Studies in English Literature* 53, no. 4 (2013): 829–51.

Lamarque, Peter. *The Philosophy of Literature.* Malden, MA: Wiley-Blackwell, 2008.

Lanser, Susan. "The Diachronization of *Jane Eyre.*" In *How to Do Things with Narrative: Cognitive and Diachronic Perspectives,* edited by Jan Alber and Greta Olson and in collaboration with Birte Christ, 109–24. Berlin: De Gruyter, 2018.

———. *Fictions of Authority: Women Writers and Narrative Voice.* Ithaca, NY: Cornell University Press, 2018. Originally published in 1992.

———. "(Im)plying the Author." *Narrative* 9, no. 2 (2001): 153–60.

———. *The Narrative Act: Point of View in Prose Fiction.* Princeton, NJ: Princeton University Press, 1981.

———. "Toward (a Queerer and) More (Feminist) Narratology." In *Narrative Theory Unbound: Queer and Feminist Interventions,* edited by Robyn Warhol and Susan Lanser, 23–42. Columbus: Ohio State Press, 2015.

Leavis, F. R. *The Great Tradition: George Eliot, Henry James, Joseph Conrad.* 3rd ed. London: Chatto & Windus, 1955. Originally published in 1948.

Leavis, F. R., and Q. D. Leavis. *Dickens: The Novelist.* London: Chatto & Windus, 1970.

Ledger, Sally. *The New Woman: Fiction and Feminism at the Fin de Siècle.* Manchester: Manchester University Press, 1997.

Levine, George. *Dying to Know: Scientific Epistemology and Narrative in Victorian England.* Chicago: University of Chicago Press, 2002.

———. *The Realistic Imagination: English Fiction from Frankenstein to Lady Chatterley.* Chicago: University of Chicago Press, 1981.

"A Lively Autobiography." *Literary World,* October 1, 1897, 227–28.

Llewellyn, Mark. "What Is Neo-Victorian Studies?" *Neo-Victorian Studies* 1, no. 1 (2008): 164–85.

Löschnigg, Martin. "Postclassical Narratology and the Theory of Autobiography." In *Postclassical Narratology: Approaches and Analyses*, edited by Jan Alber and Monika Fludernik, 255–72. Columbus: Ohio State University Press, 2010.

Lukács, Georg. *The Theory of the Novel*. London: Merlin Press, 1971. Originally published in 1916.

Lyotard, Jean-François. *The Postmodern Condition: A Report on Knowledge*. Translated by Geoff Bennington and Brian Massumi and with a foreword by Fredric Jameson. Minneapolis: University of Minnesota Press, 1984. Originally published in 1979.

MacCabe, Colin. *James Joyce and the Revolution of the Word*. 2nd ed. London: Palgrave Macmillan, 2003. Originally published in 1979.

MacDonald, Tara. "'The Heroine of a Modern Sea Epic': The New Woman Adventuress in Grant Allen's *The Type-Writer Girl*." In *Middlebrow and Gender, 1890–1945*, edited by Christoph Ehland and Cornelia Wächter, 121–37. Leiden, The Netherlands: Brill | Rodopi, 2016.

Marcus, Laura. "Feminist Aesthetics and the New Realism." In *New Feminist Discourses: Critical Essays on Theories and Texts*, edited by Isobel Armstrong, 11–25. London: Routledge, 1992.

Marcus, Sharon. "The Profession of the Author: Abstraction, Advertising, and *Jane Eyre*." PMLA 110, no. 2 (1995): 206–19.

Mascuch, Michael. *The Origins of the Individualist Self: Autobiography and Self-Identity in England, 1591–1791*. Stanford, CA: Stanford University Press, 1997.

Mason, Mary G. "The Other Voice: Autobiographies of Women Writers." In *Autobiography: Essays Theoretical and Critical*, translated and edited by James Olney, 207–35. Princeton, NJ: Princeton University Press, 1980

McCaffery, Larry. *The Metafictional Muse: The Works of Robert Coover, Donald Barthelme, and William H. Gass*. Pittsburgh: University of Pittsburgh Press, 1982.

McHale, Brian. *Postmodernist Fiction*. London: Routledge, 1987.

McKeon, Michael. "Writer as Hero: Novelistic Prefigurations and the Emergence of Literary Biography." In *Contesting the Subject: Essays in the Postmodern Theory and Practice of Biography and Biographical Criticism*, edited by William H. Epstein, 17–41. West Lafayette, IN: Purdue University Press, 1991.

Meem, Deborah T. "Eliza Lynn Linton and the Rise of Lesbian Consciousness." *Journal of the History of Sexuality* 7, no. 4 (1997): 537–60.

Mezei, Kathy, ed. *Ambiguous Discourse: Feminist Narratology and British Women Writers*. Chapel Hill: University of North Carolina Press, 1996.

Miles, Rosalind. *The Female Form: Women Writers and the Conquest of the Novel*. London: Routledge & Kegan Paul, 1987.

Miller, Jane Eldridge. *Rebel Women: Feminism, Modernism, and the Edwardian Novel*. London: Virago, 1994.

Milnes, Tim, and Kerry Sinanan, eds. *Romanticism, Sincerity and Authenticity*. New York: Palgrave Macmillan, 2010.
Moers, Ellen. *Literary Women*. Garden City, NY: Doubleday, 1976.
Murphy, James H. *Irish Novelists and the Victorian Age*. Oxford: Oxford University Press, 2011.
Nehamas, Alexander. "Writer, Text, Work, Author." In *Literature and the Question of Philosophy*, edited with an introduction by Anthony J. Cascardi, 265–91. Baltimore: Johns Hopkins University Press, 1987.
Neumann, Birgit, and Ansgar Nünning. "Metanarration and Metafiction." *The Living Handbook of Narratology* (blog), December 3, 2012, http://www.lhn.uni-hamburg.de/node/50.html.
Oulton, Carolyn W. de la L. Introduction to vol. 9 of *New Woman Fiction, 1881–1899*, vii–xvi. London: Routledge, 2016. Originally published in 1899.
Palmer, Beth. *Women's Authorship and Editorship in Victorian Culture: Sensational Strategies*. Oxford: Oxford University Press, 2011.
Parkin-Gounelas, Ruth. *Fictions of the Female Self: Charlotte Brontë, Olive Schreiner, Katherine Mansfield*. London: Palgrave Macmillan, 1991.
Pennington, Heidi L. *Creating Identity in the Victorian Fictional Autobiography*. Columbia: University of Missouri Press, 2018.
Peters, Joan Douglas. *Feminist Metafiction and the Evolution of the British Novel*. Gainesville: University Press of Florida, 2002.
Peterson, Linda H. *Becoming a Woman of Letters: Myths of Authorship and Facts of the Victorian Market*. Princeton, NJ: Princeton University Press, 2009.
———. *Traditions of Victorian Women's Autobiography: The Poetics and Politics of Life Writing*. Charlottesville: University Press of Virginia, 1999.
———. *Victorian Autobiography: The Tradition of Self-Interpretation*. New Haven, CT: Yale University Press, 1986.
Phegley, Jennifer. *Educating the Proper Woman Reader: Victorian Family Literary Magazines and the Cultural Health of the Nation*. Columbus: Ohio State University Press, 2004.
Price, Leah. "Grant Allen's Impersonal Secretaries: Rereading *The Type-Writer Girl*." In *Grant Allen: Literature and Cultural Politics at the Fin de Siècle*, edited by William Greenslade and Terence Rodgers, 129–41. Abingdon, Oxon: Routledge, 2016.
Pykett, Lyn. *The "Improper" Feminine: The Women's Sensation Novel and the New Woman Writing*. London: Routledge, 1992.
Rainey, Lawrence. "Secretarial Fiction: Gender and Genre in Four Novels, 1897–1898." *English Literature in Translation, 1880–1920* 53, no. 3 (2010): 308–30.
Sadleir, Michael. *Things Past*. London: Constable, 1944.

Sanders, Valerie. *The Brother-Sister Culture in Nineteenth-Century Literature: From Austen to Woolf.* Houndmills, Hampshire: Palgrave, 2002.

———. "'Fathers' Daughters': Three Victorian Anti-Feminist Women Autobiographers." In *Mortal Pages, Literary Lives: Studies in Nineteenth-Century Autobiography*, edited by Vincent Newey and Philip Shaw, 153–71. Aldershot, UK: Scolar Press, 1996.

Scholes, Robert. *Fabulation and Metafiction.* Champaign: University of Illinois Press, 1979.

———. "Metafiction." *Iowa Review* 1, no. 4 (1970): 100–115.

Schwartz, Hillel. *The Culture of the Copy: Striking Likenesses, Unreasonable Facsimiles.* New York: Zone Books, 2014.

Shastri, Sudha. *Intertextuality and Victorian Studies.* Hyderabad, Telangana: Orient Blackswan, 2001.

Shaw, Harry E. *Narrating Reality: Austen, Scott, Eliot.* Ithaca, NY: Cornell University Press, 1999.

Showalter, Elaine. *A Literature of Their Own: British Women Novelists from Brontë to Lessing.* Expanded ed. Princeton, NJ: Princeton University Press, 1999. Originally published in 1977.

Siegle, Robert. *The Politics of Reflexivity: Narrative and the Constitutive Poetics of Culture.* Baltimore: John Hopkins University Press, 1986.

Silver, Brenda R. "The Reflecting Reader in *Villette*." In *The Voyage In: Fictions of Female Development*, edited by Elizabeth Abel, Marianne Hirsch, and Elizabeth Langland, 90–111. Hanover, NH: University Press of New England for Dartmouth College, 1983.

Smith, Sidonie. "Resisting the Gaze of Embodiment: Woman's Autobiography in the Nineteenth Century." In *American Women's Autobiography: Fea(s)ts of Memory*, edited and with an introduction by Margo Culley, 75–110. Madison: University of Wisconsin Press, 1992.

Spacks, Patricia Meyer. *The Female Imagination.* New York: Knopf, 1975.

Sparks, Tabitha. "Absent Character: From Margaret Harkness to John Law." In *Margaret Harkness: Writing Social Engagement, 1880–1921*, edited by Flore Janssen and Lisa Robertson, 39–54. Manchester: Manchester University Press, 2019.

Stewart, Victoria. "The Woman Writer in Mid-Twentieth Century Middlebrow Fiction: Conceptualizing Creativity." *Journal of Modern Literature* 35, no. 1 (2011): 21–36.

Stonehill, Brian. *The Self-Conscious Novel: Artifice in Fiction from Joyce to Pynchon.* Philadelphia: University of Pennsylvania Press, 1988.

"Table Talk." *Literary World*, October 1, 1897, 236–38.

Thompson, Nicola Diane. "Lost Horizons: Rereading and Reclaiming Victorian Women Writers." *Women's Studies* 31, no. 1 (2002): 67–83.

Trotter, David. *The English Novel in History, 1895–1920*. London: Routledge, 1993.

Tuchman, Gaye, and Nina E. Fortin. *Edging Women Out: Victorian Novelists, Publishers, and Social Change*. London: Routledge, 2012.

Valman, Nadia. *The Jewess in Nineteenth-Century British Literature Culture*. Cambridge: Cambridge University Press, 2007.

Walker, Nancy A. *Fanny Fern*. New York: Twayne, 1993.

Warhol, Robyn R. *Gendered Interventions: Narrative Discourse in the Victorian Novel*. New Brunswick, NJ: Rutgers University Press, 1989.

Warhol, Robyn, and Susan S. Lanser, eds. *Narrative Theory Unbound*. Columbus: Ohio State University Press, 2015.

Watt, Ian. *The Rise of the Novel: Studies in Defoe, Richardson, and Fielding*. 7th ed. Berkeley: University of California Press, 1971. Originally published in 1957.

Waugh, Patricia. *Metafiction: The Theory and Practice of Self-Conscious Fiction*. London: Methuen, 1984.

———. "Postmodern Fiction and the Rise of Critical Theory." In *A Companion to the British and Irish Novel, 1945–2000*, edited by Brian W. Shaffer, 65–82. Malden, MA: Blackwell, 2005.

Weber, Brenda R. *Women and Literary Celebrity in the Nineteenth Century: The Transatlantic Production of Fame and Gender*. Farnham, Surrey: Ashgate, 2012.

Wells, Juliette. "A Note on Henry Austen's Authorship of the 'Biographical Notice.'" *Persuasions* 38, no. 1 (2017), http://jasna.org/publications/persuasions-online/vol38no1/wells-2/.

White, Hayden. *Metahistory: The Historical Imagination in Nineteenth-Century Europe*. Baltimore: John Hopkins University Press, 1973.

Woolf, Virginia. "George Eliot." In *The Common Reader*, 205–18. London: Hogarth Press, 1925.

———. *A Room of One's Own*. Orlando, FL: Harcourt Brace Jovanovich, 1981.

———. "Women and Fiction." In vol. 1 of *Virginia Woolf on Women & Writing: Her Essays, Assessments and Arguments*, edited by Michèle Barrett, 43–52. London: Women's Press, 1979.

Wynne, Deborah. *The Sensation Novel and the Victorian Magazine*. London: Palgrave Macmillan, 2001.

Zakreski, Patricia. *Representing Female Artistic Labour, 1848–1890: Refining Work for the Middle-Class Woman*. Burlington, VT: Ashgate, 2006.

INDEX

Adam Bede (Eliot), 17, 74, 102
adventure novel, 50
Aguilar, Grace, "The Authoress," 33
Aiken-Kortright, *Anne Sherwood*, 33–34
Alcott, Louisa May, *Little Women*, 80, 82
Alias Grace (Atwood), 118
All Sorts and Conditions of Men (Besant), 145, 175n63
Allen, Grant (pseud., Olive Pratt Rayner), 11, 127–40; *Rosalba*, 139; *The Type-Writer Girl*, 9, 11, 127–28, 131–40
Alter, Robert, 13–14, 17–18
Anderson, Nancy Fix, 117, 125, 171n27
Angel (Taylor), 12, 155–57
Anne Sherwood (Aiken-Kortright), 33–34
Ardis, Anne, 128, 129, 174n41
Armstrong, Nancy, 7
Arnold, Matthew, 125
Athelings, The (Oliphant), 10, 34, 91–98, 102, 105, 156
Atkinson, Juliette, 122
Atwood, Margaret, 9, 65, 165n68; *Alias Grace*, 118; *The Blind Assassin*, 39; *The Edible Woman*, 165n68; *The Handmaid's Tale*, 155
Auerbach, Erich, *Mimesis*, 6, 7
Aurora Leigh (Barrett-Browning), 5, 9, 29, 56
Austen, Henry (attributed), "Biographical Notice," 50, 163n4
Austen, Jane, 7, 13, 21, 23, 48, 50; *Northanger Abbey*, 13, 50, 147; *Persuasion*, 50; *Sense and Sensibility*, 47, 93
"Authoress, The" (Aguilar), 33

author function, 112, 170n4
autobiography: fictional, 10, 55, 58, 60, 70–71, 81–84, 118, 120, 122; form of, 52, 58, 68–69, 71, 73–74, 80, 82, 87, 107, 124; women's, 6, 20, 76, 154
Autobiography of Christopher Kirkland, The (Linton), 9, 11, 109, 116–25, 141

Babe in Bohemia, A (Frankau), 113–14
Bache, Lee Ann, 117, 123
Bachelor Girl in London, A (Mitton), 137–38
Backscheider, Paula R., 49
Baisnée-Keay, Valérie, 78
Balzac, Honoré de, 145
Barrett Browning, Elizabeth, 5, 9, 29, 51, 56, 132; *Aurora Leigh*, 5, 9, 29, 56
Barros, Carolyn, 58
Barth, John, 2
Beckett, Samuel, 2, 13
Behn, Aphra, 49
Bell, Acton, 53–54, 108. *See also* Brontë, Anne
Bell, Currer, 19, 42, 53–55, 66, 108, 111, 117, 153, 162n112. *See also* Brontë, Charlotte
Bellamy, Joyce M., and Beate Kaspar, 115
Besant, Walter, *All Sorts and Conditions of Men*, 145, 175n63
Black, Helen C., 85–86, 89
Blackburne, E. Owens, *Molly Carew*, 32–33
Bleak House (Dickens), 17, 25
Blind Assassin, The (Atwood), 39

Boardman, Kay, 26
Bonaparte, Felicia, 7, 8–9
Booth, Wayne C., 110–11
Borges, J. L., 9; "Pierre Menard, Author of the *Quixote*," 133–34
Boumelha, Penny, 94
Bowen, Elizabeth, 155
Bowles, Caroline, *Fanny Fairfield*, 32
Braddon, Mary Elizabeth, 19; *The Doctor's Wife*, 34
Brake, Laurel, 26
Breton, Rob, 171n23
Brontë, Anne, 53, 54, 108; *Agnes Grey*, 19, 53, 54; *The Tenant of Wildfell Hall*, 53, 54
Brontë, Charlotte: autobiographical interpretation of, 21–22, 23, 31, 49–69, 88, 117, 154–55; feminist criticism and, 21–22, 23, 57, 112, 153; pseudonym, use of, 29, 54–55, 108, 111–12, 117; reception of, 9, 19, 55, 56, 69, 103; woman writer, status as, 1, 32, 42, 63, 65, 92, 108, 132, 154, 157, 164n32. *See also individual works*
Brontë, Emily, 54, 108; *Wuthering Heights*, 17, 19, 53, 54
Brontë myth, 93, 102
Brontë sisters, 3, 10, 21, 93
Brookner, Anita, 23
Broughton, Rhoda, 1, 9, 10, 31, 69–90, 91; *Cometh Up as a Flower*, 9, 10, 58, 69–90, 91, 100, 118, 130, 150; *A Fool in Her Folly*, 10, 87–90; *Not Wisely but Too Well*, 86, 89; *A Waif's Progress*, 142
Burney, Fanny, 14, 41; *Evelina*, 142
Byron, Lord, 77

Caird, Mona, 22, 128
Callard, Agnes, 4, 130
canon and canonicity, 1, 7, 15, 20, 25, 36, 48, 78, 92, 130, 131, 133–34, 144, 148
canonical novel, 1, 20, 21, 25
Carey, Peter, *Jack Maggs*, 141

Carlisle, Janice, 55
Carlyle, Thomas, 19, 56, 58, 60–62, 125; *Sartor Resartus*, 9, 10, 17, 58–62, 69, 166n78, 166n26
Carter, Angela, 23
Case, Alison, 66
Castle Rackrent (Edgeworth), 76
celebrity (literary) 32, 39, 40, 93, 103, 106, 156, 164n32
Cervantes, Miguel de, 133–34
Chaucer, Geoffrey, 13
Cholmondeley, Mary, 44–45, 137
Christensen, Inger, 13, 159n24, 160n25
City Girl, A (Harkness), 11, 114
Cixous, Hélène, 21
Clarissa (Richardson), 25, 142
Clayton, Jay, 20
Colby, Vineta, 117, 163n132
Colet, Louise, 157
Conrad, Joseph, 7; *Chance*, 16
Corelli, Marie, 156
Craik, Dinah Mulock, *John Halifax, Gentleman*, 15, 160n36
Culler, Jonathan, 66, 124
Currie, Mark, 12, 13, 20, 160n25

Daudets, the, 145
David Copperfield (Dickens), 34, 75
Davies, Helen, 141
Defoe, Daniel, 7; *Moll Flanders*, 25, 142; *Robinson Crusoe*, 4, 118
De Goncourts, the, 145
Diary of a Novelist, The (Tabor), 35
Dickens, Charles, 6, 20, 33, 63; *Bleak House*, 17, 25; *David Copperfield*, 34, 75; *Dombey and Son*, 17; *Great Expectations*, 17, 141
Diviners, The (Laurence), 165n68
Dixon, Ella Hepworth, 142, 172n59
Dombey and Son (Dickens), 17
domestic novel, 1, 26, 92, 135
"Dover Beach" (Arnold), 15
Dowling, Linda C., 114

Drabble, Margaret, 65; *The Waterfall*, 65–66, 168n68
Dr. Philips, A Maida Vale Idyll (Frankau), 11, 113–34
DuPlessis, Rachel Blau, 22

Easley, Alexis, 26, 27
Edgeworth, Maria, 21
education, 18, 52, 57, 76–77, 91, 118–19, 121, 122, 125, 131, 138; Victorian women's, 19, 57, 65, 76, 121
Edwardian era, 156
Egerton, George, 129
Ehland, Christoph, 135, 176n7
Eliot, George, 1, 3, 6, 7, 10, 19, 21, 24, 27, 48, 51, 78, 98, 101–2, 105, 107–9, 111–12, 163n132; *Adam Bede*, 17, 74, 102; *Middlemarch*, 15, 17, 45, 163n132; *The Mill on the Floss*, 102, 111; *Scenes of Clerical Life*, 102, 112; *Silas Marner*, 102; "Silly Novels by Lady Novelists," 29, 98, 101
Engels, Friedrich, 114
Evans, Marianne/Mary Ann. *See* Eliot, George
Evelina (Burney), 142
experimental novel, 11, 19, 24, 44, 55, 105

Faber, Lindsey, 89
Fanny Fairfield (Bowles), 32
feminist criticism, 21–27, 48, 52, 55, 112, 122, 123
feminist narratology, 3, 6, 23
Flaubert, Gustave, 6, 110, 111, 145, 157; *A Sentimental Education*, 110
Flint, Kate, 78
Fortin, Nina E., and Tuchman, Gayle, 170n1
Foucault, Michel, 112, 170n4
Fowles, John, 2, 12; *The French Lieutenant's Woman*, 12, 16, 160n26
Frankau, Julia (pseud., Frank Danby), 11, 109, 112–14, 116, 123; *A Babe in Bohemia*, 113–14; *Dr. Philips, A Maida Vale Idyll*, 11, 113–14
Frankenstein (Shelley), 64
Fraser, Hilary, 26
Freedgood, Elaine, 2
free indirect discourse, 46, 141, 149
Freidman, Ellen G., 21, 22, 24
French feminist theory, 21–22, 128
French Revolution, the, 14, 166n26
Freud, Sigmund, 2
Freudianism and Freudian psychoanalysis, 21, 130
Fuchs, Miriam, 21, 22, 24

Gaddis, William, 2
Galchinsky, Michael, 114
Gallagher, Catherine, 50
Gardiner, Judith Kegan, 23
Gaskell, Elizabeth, 1, 18, 21, 27, 57, 117; *The Life of Charlotte Brontë*, 57, 92, 93, 108, 117; *Mary Barton*, 18; *North and South*, 18
Gass, William, 2, 12
Genette, Gerard, 118, 149
genius (literary), 10, 29, 32–35, 38, 40, 43–44, 51, 92–94, 102, 105, 153–54, 156
Gibson, Anna, 60
Gilbert, Pamela, 167n34
Gilbert, Susan M., and Sandra Gubar, 21–22, 25, 51, 60, 109
Ginsburg, Michael Peled, 112
Gissing, George, 101, 135; *New Grub Street*, 15, 34, 35
Goethe, Johann Wolfgang von, 6
Golden Notebook, The (Lessing), 12
Grand, Sarah, 22, 128, 129, 148
Gray, Nancy, 23
Great Expectations (Dickens), 17, 141
Greene, Gayle, 65, 165n68
Greg, W. R., 50
Gubar, Sandra, and Susan M. Gilbert, 21–22, 25, 51, 60, 109

Hall, Anna Maria (Mrs. S. C. Hall), 39; *A Woman's Story*, 39–41, 44, 48
Hardy, Thomas, *Jude the Obscure*, 15, 35
Harkness, Margaret (pseud., John Law), 11, 109, 112, 114–16, 123, 171n23, 171n24; *A City Girl*, 11, 114; *In Darkest London*, 114; *A Manchester Shirtmaker*, 114; *Out of Work*, 114, 115
Harraden, Beatrice, *Ships That Pass in the Night*, 35
Haugom Olsen, Stein, 56
Heilmann, Anne, 22, 127–28, 174n41
Heller, Tamar, 87
Henry, Peaches, 123
heroine, 3, 12, 22, 47, 72, 81, 87, 89, 91–92, 94, 154; as autobiographer, 1, 10, 70, 74, 81, 86, 87; narrator, 70; tragic, 10, 81–82, 146; as writer/novelist, 1, 4, 9, 11, 27–36, 39, 66, 69, 106, 126–52
historical novel, 16
historical present, 74–75, 155
historiographic metafiction, 12, 79, 118
History of Miss Betsy Thoughtless, The (Haywood), 49
Holdsworth, Annie, *The Years That the Locust Hath Eaten*, 145–46
Hunt, Linda, 114
Hutcheon, Linda, 12, 13, 79, 118, 134, 160nn25–26, 173n27

Idylls of the King (Tennyson), 77
implied author, 110–11, 117, 170n4
In Darkest London (Harkness), 114
Irigaray, Luce, 21

Jack Maggs (Carey), 141
Jacobus, Mary, 21
Jaffe, Audrey, 7, 16, 27
James, Henry, 7, 51; *The Portrait of a Lady*, 142
Jameson, Fredric, 77
Jane Eyre (C. Brontë), 9, 19, 25, 49, 52, 53, 66, 106, 112, 153–54; autobiographical form of, 53, 55–56, 59, 74, 88, 112, 154; compared to *Nigel Bartram's Ideal*, 42, 44
Jane Eyre (character), 22, 59, 74, 109, 111, 154
John Halifax, Gentleman (Craik), 15, 160n36
Johnson, Patricia, 57
Johnstone, Christian, 27
Joyce, James, 2, 13, 14
Judd, Catherine A., 29, 108
Jude the Obscure (Hardy), 15, 35

Kaspar, Beate, and Joyce M. Bellamy, 115
Kelleher, Margaret, 170n61
Kornbluh, Anna, 8
Kreilkamp, Ivan, 54
Kristeva, Julia, 10, 21

Lady Chatterley's Lover (Lawrence), 8, 25
Lamarque, Peter, 110, 112, 122, 170n4
Lanser, Susan S., 19, 22, 24, 49, 111, 117, 125
Laporte, Charles, 56, 159n9
Laurence, Margaret, 65, 165n68
Law, John. *See* Harkness, Margaret
Lawrence, D. H.: *Lady Chatterley's Lover*, 25; *The Rainbow*, 25
Leavis, F. R., 7, 48
Ledger, Sally, 128, 129, 135
Lehmann, Rosamund, 155
Lessing, Doris, 65, 165n68; *The Golden Notebook*, 12, 165n68
Levine, George, 7, 8, 20, 27
Levy, Amy, 114; *The Romance of the Shop*, 142
Liddell, Robert, 157
Life and Opinions of Tristram Shandy, Gentleman, The (Sterne), 2, 12, 13, 180n25
Life of Charlotte Brontë, The (Gaskell), 57, 92, 93, 108, 117
Linton, Eliza Lynn, 11, 31, 109, 116–26, 141, 171n127; *The Autobiography of*

Christopher Kirkland, 11, 109, 116–26; Lizzie Lorton of Greyrigg, 116; Patricia Kemball, 116; The Rebel of the Family, 116
Little Women (Alcott), 80, 82
Living Handbook of Narratology (LHN), 2
Lizzie Lorton of Greyrigg (Linton), 116
Llewellyn, Mark, 127, 165n67, 172n1, 173n27
London Review, 84
Löschonigg, Martin, 73
Loy, Mina, 23
Lukács, Georg, 7, 48
Lyotard, Jean-François, 120–21

MacCabe, Colin, 111
MacDonald, Tara, 125
Manchester Shirtmaker, A (Harkness), 114
Mansfield, Katherine, 153
Marcus, Laura, 24
Marcus, Sharon, 111–12
"Mariana" (Tennyson), 82–83
Martineau, Harriet, 27, 98, 129, 173n12
Marxism, 7, 130
Mary Barton (Gaskell), 18
"Mary Gresley" (Trollope), 29–31
McCaffery, Larry, 159n24
McEwan, Ian, Atonement, 149
McKeon, Michael, 4
Meem, Deborah T., 124–25
melodrama, 10, 39, 46–47, 80, 82, 89, 97, 156
Merrick, Leonard, 114
metafiction: formal definition of, 1, 12, 13, 28; historiographic, 12, 79, 118; narcissistic, 16–17; as a neo-Victorian technique, 127–28; as a postmodern technique, 3, 12, 13, 14, 16, 20, 24, 65; reflexive, 8, 16–18
Meteyard, Eliza, Struggles for Fame, 33–34
Mezei, Kathy, 23
middlebrow, 135, 155
Mill, John Stuart, 19
Miller, Anita, 175n88

Mill on the Floss, The (Eliot), 102, 111
Milton, John, 77
mimeticism, 2, 3, 7, 8, 13, 16, 18, 27
Mitton, Geraldine, A Bachelor Girl in London, 137–38
modernism, 3, 6, 23, 24
Moers, Ellen, 3, 51
Moll Flanders (Defoe), 25, 142
Molly Carew (Blackburne), 32–33
More, Hannah, 76
Mrs. Dalloway (Woolf), 25

narrative metalepsis, 144
Nehemas, Alexander, 28–29, 56
neo-Victorian novel, 11, 127–51
Newgate novel, 16, 50
New Grub Street (Gissing), 15, 34–35
new historicism, 16
new woman, 1, 11, 22, 27, 32, 36, 48, 127–30, 134, 137
new woman novel, 1, 11, 32, 36, 124, 126–51
Nigel Bartram's Ideal (Wilford), 41–44, 48
noncanonical novel, 26, 28, 31, 35
North and South (Gaskell), 18
Northanger Abbey (Austen), 13, 50, 147
North British Review, 29
novel, periodic and thematic categories of: adventure, 50; canonical, 1, 20, 21, 25; experimental, 11, 19, 24, 44, 55, 105; historical, 16; modernist, 153; nautical, 50; neo-Victorian, 1–51; Newgate, 16, 50; new woman, 1, 11, 32, 36, 124, 126, 127–51; noncanonical, 26, 28, 31, 35; postcolonial, 1; postmodern, 39, 79, 110, 118, 121, 160n26; sensation, 1, 26, 33, 41, 42, 46, 47, 100, 114, 120, 137, 176n90; sentimental, 1, 2, 11, 15, 16, 39, 47, 85, 171n23. See also Victorian novel

Oliphant, Margaret, 10, 39, 91–105; The Athelings, 10, 34, 91–105, 156

Oulton, Carolyn W. de la L., 46, 163n32, 174n41
Out of Work (Harkness), 114

Palmer, Beth, 26, 129
Pamela (Richardson), 4
Pantner-Downs, Mollie, 155
Parkin-Gounelas, Ruth, 52
pastiche, 77
Paston, George. *See* Symonds, Emily Morse
Patricia Kemball (Linton), 116
Pendennis (Thackeray), 34
"Pierre Menard, Author of the *Quixote*" (Borges), 133–34
Pennington, Heidi, 60–61
periodical press, 5, 25, 27, 33, 113
Peters, Joan Douglas, 25
Peterson, Linda, 20, 71, 92–93, 104, 163n132
Phegley, Jennifer, 26
poetry, 5, 52, 93, 136
Portrait of a Lady, The (James), 142
postcolonialism, 25
postcolonial novel, 1
postmodernism, 3, 6, 12, 13, 14, 17, 20, 24, 77, 78, 118–20, 128, 133, 161n49
postmodern novel, 1, 2, 11, 13, 15, 18, 20, 39, 61, 79, 110, 118, 121, 128, 160n26
poststructuralism, 113, 158
poverty, 36, 145
Price, Leah, 134, 140
print culture, 26
professional and professionalism, 4, 6, 10, 28, 30, 34, 50, 90, 92, 96–98, 100, 117, 135, 145; Victorian women writers, 26–28, 36, 43, 91–92, 99, 106, 108, 111–12, 123, 138, 140, 151
pseudonyms and pseudonymity, 10–11, 29, 37, 50, 54, 89, 99, 108–26, 127, 129, 140, 150, 166n78
publishing industry, 5, 10, 18, 26, 92, 93, 97–98, 104, 105, 108–9, 123, 135, 144
Pykett, Lynn, 128

Rainbow, The (Lawrence), 25
Rainey, Lawrence, 136, 137
Rayner, Olive Pratt. *See* Allen, Grant
reader, the, and readers, 12, 25, 26, 35, 43, 44, 52, 55–61, 65–69, 73–74, 80–81, 92, 94, 95, 97, 98, 101, 107, 112, 118, 120–21, 125, 126, 133, 138, 143, 144, 155–56; implied reader, 67–69, 71, 74, 78, 80–81, 83; Victorian readers, 19, 26, 37, 38, 72, 86, 105, 106, 123, 126, 140, 142, 174n2
realism: domestic, 1, 92; as literary movement, 6–19, 25, 47, 100, 112, 129, 135, 144, 148; as literary technique, 7, 14, 20, 23, 27, 45, 62, 68–69, 80, 84, 88, 98, 102, 105–6, 127–28, 131–33, 145; urban, 101, 135
realist novel, 1, 3, 7, 13, 20, 48, 55, 68, 107, 112, 149
Rebel of the Family, The (Linton), 116
Red Pottage (Cholmondeley), 36, 44–47, 137, 163n132
reflexive fiction. *See* metafiction
res gestae, 71
Richardson, Dorothy, 3, 24, 153
Richardson, Samuel, 13; *Clarissa*, 25, 142; *Pamela*, 4; *Sir Charles Grandison*, 94, 169n13
Riddell, Charlotte, 1, 10, 31, 91–107; *Struggle for Fame*, 4, 5, 10, 33–34, 91–107, 124, 156; *Too Much Alone*, 104
Rigby, Elizabeth, 106
Robbe-Grillet, Alain, 2
Robinson Crusoe (Defoe), 4, 118
romanticism, 8, 93
Romeo and Juliet (Shakespeare), 133
Room of One's Own, A (Woolf), 154–55
Rosalba (Allen), 139
Rossetti, Christina, 27
Rouges-Macquart, Les (Zola), 116
Ruth Hall (Willis), 36–39, 44, 48

Sadleir, Michael, 85, 89
Sartor Resartus (Carlyle), 9, 10, 17, 58–62, 69, 166n78, 166n26

satire, 10–11, 17, 114, 136
Scenes of Clerical Life (Eliot), 102, 112
Schlegel, Freidrich, 8
Scholes, Robert, 12, 160n25
Schreiner, Olive, 21
Schwartz, Hillel, 131
Scott, Sir Walter, 6, 77
sensation novel, 1, 26, 33, 41, 42, 46–47, 100, 114, 120, 137, 176n90
Sentimental Education, A (Flaubert), 110
sentimental novel, 1, 2, 11, 15, 16, 39, 47, 85, 171n23
Shakespeare, William, 13, 80; *Romeo and Juliet*, 133–34
Shastri, Sudha, 128
Shaw, Harry E., 7
Shelley, Mary, 21; *Frankenstein*, 64
Shields, Carol, *Swann: A Mystery*, 39, 65
Shirley (Brontë), 53, 55–56
Showalter, Elaine, 3, 25, 51, 129, 163n132
Sidgwick, Cecily, 114
Siegle, Robert, 15–18
Silas Marner (Eliot), 102
Slaughterhouse Five (Vonnegut), 79
Sir Charles Grandison (Richardson), 94, 169n13
Southey, Robert, 32, 57, 77, 162n84, 164n32
Spacks, Patricia Meyer, 52
Spectator, 85
Stein, Gertrude, 3, 24, 153
Stendhal, Henri, 6
Stephen, Leslie, 51, 156
Sterne, Laurence, 12, 14, 165n67, 172n1; *The Life and Opinions of Tristram Shandy, Gentleman*, 2, 12–13, 160n25
Stonehill, Brian, 20
Stowe, Harriet Beecher, 33
structuralism, 78, 158
structural materialism, 14
Struggle for Fame, A (Riddell), 4, 5, 10, 33, 34, 91–107, 124, 156
Struggles for Fame (Meteyard), 33–34
surface reading, 16

surfiction. *See* metafiction
Swann: A Mystery (Shields), 39, 65
Symonds, Emily Morse, 150, 153; *A Writer of Books*, 11, 127–28, 138, 141–51, 153

Tabor, Eliza, *The Diary of a Novelist*, 35
Taylor, Elizabeth, 11; *Angel*, 12, 155–57
Tennyson, Alfred, Lord: *Idylls of the King*, 77; "Mariana," 82–83; "The Lord of Burleigh," 77
Thackeray, William Makepeace, 16, 63, 110–11; *Pendennis*, 34; *Vanity Fair*, 16, 17
Thatcher, Margaret, 17
thing theory, 16
Thompson, Nicole Diane, 26
Times (London), 86
Tinsley, William, 104
Tipping the Velvet (Waters), 141
Too Much Alone (Riddell), 104
Tower of London, The (Ainsworth), 78
Trollope, Anthony: "Mary Gresley," 29–31; *The Way We Live Now*, 34–35
Trollope, Frances, 21
Tuchman, Gayle, and Nina E. Fortin, 170n1
Type-Writer Girl, The (Allen), 9, 11, 127–28, 131–40

Valman, Nadia, 114
Vanity Fair (Thackeray), 16, 17
Velleman, David, 130
Victorian novel, 2–4, 7–8, 9, 10, 16, 17, 19, 20, 21, 24, 26, 58, 127, 128, 142, 153, 158
"Victorian values," 17
Victorian women, 1, 20, 25–28, 57, 109, 123, 155
Victorian women novelists, 1, 2, 11, 12, 21; as "lady novelists" 10, 29, 156; self-expression of, 3, 5, 9, 57, 74, 154, 158; "silenced," 3, 21, 28, 29
Victorian women writers, 1, 3, 10, 11, 19, 21, 26, 28, 49, 52, 88, 91, 108, 109, 110, 112
Villette (C. Brontë), 9, 17, 49–69, 71, 91, 150, 157
Vonnegut, Kurt, 9; *Slaughterhouse Five*, 79

Wächter, Cornelia, 135, 176n7
Ward, Mary Augusta, 1
Warhol, Robyn, 18, 22
Warren, Robert Penn, *World Enough and Time*, 16
Waterfall, The (Drabble), 65–66, 165n68
Waters, Sarah, *Tipping the Velvet*, 141
Watt, Ian, 7, 51
Waugh, Patricia, 13, 14–15, 17, 20, 160nn24–25, 161n49
Way We Live Now, The (Trollope), 34–35
Weber, Brenda R., 97
West, Rebecca, 153
Westminster Review, 53, 101
White, Hayden, 78
Wilford, Florence, *Nigel Bartram's Ideal*, 41–44, 48
Willis, Sara Payson (pseud., Fanny Fern), 36–39; *Ruth Hall*, 36–39, 44, 48
Wollestoncraft, Mary, 23
Woman's Story, A (Hall), 39–41, 44, 48
women, 66, 71, 76, 88, 101, 108–10, 112–13, 116–17, 122–25, 126, 131, 134, 140–41; as artists and writers, 1, 3, 10, 11, 19, 21, 26, 28, 49, 52, 65, 88, 91, 105–6, 108, 109–10, 112, 137, 140–41, 145; traditional roles of, 66, 117; women's genius, 10, 29, 32–35, 38, 40, 43, 44, 51, 92–94, 102, 105, 153, 156. *See also* Victorian women
Woolf, Virginia, 2, 3, 11–14, 22–24, 153–54; *Mrs. Dalloway*, 25; *A Room of One's Own*, 154–55
Wordsworth, William, 77
World Enough and Time (Warren), 16
Writer of Books, A (Symonds), 11, 127–28, 138, 141–51, 153
Wynne, Deborah, 26

Years That the Locust Hath Eaten, The (Holdsworth), 145–46
Yonge, Charlotte, 1

Zakreski, Patricia, 26–27
Zola, Émile, 116, 135; "The Experimental Novel," 113; *Les Rouges-Macquart*, 116

Recent books in the
VICTORIAN LITERATURE AND CULTURE SERIES

Narrative and Its Nonevents: The Unwritten Plots That Shaped Victorian Realism
Carra Glatt

Strangers in the Archive: Literary Evidence and London's East End
Heidi Kaufman

Evangelical Gothic: The English Novel and the Religious War on Virtue from Wesley to "Dracula"
Christopher Herbert

Reading with the Senses in Victorian Literature and Science
David Sweeney Coombs

Parting Words: Victorian Poetry and Public Address
Justin A. Sider

The Physics of Possibility: Victorian Fiction, Science, and Gender
Michael Tondre

Willful Submission: Sado-Erotics and Heavenly Marriage in Victorian Poetry
Amanda Paxton

Pirating Fictions: Ownership and Creativity in Nineteenth-Century Popular Culture
Monica F. Cohen

Mathilde Blind: Late-Victorian Culture and the Woman of Letters
James Diedrick

Poetry and the Thought of Song in Nineteenth-Century Britain
Elizabeth K. Helsinger

The Antagonist Principle: John Henry Newman and the Paradox of Personality
Lawrence Poston

Personal Business: Character and Commerce in Victorian Literature and Culture
Aeron Hunt

Second Person Singular: Late Victorian Women Poets and the Bonds of Verse
Emily Harrington

The Ghost behind the Masks: The Victorian Poets and Shakespeare
W. David Shaw

Victorian Poets and the Changing Bible
Charles LaPorte

Liberal Epic: The Victorian Practice of History from Gibbon to Churchill
Edward Adams

Supposing "Bleak House"
John O. Jordan

Feeling for the Poor: Bourgeois Compassion, Social Action, and the Victorian Novel
Carolyn Betensky

The Science of Religion in Britain, 1860–1915
Marjorie Wheeler-Barclay

Reading for the Law: British Literary History and Gender Advocacy
Christine L. Krueger

www.ingramcontent.com/pod-product-compliance
Lightning Source LLC
Chambersburg PA
CBHW020906230426
43666CB00008B/1336